ner

in

ng

'003

20

D1421976

PROFESSIONAL SKILLS FOR COUNSELLORS

The *Professional Skills for Counsellors* series, edited by Colin Feltham, covers the practical, technical and professional skills and knowledge which trainee and practising counsellors need to improve their competence in key areas of therapeutic practice.

Titles in the series include:

Counselling, Psychotherapy and the Law
Peter Jenkins

Contracts in Counselling
Charlotte Sills (ed.)

Counselling Difficult Clients
Kingsley Norton and Gill McGauley

Learning and Writing in Counselling
Mhairi MacMillan and Dot Clark

Counselling and Psychotherapy in Private Practice
Roger Thistle

Referral and Termination Issues for Counsellors
Anne Leigh

The Management of Counselling and Psychotherapy Agencies
Colin Lago and Duncan Kitchin

Group Counselling
Keith Tudor

Practitioner Research in Counselling

John McLeod

SAGE Publications
London • Thousand Oaks • New Delhi

SAGE Publications Ltd
6 Bonhill Street
London EC2A 4PU

SAGE Publications Inc.
2455 Teller Road
Thousand Oaks, California 91320

SAGE Publications India Pvt Ltd
32, M-Block Market
Greater Kailash – I
New Delhi 110 048

British Library Cataloguing in Publication data

A catalogue record for this book is available
from the British Library

ISBN 0 7619 5762 6
ISBN 0 7619 5763 4 (pbk)

Library of Congress catalog card number 99–71228

Typeset by Mayhew Typesetting, Rhayader, Powys
Printed in Great Britain by Biddles Ltd, Guildford, Surrey

For Julia

Contents

Introduction

I am an academic who is also a counsellor. For several years, I have worked with counsellors who have been carrying out research projects in the context of meeting the requirements for the award of a Masters degree or Doctorate. It has seemed to me that, in an academic environment, some of these experienced counsellors have denied their own awareness and experience in a desire to meet what they perceive to be the requirements of the degree, and have produced work that is technically competent yet dry and lifeless. Others have been unwilling or unable to set aside their practitioner identity, and have struggled long and hard to use their research project as a means of exploring and questioning their beliefs and assumptions, or as a vehicle for creating a new understanding of some aspect of their practice. What I have found is that this latter type of participation in inquiry can be a liberating and transforming experience. Other avenues for learning about counselling, such as training and supervision and even personal therapy, have become increasingly regulated and dominated by orthodoxy. Doing passionate research involves a process of questioning these orthodoxies and achieving personal understanding. The practitioner researcher develops a relationship with the research literature and research methodologies which, I would argue, transfers effectively into the counselling setting itself. He or she is no longer defined and controlled by dominant cultural narratives or knowledges, but is more able to resist them and find alternative voices.

Why should counsellors do research? Recent years have seen a steady increase in interest in the role of research in relation to counselling (Barker, Pistrang and Elliott, 1994; McLeod, 1994b). Partly this trend has reflected the movement toward locating counselling training in universities. Partly it can be attributed to the increasing professionalisation of counselling, and the tendency for professions to define themselves around a distinct knowledge base. It can also be seen as a by-product of the demand of both consumer/user groups and government funding

agencies for accountability, for concrete evidence of the effectiveness and benefits of human services. Finally, involvement in
research can be intrinsically satisfying for counsellors, and can
help to promote competence and enhance professional development (McLeod, 1997).

There are therefore several reasons why counselling and
counsellors have been becoming more involved in research. This
book takes as its starting point the counsellor's engagement in
practical action, and the questions thrown up by the activity of
doing counselling. Practitioner research is about what you need
to know in order to do the job better, or to be able to keep doing
the job.

This book is designed to facilitate access to resources. In the
Appendix, and in specific chapters, there are suggestions about
what to read next, and where these sources of information can
be found. Throughout the book there are lots of references to
examples of research studies. It is a good idea to get into the
habit of reading these articles not just for their content but also
for their process – how was the research done? How could it
have been done better? Does it yield practical knowledge, and if
not, why not? Throughout most of the chapters, there is con-
siderable focus on *skills*. As in any other area of life, skills can
only be acquired through practice and experience. There is no
substitute for actually *doing* research, for being involved.

The primary aim of this book is to establish *practitioner
research* as a distinctive and essential strand of research activity.
The book is intended for counsellors, psychotherapists and
members of allied therapeutic professions such as social work,
clinical psychology, psychiatric nursing, the ministry and psychiatry who seek to integrate research into their practice. Readers
whose previous training has included an introduction to research
methods may wish to skip the chapters on technical aspects of
research, for example analysing data. However, my hope is that
the book may help even those with some previous research
experience to re-evaluate the role and meaning of research from
a practitioner perspective.

Acknowledgements

In writing this book I have been aware of the enormous debt I
owe to the many people who have taught me about the

relationship between research and therapy, particularly all the students over the years on the MA in Counselling Studies at Keele University. For their intellectual support and challenge around research matters I would particularly like to thank Lynne Angus, Sophia Balamoutsou, Linda Berman, Dee Danchev, Robert Elliott, Judith Fewell, Alison McCamley Finney, Stephen Goss, Soti Grafanaki, Colin Kirkwood, Gordon Lynch, Linda Machin, Dave Mearns, David Rennie, John Sherry and Les Woods. My wife Julia, and daughters Kate, Emma and Hannah have been a constant source of love, encouragement and reminders of the need to 'get a life' that transcends both research and practice.

1

The Nature of Practitioner Research in Counselling

Do you sometimes read research articles in counselling and psychotherapy journals and think that these articles seem to bear no relationship to what you do as a counsellor?

In your work as a counsellor, do you find that there are times when you just feel that you do not know why something is happening, and really want to know more?

Do you occasionally think that it would be useful to know more about how other counsellors deal with similar clients or problems, and what is or is not effective for them?

When you read theoretical books and articles, do you sometimes have the sense that what you are being offered is little more than an uncritical rendering of what Freud, Rogers, Winnicott or other legendary figures wrote many years ago? Do you have a sense that these books are telling you what you already know?

Has your growing experience as a counsellor revealed to you the existence of paradoxes or contradictions in your approach?

If your answers to these questions are 'yes', then it may be that you are ready to embark on practitioner research. The aim of this chapter is to provide an outline of the main features and principles of practitioner research in counselling. Later chapters examine different areas of application of this approach.

There has been a significant increase in the volume of counselling research over the last 20 years. However, although more research is being carried out and published, it is hard to see that it is making much of an impact on practice. The circulation of research journals is meagre, in relation to the number of active counsellors. In surveys of psychotherapists in the USA (Morrow-Bradley and Elliott, 1986; Cohen et al., 1986), books and articles on research were given low ratings in terms of relevance for practice, in comparison with sources of information and learning such as colleagues, supervisors, personal therapy and clients. Given that psychotherapists in the USA undergo a highly research-oriented training, leading to the award of PhD, it seems certain that counsellors and psychotherapists in other countries would report even lower levels of use of research information. All in all, there is little evidence in counselling of concrete examples of policy and practice being influenced by research. This is not the situation in other human service professions, such as nursing, medicine and social work, where research results can result in quite basic reappraisal of areas of practice. In counselling and psychotherapy, by contrast, there would appear to be a distinct gap between research and practice.

The research–practice 'gap' can be understood in part as arising from the different preoccupations and needs of practitioners and researchers. Counsellors engaged in clinical activity necessarily focus mainly on the issues presented by individual clients, and can find it difficult to apply findings or conclusions derived from research on groups or populations. Also, research results are seldom precise enough to be applied in individual cases. A clinician needs to know what to do *now*, with this specific client, whereas research studies on the whole yield knowledge that is generalised and schematic.

The 'gap' can only be partially explained by the contrasting roles of practitioner/clinician and researcher. The question can be asked – why are researchers not more interested in practice? Over the course of the twentieth century, the advancement of scientific knowledge has been associated with a clear distinction between 'pure' and 'applied' scientific research. 'Pure' research is given higher status and value within the academic community, particularly research which corresponds to the methods and assumptions of the natural sciences, such as physics and chemistry. Within society, universities have historically been the location for most scientific inquiry, and anyone working within a university has received strong signals that theory and pure research is rewarded, while applied research and community work is a marginal activity. There has therefore been a strong 'pull' away from practice-oriented research in university staff and in the students they supervise and teach. This situation is changing. The new information technologies mean that both knowledge and knowledge skills are distributed more widely across society. No longer does one need actually to visit a university library in order to keep up to date with the published literature. The higher education system itself has become more differentiated, with some universities or departments explicitly prioritising applied work. There is also a greater breadth of channels for disseminating research findings. So, although there are still strong forces that devalue practitioner research, there are also important trends in the opposite direction.

The majority of studies that are published in counselling journals are not primarily motivated by immediate practical or clinical questions. A great many published studies in the counselling literature are derived from PhD research carried out by students on clinical or counselling psychology programmes in the USA. The priority for these students is to do research that demonstrates their competence in critical academic thinking and analysis of data. The clinical competence and awareness of these students are assessed in other ways, and there is no requirement that their dissertation research should enhance their practice. Another group of published studies is generated by the activities of people in academic positions in universities. Almost all of these people are to a greater or lesser extent practitioners, but their clinical role is secondary to their academic role. As academics, they are expected to contribute to what I would call 'big' research. There are two kinds of 'big' research. First, and most common, there are individuals or groups of academics who work over many years to establish the validity of the particular methodological or theoretical perspective with which they are identified. Beutler and Crago (1991), Dryden (1996) and Hoshmand and Martin (1994) give examples of this type of research programme. Second, there are government-funded research groups which conduct studies of issues considered to be crucial to social and health policy-making.

The best recent example of this type of programme has been the large study in the USA, sponsored by the National Institute of Mental Health, comparing the effectiveness of brief psychotherapy and drug treatment for patients suffering from depression (Elkin, 1994).

'Big' research is always conducted within a political context. There is fierce competition for research funding in all countries, and policy-oriented research studies have to be set up in a way that will be persuasive to those who hold the purse-strings. Even programmes of research which attract little or no funding can be associated with high levels of competitiveness, as researchers wield publications and conference presentations in a battle for prestige and status within the research community. The point here is that, for many researchers who publish their work in counselling journals, relevance for practice can be relatively low on their agenda. At the risk of exaggeration, it could be said that the priority for doctoral students is to get their degree, for academic researchers it is to gain the esteem of their professional peers, and for policy researchers the priority is to press the right buttons to keep the funding flowing.

One of the aims of this book is to challenge the domination of counselling research by researchers. In the end, counselling is a practical activity. *Practitioner research* is research carried out by practitioners for the purpose of advancing their own practice. Some of the key characteristics of practitioner research in counselling are:

- the research question is born out of personal experience and a 'need to know';
- the goal of the research is to produce knowledge that makes a difference to practice;
- throughout the research, the investigator uses his or her reflexive self-awareness to gain access to the underlying or implicit meanings of the study;
- each research project is relatively limited in scope, to fit the realities of the time and resources available to someone who is primarily a practitioner;
- the researcher actively addresses the moral and ethical issues associated with the combination of researcher and practitioner roles, and with a process of inquiry into the experience of perhaps vulnerable or fragile informants;

- the research is designed in such a way as to enhance and facilitate the counselling process;
- the researcher retains 'ownership' of the knowledge that is produced; the findings represent subjective, personal knowing as well as objective, impersonal or 'factual' knowledge;
- the results of research are written and disseminated in ways that are consistent with the principles and values of practitioner research outlined above.

The practical implications of these statements are explored in the following chapters. Some of the main differences between practitioner research and 'big' research are highlighted in Box 1.1.

It is important to avoid any urge to characterise one approach as 'right' and the other as 'wrong'. Both of these approaches to inquiry have a part to play in advancing knowledge and understanding about counselling. Linehan (1997) has argued that the development of any new form of mental health intervention should follow three stages. Stage 1 consists of the *discovery* and pilot evaluation of new treatments. Stage 2 concentrates on evaluating the efficacy of these approaches in controlled situations. This stage focuses on the task of *verifying* whether or not approaches that appear to have potential actually represent an improvement on previously available therapeutic methods. Stage 3 then addresses issues arising from the *application* of these approaches in a variety of settings and contexts. Crucial questions arising at this stage also include the effectiveness of methods of training and supervising practitioners using the new approach. This model of stages of treatment research suggests complementary roles for practitioner-researchers and full-time university-based research teams. In counselling, virtually all new ideas have emerged from discoveries made by practitioners. There is therefore a key role for practitioner-researchers in describing and documenting new ideas and techniques, and carrying out small-scale pilot studies or case studies into these innovative approaches. At stage 3 of the model, practitioners again have an invaluable role to play in reporting on the applicability of new approaches in their own work settings, and in monitoring the effectiveness of training and supervision provision. It is really only in stage 2 that large-scale outcome studies are logically necessary. Linehan (1997) suggests that in the past, therapy research has placed too much weight on stage 2

Box 1.1

Practitioner research and 'big' research: differing emphases

Mainstream, 'big' research	*Practitioner research*
mainly positivist, quasi-experimental, quantitative	methodologically pluralistic, using quantitative and qualitative methods as appropriate
written up non-reflexively, in standard journal article format	use of a wider range of communication formats, including first-person reports
research teams staffed by employees who do not necessarily share a passionate commitment to the research concept	researcher or group of researchers display high level of 'ownership' of the topic
usually large samples of subjects	usually intensive analysis of small samples
externally funded or assessed	supported from personal or local resources
verificationist, hypothesis-testing	heuristic: goal of generating new insights
emphasis on theoretical and methodological issues	emphasis on the development of practical understandings

---

'big' research, to the neglect of the more preparatory earlier stage of discovery-oriented research, with the result that a great deal of public money has been spent on evaluating approaches that have not been adequately described, standardised or pilot tested.

The Linehan (1997) model makes it clear that there is an essential role for practitioners within the field of counselling research. Her model also specifies the stages in the research cycle where practitioners can do useful work, and the stage at which a more resource-intensive strategy is required.

The knowledge-in-context model

Most research in counselling and psychotherapy is written in such a way as to make claims for the general truth of the results and conclusions that it generates. This approach to research is based on a mainstream, 'positivist' approach which assumes that there is no fundamental difference between the knowledge produced by the physical sciences, such as physics, chemistry and biology, and the human sciences such as sociology, psychology or anthropology. For positivists, there exists an objective reality, and the goal of research is to act as a 'mirror' to that reality in as objective and reliable a fashion as possible. A good summary of the key features of positivism can be found in von Wright (1993) and Kolakowski (1993). Institutionally, research into counselling and psychotherapy has been located in psychology and psychiatry departments which have strongly favoured a positivist, quantitative mode of inquiry.

In recent years, there has been a growing chorus of objections to the positivist approach to research in counselling and psychotherapy, from writers such as Polkinghorne (1991) and Rennie (1994d), and many others. It is important to acknowledge, however, that none of these criticisms is new. The voice of *human science* (to use the term coined by the philosopher Wilhelm Dilthey) or *qualitative research* (the currently favoured label) has always existed in opposition to the positivist model. There is nothing new or 'progressive' about non-positivist approaches to knowledge. In fact, the human science style of inquiry draws on very old traditions, such as hermeneutic interpretation of texts, the study of rhetoric, and philosophical debate. A more appropriate perspective on what has happened in the social and human sciences is that the tremendous success of experimental methods and statistics which was first made possible by advances in statistical theory, and was then given further impetus by the invention of calculating machines, computers and finally PCs, has led to an understandable fascination with the potential of quantitative methods. These methods have also been appropriated to the interests of powerful political groups (statistics originated from the need to measure the possessions and income of the state). What seems to have happened in recent years is that more of a balance has been achieved, in which the strengths and limitations of both quantitative and interpretive approaches are acknowledged.

It seems to me that one of the crucial understandings which has emerged as the magic spell cast by positivism has gradually dissipated, is the recognition that a reductionist, hypothesis-testing model is fundamentally flawed as an approach to constructing *practical* knowledge of persons. To carry out research that is relevant to practice, it is necessary that investigations are placed in a context of practice. Virtually all academics and researchers who carry out investigations of counselling outcome and process are themselves practitioners. If you ask these people to talk about the relationship between research and practice in their own work, you will usually find that the discipline of collecting and analysing research data on topics of interest has had a huge impact on what they do as practitioners. But, when these same researchers write up what they have found, they are all too often constrained by the perceived demands of the academic establishment to report their results in an abstract, impersonal and disembodied style. The effect of this is to make it impossible for the reader to understand why the researcher did the research in the first place, what it meant to him or her, and how it influenced their subsequent practice.

If research in counselling is to be usable and applicable, it needs to be presented as knowledge-in-context. Research findings that are written as if by a voice from nowhere are no use to us. To be able to decide whether research findings are applicable to our work situation, we need to know a lot about the situation in which they were produced. We need to know about the motivation of the person who carried out the research, what he or she learned, and their process of arriving at new understandings. We also want to know about what the researcher did not learn, and the areas of ambiguity that still exist for him or her. In a research report, the counselling approach used, and the clients involved, should be recognisable in terms of counselling interventions we might use, and clients we might work with. My prediction is that, when research reports are written with these criteria in mind, then practitioners will enjoy reading them, will be informed by what they read, and that the research–practice gap will gradually disappear.

But to produce research reports of this kind means reconceptualising the research process. For too long the research literature in counselling and psychotherapy has been dominated by the methods and assumptions of psychology and medicine. These methods and assumptions have their place in counselling research, but represent only one way of knowing and telling. In the social sciences there are many other traditions that are of value to counselling researchers, encompassing a concern with reflexivity, a willingness to produce detailed ethnographic descriptions of experience and human action, systematic analysis of single cases, and use of different forms of writing. Some of these alternative approaches are described in the following chapters. When applied to counselling research, what they produce is a type of research characterised by a 'situated' or 'local' knowledge, rather than an attempt to construct abstract universal truths. This kind of research yields knowledge-in-context, where the context includes not only the personal experience and intentionality of the researcher, but also their social, cultural, political and historical world.

The scientist-practitioner model

It is important to be aware of both the similarities and differences between the knowledge-in-context practitioner research approach being described here, and the *scientist-practitioner* model which is frequently cited in the counselling and psychotherapy literature (see, for example, Barlow, Hayes and Nelson, 1984). The notion of the scientist-practitioner emerged during the 1950s in the USA as part of various discussions that led to the formation of the profession of clinical psychology. At a series of conferences held to bring together the views both of clinicians and of academic psychologists, a consensus developed that it was desirable that those who called themselves clinical *psychologists* should practice in a way that was informed by scientific research, and should also carry out their clinical work in a style that was consistent with scientific scrutiny and contributed to the generation of valid scientific data. In reality, what this meant was that clinical psychology training was based in universities, that research skills and completing a research thesis became important components of that training, and that clinicians were encouraged to publish research studies. The research genre that is particularly associated with the scientist-practitioner model is the 'n = 1' single subject case study design (see Chapter 2). This is a form of research in which the pattern of change in a client is followed up by administering a standard measurement instrument, or making observations of the client's behaviour, at regular intervals.

It is clear that the concept of the scientist-practitioner is embedded in the cognitive-behavioural approach to therapy which has dominated American (and to some extent, British) clinical psychology. It is similar to the approach being advocated in this book in so far as it takes the position that it is valuable for practitioners to be actively engaged in research. However, the knowledge-in-context perspective incorporates a somewhat broader view of research, drawing on the contributions of many different research traditions, and requires consideration of both the social and organisational setting of the research, and the identity and reflexive responsiveness of the researcher. Also, while the scientist-practitioner model suggests that data collection should be integrated with client work as a matter of routine, the angle taken in this book is that while that type of case study research can be valuable, it is only one among many research strategies, and may not be appropriate for all counsellors or counselling agencies.

The moral dimension of practitioner inquiry

One of the limitations of the scientist-practitioner model is that, in espousing a conventional scientific approach, it necessarily must adopt at the same time a stance of value neutrality in relation to social issues. The value base of mainstream scientific inquiry emphasises such principles as rationality, objectivity and rigour, in the service of advancing human well-being through the accumulation of knowledge. The passion, partiality or interest of the scientist is supposed to be fenced off and kept to one side, to avoid the introduction of subjective 'bias' into the process of collecting and analysing 'data'. Now, while there have been and will continue to be great debates within the social science community over the role of values in social inquiry, there are perhaps some brief observations that can be made here on this topic. First, it will be very clear to any counsellor or psychotherapist that the attempt to draw a fixed line between the rational aspects of human experience on the one hand, and the emotional and interpersonal on the other, is doomed to failure. Everything that we do, even in the role of scientist, is shaped by our world-view, motivations, attachments, sense of self and so on. From a therapist's perspective, the choice of becoming a scientist, or the choice of method and area of study, are all shaped by factors of personal history. There is just no way of creating a wholly rational enclave. The second point that can be made is that, even if a *mainly* value-free space can be constructed within which to pursue the 'natural' sciences such as chemistry or biology, such an approach to the human or social sciences would run the risk of missing the point. The actual subject matter of the human sciences is intrinsically linked to the core question of 'how should we live our lives?' The emergence and expansion of the social sciences and psychology in the twentieth century can be seen as a reaction to the eclipse of religious certainties and communal traditions in Europe, and the need to create another cultural arena within which a conversation about alternative notions of the 'good' could be carried forward.

The relevance of these issues to practitioner research in counselling can be appreciated through consideration of a recent paper by Christopher (1996), in which he outlines what he calls the 'inescapable moral visions' of counselling. The emphasis on passion, values and committed 'partiality' in research is informed by recent developments in feminist research methods (see Mies, 1993; Olesen, 1994).

Some of the implications of accepting that there is a moral dimension to practitioner inquiry can be briefly sketched out here, and will be expanded in later sections of the book:

- when carrying out an evaluation of the effectiveness of a counselling service, a moral perspective requires that the consequences of the evaluation for different 'stakeholders' are anticipated in advance;
- a legitimate aim of research is to empower users of services;
- it is helpful for readers of research to know about the values of a researcher/author in relation to the issues about which he or she is writing;
- when developing a critique of the literature on a topic, it is necessary to take account of the political context within which the research was carried out;
- it is legitimate in research to take a stance of 'conscious partiality', for example to argue from an anti-oppressive position in relation to racism or sexism;
- research encompasses analysis of the moral issues faced by practitioners.

These are just some of the moral themes that run through practitioner inquiry. To begin to be able to address these issues, it is necessary for counsellors undertaking research to explore their values, and to locate themselves within the moral traditions of their culture. It is also necessary for the counselling and psychotherapy community as a whole to become more active in maintaining a moral discourse that will facilitate this kind of discussion. For too long, moral issues in counselling have been relegated to the realm of codes of professional ethics. While professional ethical codes are undoubtedly necessary, they represent a somewhat static and rigid format within which to explore moral concerns. Good examples of how moral considerations can be made relevant to counselling as a whole, and not merely to the regulation of professional conduct, can be found in Christopher (1996) and Cushman (1995).

It is perhaps worth noting that one of the few areas of counselling where research has made a tangible impact on practice has been in the moral domain. Over the last 20 years, counsellors have become much more aware of ethical issues, and professional associations have become much more effective in responding to ethical breaches. This whole movement has been greatly influenced by the findings of research studies carried out by Masson (1988), Pope and Bouhoutsos (1986) and others.

Practitioner research as heuristic inquiry

An approach to research that has much to offer counselling practitioners is the *heuristic inquiry* model developed by Moustakas (1967, 1990a, b). The general process of heuristic research can be described as arising from some aspect of practice or personal engagement with the world:

> Heuristic inquiry is a process that begins with a question or problem which the researcher seeks to illuminate or answer. The question is one that has been a personal challenge and puzzlement in the search to understand one's self and the world in which one lives. The heuristic process is autobiographical, yet with virtually every question that matters there is also a social – and perhaps universal – significance. (Moustakas, 1990a: 15)

In his books and articles on heuristic research, Moustakas outlines a research process that is similar to a personal journey. There is an immersion in the research question, which leads into a period of personal struggle, a 'passionate, disciplined commitment to remain with a question intensely and continuously until it is illuminated or answered' (p. 15). Following illumination, the new insights need to be verified against external observations, and brought together into a new synthesis or statement of understanding.

Although some of Moustakas' writing adopts a humanistic psychology rhetoric that will not be to everyone's taste, I would suggest that, perhaps better than anyone else, he captures the challenge of knowing that is intrinsic to personal research. His focus is not on method or technique, but on the *need to know* and the sense of being driven on and on until some clarity is achieved. And again, perhaps also more than anyone else, he is willing to acknowledge just how emotional and passionate this kind of struggle can be.

The question of validity in practitioner research

The issue of validity represents a fundamental and recurring problem in research. How can we know that the findings reported in a study are reliable and true? If our practice, or policy decisions, are to be informed by research, then it is important to have confidence that the results of the research we use are based in reality rather than distorted by the individual fantasies and biases of those who carried out the research.

A great deal of time, thought and effort has been devoted to the problem of validity in research. Within the tradition of quantitative research, which relies on numbers and statistics, there are well-established techniques for estimating the reliability and validity of measurements and the extent to which they can be generalised. Information on quantitative validity criteria can be found in any of the textbooks listed in the Appendix. In qualitative research, which relies on the analysis of written or spoken verbal accounts of experience, a rather different set of validity criteria have needed to be developed. The clearest statement of how the concept of validity can be addressed in qualitative research is in a paper by Stiles (1993).

Practitioner research draws upon a wide range of established qualitative and quantitative methods (introduced in the following chapters), and therefore needs to make use of the appropriate validity criteria associated with these approaches. However, there are additional criteria which apply to practitioner research. It has already been suggested that to be able to develop knowledge that enriches practice, it is necessary to be as explicit as possible about the organisational and personal context within which the research was carried out. This principle leads to the following criteria for practitioner research:

■ a good practitioner research study will provide sufficient descriptive detail of clients, counsellors, the counselling approach, setting, social and political context, etc., for readers to be able to make informed judgements regarding the similarity and applicability of the study to their own practice;
■ a good practitioner research study will provide sufficient information on the personal engagement of the researcher(s) in the study, and their heuristic process, for the reader to be able to make a judgement concerning authenticity, 'owner-ship' and personal integrity.

The first of these criteria might be called (in the absence of any better label) *descriptive* validity. It is similar to the notion of 'ecological validity' used in experimental research, and to the stance taken by many qualitative researchers (see Wolcott, 1994) that a good study depends first and foremost on accurate and sensitive description of the phenomena being investigated. The second of these criteria might be called *personal* validity, in that it reflects the personal trustworthiness or credibility of the researcher. A notion of personal validity is abhorrent to many researchers and academics, who would wish to assert very strongly that it is adherence to a set of rational procedures, along with critical counter-checking of observations by other research-ers, that leads in the end to valid knowledge.

It is important to be clear that the criterion of personal validity does not stand on its own, but is one source of value alongside several others. If a study was to be written up that relied solely on claims to personal integrity and authenticity, without backing up its results in any other way, it would be unlikely to be seen as convincing or credible. A study that relied only on personal validity would come across as if the writer was saying 'This is true because I say it is true, or because I *know* it to be true.' There is no space here for ambiguity, alternative interpretations, or dialogue. On the other hand, at present most studies are written up in a way that gives little or no space for personal validity to be established. I would wish to argue that this greatly diminishes the value of these studies in relation to practice. It seems to me that when a researcher or scholar has inquired deeply into a topic over a period of time, and can be seen to have undergone some version of the stages of heuristic inquiry described by Moustakas (1990a), then inevitably there is *some truth* in what they have to say. Their findings or conclusions are respectable, in the sense of demanding our respect. We may disagree with their conclusions, but if the researcher has provided enough contextual detail then we should be able to arrive at an understanding of how our different views of a situation may co-exist or complement each other. An absence of personal and contextual information can make it impossible ever to gain this kind of level of appreciation of a study.

These practitioner-researcher validity criteria have implications for the way that research is read and critiqued. In conventional 'scientific' research there is a tendency to treat research papers as 'fact modules'. Many reviews of the research literature are organised around statements such as 'Brown (1997) showed that . . .', where the key findings of an (imaginary) Brown (1997) study can be summed up in a few words. The technique of *meta-analysis* (see Bergin and Garfield, 1994) is a means of adding up the findings of many studies by looking purely at their statistical results. If research is written in such a way as to reflect the practitioner-oriented principles described in this chapter, it becomes impossible to regard results as being capable of summary in brief 'sound-bite' form. Developing a critique and summary of a set of papers on a particular issue will require entering into the work of these authors, and arriving at a critical interpretation that reflects the contextual and often ambiguous nature of what they have found.

The relationship between practitioners and full-time researchers

The central argument of this book is that developing a distinctive tradition of practitioner research or practitioner inquiry would strengthen counselling. To create such a tradition requires re-negotiating the types of relationship that exist between practitioners and full-time researchers in universities. At the moment, research-active staff in universities, for the most part see their role as either being that of doing their own research or as teaching research methods to practitioners (who are seen as 'students' rather than as collaborators). The research methods that are taught are heavily influenced by the assumptions and techniques of psychology. For example, all the main counselling research textbooks listed in the Appendix are written by psychologists, and what they recommend are research strategies that will produce papers that can be published in conventional psychological journals.

The intention of this book is to turn around the relationship between practitioners and academics, so that academics become consultants and resource providers but practitioners remain in control of their process of personal inquiry. It seems to me that, once the hegemony of statistical methods is overthrown and the principle of methodological pluralism (Howard, 1983) is accepted, there are so many methodologies that can potentially be applied in counselling research that it will be beyond the scope of a single training course to cover them. In a situation where there are so many alternative genres of research, who decides? My answer to this question is that when a practitioner brings to a research project his or her passionate need to know, and personal commitment of time and resources, then he or she must choose the method. One of the key issues centres around having a sense of what kind of research 'product' will make a difference, will have an impact on practice. Only the practitioner, or group of practitioners working together in an agency or clinic, will know this. Another criterion for practitioner research is that the results of the inquiry remain grounded in practice in a form that the practitioner is able to 'own' these results. Again, this can only happen when practitioners are engaging in research that flows from their everyday activity and purposes as counsellors, rather than being imposed from outside.

Practitioner research in counselling and psychotherapy draws upon existing research methods, but integrates these methods with the ways of knowing that counsellors already possess – reflexivity, collaborative sense-making, finding meaning in feeling. This kind of work leads to a different approach to doing research and writing up research reports. So far, there are relatively few examples of a distinctive practitioner tradition in counselling and psychotherapy research, outside of psycho-analysis. At present, practitioner studies tend to be found around the edge of the research literature. Some examples of well-known and readily accessible published studies which show the potential for research and practice to gain from each other are:

- The work of Carl Rogers and his colleagues in the 1950s and early 1960s. During this period, the foundations of person-centred counselling were established through a constant interplay between theory, research and practice. The book which illustrates the practitioner basis of this research most clearly is Rogers and Stevens (1968).
- The analysis of the social, historical and cultural origins of psychotherapy carried out by Philip Cushman. Here, it is possible to see how a practising therapist has struggled to make sense of some of the contradictions and limitations of his profession by constructing a compelling account of how psychotherapy has reflected and amplified social forces in the USA, yet has continually denied the social implications of therapeutic practice. The book which brings all this together is Cushman (1995).
- The qualitative studies of the client's experience of therapy carried out by David Rennie and his colleagues through the 1980s and 1990s. Most of the published papers arising from this research do not particularly focus on implications for practice. However, Rennie's (1998) recent book clearly shows the interplay between the research and his practice as a counsellor and trainer.
- The development of *process-experiential* therapy has been built around a process of examining personal practice through research. The book which most clearly exemplifies the interconnectedness of research and practice in this approach to counselling is Greenberg, Rice and Elliott (1993). One of the most interesting things about this set of studies lies in the way that those involved needed to work out practice-sensitive methods of inquiry that would allow them to learn about what *really* happened when they used their approach with clients. The research techniques of task analysis (Greenberg, 1984b, 1992) and comprehensive process analysis (Elliott, 1984) opened up new aspects of the therapeutic process.

There are some common themes running through these examples of practitioner research. First, all of these practitioner-researchers found the need to develop new methods of inquiry

---

Box 1.2

Practitioner research: some exemplar studies

1   For several years, Eric Hall and his colleagues in the Centre for Human Relations at the University of Nottingham have been running Masters courses in counselling and human relations which emphasise the use of experiential group work. In Hall et al. (1997), they report on the results of a survey of participants' perceptions of the impact of different types of group workshop. In their analysis of this data they focus particularly on the question of whether development groups can harm as well as help participants.

2   Peter Dale is a counsellor employed by a national voluntary organisation which works with child abuse issues. Interested in gaining a better understanding of how adults who were abused as children view counselling services, he carried out interviews with child abuse survivors and their counsellors. It was clear that some clients had received counselling which was damaging, although others had benefited greatly. There was a diversity of experiences in the client group, which called into question the meaningfulness of 'child abuse survivor' as a way of categorising such people. This research is reported in Dale, Allen and Measor (1998).

3   How confident and competent are counsellors in responding to the needs of clients who report problems in the area of alcohol misuse? Alcohol abuse is a major social and health issue, and yet few generic counsellors appear to have received training in this area. Wheeler and Turner (1997) explored the extent of this deficit in counsellor competence through a questionnaire distributed to a large number of counsellors in the Midlands, and make useful recommendations for training and practice.

---

that would allow them to study what they knew to be important. They did not merely adopt 'off the shelf' pre-existing methods. Second, all of them used theory as a means both of guiding their research and of knitting together what they found. These were not mere blind 'fact-finding' exercises. Third, all of them have, to a greater or lesser degree, been open about the personal meaning of their work. All of them have written reflexively about their research and placed it in context.

The research by Rogers, Rennie, Cushman and others has achieved international recognition, while remaining firmly based in practice concerns. Some examples of smaller-scale, yet equally valuable, studies by practitioners are presented in Box 1.2.

Conclusion

The aim of this chapter has been to introduce some of the central features of practitioner research in counselling, and to explain why such an approach is necessary. In later chapters, these themes will be traced through the different phases of a research study: refining a question, designing the study, collecting and analysing data, and writing. There is also, in the next chapter, an exploration of the different types, or *genres* of research which comprise the contemporary knowledge base of counselling and psychotherapy, and a discussion of the extent to which existing research genres can contribute to a practitioner-oriented approach.

Further reading

The items on the reading list below explore different aspects of the tensions and debates that have existed between research and practice in counselling. Dryden (1996) contains chapters by a number of well-known researchers who were asked to 'spell out the practical applications of their findings'. As Dryden (1996: xi) noted, 'virtually all contributors had difficulty with this task'. The other papers in the list examine how and why this difficulty has arisen, and what can be done about it. Pilgrim (1983) is particularly trenchant in his criticisms of the inadequacy of mainstream approaches to research.

Dryden, W. (ed.) (1996) *Research in Counselling and Psychotherapy: Practical Applications.* London: Sage.

Elliott, R. (1983) 'Fitting process research to the practising psychotherapist', *Psychotherapy*, 20 (1): 47–55.

Firth, J., Shapiro, D. and Parry, G. (1986) 'The impact of research on the practice of psychotherapy', *British Journal of Psychotherapy*, 2 (3): 169–79.

Gendlin, E. (1986) 'What comes after traditional psychotherapy research?' *American Psychologist*, 41 (2): 131–6.

Henry, W.P. (1998) 'Science, politics, and the politics of science: the use and misuse of empirically validated treatment research', *Psychotherapy Research*, 8: 126–40.

McLeod, J. (1994) 'The research agenda for counselling', *Counselling*, 5 (1): 41–3.

Mellor-Clark, J. and Shapiro, D. (1995) 'It's not what you do . . . it's the way that you do it: the inception of an evaluative research culture in Relate Marriage Guidance', *Changes*, 13 (3): 201–7.

Morrow-Bradley, C. and Elliott, R. (1986) 'Utilization of psychotherapy research by practising psychotherapists', *American Psychologist*, 41 (2): 188–97.

Parry, G. (1992) 'Improving psychotherapy services: applications of research, audit and evaluation', *British Journal of Clinical Psychology*, 31: 3–19.

Rennie, D.L. (1994) 'Human science and counselling psychology; closing the gap between science and practice', *Counselling Psychology Quarterly*, 7: 235–50.

Safran, J.D., Greenberg, L.S. and Rice, L.N. (1988) 'Integrating psychotherapy research and practice: modeling the change process', *Psychotherapy*, 25: 1–17.

Strupp, H.H. (1989) 'Psychotherapy: can the practitioner learn from the researcher?' *American Psychologist*, 44: 717–24.

Treacher, A. (1983) 'On the utility or otherwise of psychotherapy research', in D. Pilgrim (ed.) *Psychology and Psychotherapy: Current Trends and Issues*. London: Routledge and Kegan Paul.

2

Types of Research

One of the great strengths of counselling and psychotherapy research at the present time lies in the degree of acceptance of *methodological pluralism* (Howard, 1983; Goss and Mearns, 1997 a, b). Here, the idea of 'pluralism' refers to diversity in research methods. A search of the published literature reveals statistical papers alongside qualitative and narrative studies, and large-scale surveys or experiments alongside single-case studies or small-scale intensive interview investigations. In contrast to the situation in the 1970s and even 1980s, in which the vast majority of research output relied on quantitative methods, there is now much more openness and diversity in the type of studies that are being carried out. This is undoubtedly conducive to the production of creative, interesting and relevant research. On the other hand, the range of different research models or genres that are currently being employed can be confusing for novice researchers. It can sometimes seem as if there are just too many choices.

The aim of this chapter is to review the research genres that are most widely used by counselling researchers. There are at least three reasons why it is important to be aware of the distinctions between different styles or genres of research:

- Different research genres represent distinctive traditions of inquiry, each of which has its own logic for justifying the methodological stance and choices that its adherents have adopted. What may seem reasonable and valid in one genre may make little sense in another. For example, in a quantitative outcome study it is a good idea to obtain as large a sample of subjects as possible. In a qualitative process study,

---

Box 2.1

Major genres of counselling research

quantitative outcome studies
client satisfaction studies
qualitative outcome studies
quantitative process studies
qualitative process research
surveys
clinical case studies
'n = 1' single case studies
research on practitioners
cultural/historical studies
economic/cost-effectiveness research
compiling protocols and treatment manuals

---

by contrast, a large sample would almost inevitably lead to a superficial and unsatisfactory analysis and set of conclusions.
- Although there are some general research skills that are common to all modes of inquiry (e.g. a capacity to draw conclusions from data), each research genre is associated with its own distinctive set of skills and knowledge base.
- When designing and carrying out a piece of research, it is usually sensible and desirable to locate it within a single genre, rather than trying to combine approaches. Mixing methods can be valuable in some instances, but runs the danger of producing a piece of work that does not really meet the criteria for any of its constituent methods, and can end up seeming to be just a muddle. Particularly when beginning research, it is advisable to stick to a single genre.

Box 2.1 provides a list of the research genres that are most frequently employed within counselling and psychotherapy research. Choosing a research design or genre for any particular study is always problematic. It is essential to recognise that each method has its own intrinsic strengths and weaknesses: there can be no 'perfect' piece of research.

Although there is a complex array of alternative styles or genres of research, it is also possible to make a rather more simple and sweeping distinction between *quantitative* and *qualitative*

Box 2.2

Contrast between different research traditions

Qualitative/'new paradigm' approaches	*Traditional/experimental quantitative approaches*
holistic	reductionist
elucidate meanings	measurement of variables
sensitive, accurate description	statistical techniques
look for categories actually used by people	impose researcher's categories
inductive	deductive
heuristic	theory-testing
seek authenticity	seek validity and reliability
seek to minimise illusion	seek to minimise error
reflexive	other-directed
researcher as tool	techniques as tools
co-informants/collaborators	research 'subjects'
negotiation of outcomes	outcome decided by researcher
research design evolves	rigid initial research design
methods: interviews, open-ended questionnaires	methods: experiments, questionnaires, coding schemes
research genres: qualitative, grounded theory, narrative, phenomenological, human inquiry, feminist	research genres: quantitative outcome and process studies, surveys

---

approaches to research. Some of the key characteristics of each of these broad approaches or 'paradigms' are listed in Box 2.2. It is important to recognise that the qualitative and quantitative research traditions are located in contrasting, and competing, philosophical perspectives. Quantitative research is based on what is known as a *positivist* view of science, which assumes the existence of a knowable objective reality. Qualitative research is derived from a *social constructionist* perspective (Gergen, 1985; 1994) which regards the reality we experience as created by the actions, beliefs and cultural history of a group of people: there is no single 'objective' truth but instead a variety of 'local' knowledges or truths. These two philosophical perspectives are clearly quite different from each other, and they translate into very distinctive research traditions. It is not at all easy to carry out research that bridges the quantitative–qualitative divide, and so most researchers concentrate their efforts on conducting *either* quantitative *or* qualitative research, but not both at the same time. On the other hand, it is possible to argue that positivist objectivity and social constructionist relativism reflect contrasting, but equally valid aspects of the human condition, and that a truly adequate form of counselling research would honour both of these viewpoints and attempt to integrate quantitative and qualitative methods. Indeed, this is possible (see Brannen, 1992). The tension between the quantitative and qualitative traditions is discussed in more detail in McLeod (1994b).

In the following sections of this chapter, the type of research that is carried out within different genres is described through the use of exemplar studies. References are also given about where to gain further information about how to carry out research studies within each of the genres.

Quantitative outcome studies

Outcome studies focus on the *effectiveness* of counselling by measuring change in key variables (e.g. levels of anxiety, depression, self-esteem) before and after counselling (and at follow-up if possible). The issues involved in carrying out quantitative outcome studies are examined in more detail in Chapter 9, and some of the statistical skills required in this kind of work are described in Chapter 7. It is difficult for practitioners to carry out the more ambitious forms of outcome study (such as randomised controlled trials – see Chapter 9) because these methods require substantial numbers of 'subjects' and a fairly high degree of control over the research situation (for example, randomly allocating clients to different treatment conditions, requiring counsellors to adhere to a 'treatment manual'). Quantitative outcome studies tend to have little or no place for reflexive self-awareness on the part of the researcher-practitioner. The aim is, instead, to aspire to a detached, 'objective' approach to data collection. Practitioners interested in carrying out studies of the effectiveness of their work may find it more meaningful to carry out a *client satisfaction* study or an '*n = 1*' study (both described below). However, groups of practitioners can work together to pursue *naturalistic* quantitative outcome studies. These are studies which measure variables before and after counselling, and at follow up, but where clients are not selected on the basis of diagnostic category or artificially allocated to different treatment groups. In Britain, the best examples of quantitative outcome research are the Sheffield studies conducted by David Shapiro, Michael Barkham and their colleagues (Shapiro et al., 1990), which compared the effectiveness of psychodynamic-interpersonal and cognitive-behavioural approaches to therapy. There have also been several studies of the outcomes of counselling in primary care. Hemmings (1997) and Friedli et al. (1997) are examples of randomised controlled trials of counselling in primary care; Baker et al. (1998) is an example of a naturalistic outcome study in this setting. Wilson et al. (1997) is an interesting example of a naturalistic outcome study of student counselling.

Further information about outcome measures used in this type of research can be found in Chapter 6. It is important to keep in mind that some of the most convincing outcome measures are not questionnaire-based but rely on counting actual behavioural outcomes (see section below on n = 1 studies).

Client satisfaction studies

A client satisfaction study is a piece of research which attempts to evaluate the benefits of counselling by asking clients to complete a questionnaire once they have finished seeing their counsellor. Although such questionnaires may often include items which ask clients to rate many different aspects of behavioural change, there is a tendency for clients to respond mainly in terms of their overall *satisfaction* with the therapy. So, while the researcher may be interested in different elements of the therapy such as the client's relationship with the counsellor, his perceptions of the environment and administration of the counselling agency, and the extent to which his problems have been ameliorated or got worse, in reality the answers clients give are heavily influenced by a general satisfaction factor. Moreover, clients usually give very positive ratings. This may be because they have genuinely been helped, but alternatively these ratings may result from gratitude at having someone listen to them and take them seriously for several hours (perhaps a rare experience in our society), or because less satisfied clients are less likely to complete questionnaires. For whatever reason, client satisfaction data tends to be skewed to the positive end of the scale, which can make it difficult to discriminate between sub-groups of more or less satisfied clients, or tease out those factors which contribute to good outcomes. Various efforts have been made by researchers to encourage clients to make more balanced responses, or to be more open about their criticisms of counselling (see Leiper and Field, 1993; McLennan, 1990). Despite these methodological problems, there are some very positive features of satisfaction studies. They are inexpensive and unobtrusive, and give all clients a chance to have their say. All counsellors and counselling agencies should be collecting satisfaction data, as a basic form of accountability, no matter what other types of research they are carrying out. Further information on the mechanics of designing satisfaction questionnaires can be found in Chapter 9. A useful example of a client satisfaction study is the Sloboda et al. (1993) study of workplace counselling.

Qualitative outcome studies

Quantitative outcome studies, whether using standardised measures of anxiety, depression or self-esteem, or employing satisfaction questionnaires, always have the limitation that the experience of the client is forced into categories or constructs chosen by the researcher. This may be administratively convenient, or theoretically justifiable, but it does mean that the picture that emerges from quantitative studies of whether clients benefit or not from counselling is necessarily somewhat abstract and over-simplified. An alternative approach is to *ask* clients about their counselling, collecting their accounts or stories. However, although the *qualitative* approach to counselling research (described more fully in Chapter 8) has been more widely used in recent years, there is still a lack of published qualitative outcome studies. This is a pity, because the 'discovery-oriented' nature of qualitative research has the potential to yield outcome information that could be highly relevant to practice. In principle, qualitative outcome research data can be collected through interviews, focus groups or personal journals kept by clients. Possibly the only readily accessible version of a qualitative outcome study currently available is Howe's (1989) research which involved interviewing people who had completed family therapy. This is not a piece of practitioner research, since Howe was an independent academic evaluator invited in by the family therapy clinic, but it does illustrate an approach to evaluation research which many practitioners would find useful and interesting. Clearly, one of the issues associated with practitioner qualitative outcome studies is that, in most circumstances, it would not be sensible for a counsellor to conduct follow-up interviews with her own clients. Clients might find it more difficult to express their criticisms of counselling to the person who had been their therapist. Also, meeting their therapist again might run the risk of re-entering an actual therapeutic process, which might not be helpful. Some practitioners use the notion of the client as 'consultant' to encourage client feedback after therapy (White and Epston, 1990). In other cases, colleagues from the same agency interview each other's clients (Bischoff et al., 1996). The classic texts on qualitative evaluation (Guba and Lincoln, 1989; Greene, 1994, 1998; Patton, 1990) say nothing about therapy research, but are nevertheless essential reading for anyone seeking to carry out a qualitative outcome study.

Quantitative process studies

Process research seeks to examine the influence of the crucial elements or ingredients of counselling. While outcome studies aim to look at whether counselling is effective, process research focuses on *how* it is effective, what makes it 'work'. In general, process research confronts researchers with some major methodological and ethical problems. For a start, the process of counselling is enormously complex, and disentangling the multiple levels of what is going on (cognitively, emotionally, behaviourally, interpersonally, and so on) can be difficult. Further, access to the process of counselling requires somehow getting a hold of what is happening *during* sessions. While outcome research can be carried out by gathering data before counselling has started, and then once it is finished, process studies involve a journey into the *interior* of therapy (McLeod, 1994b). Such a journey is clearly ethically sensitive. Researchers seeking to measure or quantify the process of counselling have developed two strategies for collecting data. The first is to record sessions and then later to analyse the process data captured in these recordings, or in transcripts based on them. The most widely used method of analysing tapes has been to get teams of people to rate the occurrence, or intensity, of certain factors of interest. Examples of this approach would be the work of Carl Rogers and his colleagues (see Gendlin and Tomlinson, 1967), who rated levels of empathy and depth of experiencing from audio recordings, or Luborsky et al. (1986), who analysed patterns of transference interpretation from transcripts of therapy sessions. Within this style of research, it is essential to use at least two, and preferable three or more, raters to overcome the problem of rater bias. Levels of inter-rater agreement or reliability can be checked, with the consequence that the researcher can be reasonably confident that he or she has in fact measured the 'true' level of empathy or transference actually occurring in the session. These raters need to be trained and rewarded, which can make this kind of research time-consuming and expensive. Hill (1991) provides an excellent guide to using raters in process studies. The other approach to gathering quantitative process data has been to invite clients and/or counsellors to complete questionnaires at the end of sessions. This is a much easier way of gathering data, but of course it relies on the capacity of therapist and client to remember what happened in a session. Also, levels of a process variable such as empathy may vary dramatically across the course of a single session, and a client's rating of the 'average' amount of empathy in that session may therefore not be very informative. Despite these limitations, session ratings and post-session questionnaires have yielded some important insights into the process of counselling, particularly the role of the therapeutic alliance (see Orlinsky, Grawe and Parks, 1994). Many of these studies can be described as 'process-outcome' studies, because the researcher is interested in how specific processes are related to outcome, for example whether high counsellor empathic responding ratings are predictive of good positive therapeutic change. Further details on some of the techniques used in this type of research can be found in Chapter 10.

Qualitative process research

One of the criticisms that can be made in relation to quantitative process studies is that they do not represent a satisfactory method of capturing both the complexity of therapeutic process and also the covert nature of much of what happens on a moment-to-moment basis. The experience of being in a counselling session, as counsellor or client, is that of being immersed in what is happening and of not being consciously aware of many aspects of the process. A new generation of qualitative researcher has, therefore, attempted to develop techniques that would make it more possible to open up the process of counselling in ways that would allow more of this complex experience to be explored. There have been four main qualitative approaches which have been used. First, some researchers have worked qualitatively with session transcripts. Rather than imposing a researcher-defined coding scheme on the transcript, however, these researchers have looked in a more open-ended way at the use of language within the session, and at how the interaction between counsellor and client is mediated by language. Examples of this kind of approach include McLeod and Balamoutsou (1996), who have studied the process by which a client told his story in an initial session. Davis (1986), also working with a transcript of an initial session, analysed the way in which the counsellor redefined a client's way of describing her problem. Madill and Barkham (1997) examined the negotiation of cultural meaning in a single case of successful psychodynamic counselling. The McLeod and Balamoutsou (1996) study was influenced by a method of qualitative research known as *narrative analysis* (Riessman, 1993); the Davis (1986) and Madill and Barkham (1997) studies were based on the method of *discourse analysis*. A second method of collecting qualitative data on therapeutic process has been the use of post-session interviews. Researchers such as Maluccio (1979) have interviewed clients about their experiences during counselling. A third method, which is similar to interviews, has been to ask clients to complete open-ended questionnaires (written accounts) about their experiences or perceptions of different aspects of process. Examples of this type of study are Hill et al. (1996) and Bachelor (1988). A fundamental limitation of post-counselling interviews or open-ended questionnaires is that clients and counsellors may not have a very clear recollection of precisely how they felt at points during a session. This problem has led to the development of a third important qualitative process method, known as Interpersonal Process Recall (Elliott, 1986). This method involves taping a counselling session, and then playing back the tape (or a portion of it) to the client or counsellor within 24 hours. Listening to the tape within this time period is believed to stimulate the recall of the person being interviewed, thus yielding much more detailed, richer qualitative accounts of what was going on during specific moments of the counselling session. Examples of studies which have used IPR are Angus and Rennie (1988, 1989), Elliott (1983a; Elliott and Shapiro, 1992) and Rennie (1990, 1992, 1994a, b, c). One of the common features of any type of qualitative process research that involves interviewing people is the challenge of analysing what people say in these interviews. The two most widely used approaches for making sense of open-ended interview data are grounded theory analysis (Glaser and Strauss, 1967; Strauss and Corbin, 1990; Rennie, Phillips and Quartaro, 1988) and phenomenological analysis (Becker, 1992; Moustakas, 1994). Because of the depth of information that qualitative methods generate, it is only possible to work with data from quite small numbers of research participants or informants. Some of the studies cited in this section are based on data from single cases. Others (for example the studies by David Rennie and by Clara Hill and her colleagues) are based on material from 10–20 cases.

Qualitative process studies are highly relevant to the interests of most practitioners, because they help to develop a sensitive understanding of the nuances of the therapeutic process. People who carry out this type of qualitative research also find that the actual experience of doing the research greatly contributes to their growth as therapists.

Surveys

The survey method is designed for the study of attitudes or beliefs representative of particular social groups. The survey is a well-established method within the social sciences, and there are many excellent books that explain the issues associated with designing and conducting surveys (see Robson, 1993). Essentially, a survey comprises a fixed set of questions which are asked in a standardised fashion, either through the medium of a paper-and-pencil questionnaire (sometimes now also in computerised form) or (less often) through a face-to-face interview. Accurate sampling, usually involving substantial numbers of respondents, is required in order to ensure the generalisability of survey findings. Surveys have been widely used in practitioner-oriented counselling research. There are many examples of surveys which have been carried out into different aspects of counselling. Radley, Cramer and Kennedy (1997) sent questionnaires to 484 General Practitioners in the county of Leicestershire, to explore their attitudes toward the use of counsellors. West and Reynolds (1995) conducted a survey of perceptions of counselling among employees in two hospitals. Liddle (1997) surveyed gay and lesbian users of counselling and psychotherapy about their experiences of therapy. Aubrey, Bond and Campbell (1997) conducted a survey of counsellors working in primary care settings, exploring their perceptions of which categories of patients were suitable or not suitable for counselling. All these studies represent good examples of the issues involved in designing, administering and analysing survey questionnaires.

Clinical case studies

Clinical case studies are reports of single cases based on notes taken by the counsellor after sessions. This kind of case study probably comprises the single most widely used genre of practitioner research, particularly within the psychodynamic approach. The clinical cases written up by Freud, Jung and their colleagues represent the foundations of psychoanalysis and psychodynamic counselling, and journals influenced by these traditions still publish substantial numbers of these articles. The strength of this type of study is that it does not require any data collection over and above the notes that a practitioner would normally keep, and it allows therapists the opportunity to reflect on their practice. There are, however, some serious methodological problems associated with this form of research. First, as Spence (a psychoanalyst) has pointed out, the translation from what actually happens in a session into a set of post-session process notes and then into a case report requires a substantial amount of selection and 'smoothing' of the data (Spence, 1989). The basic case information gets narrowed and selected at every stage, with the result that the eventual reader of the case study can do little else but believe the author's assertion that 'this is the way it was': there is no independent text or source of data as there would be with a recording, interview or questionnaire. The second problem with clinical case studies lies in the ethical principle of informed consent. In all the other research approaches described in this chapter, the client is asked *in advance* whether he or she is willing to participate in a study. By contrast, in a clinical case study it is more usual for the practitioner only to decide to use the case either when it has begun, or when the therapy has been

completed. In either of these situations, seeking informed consent
is far from straightforward. How free is the client to withhold
consent from their therapist? Sometimes, practitioners write up
clinical cases without seeking informed consent. Clients can
become very hurt and angry by this. Alternatively, practitioners
may seek to conceal the identities of clients by radically changing
or 'fictionalising' the case material. This is more ethically justifiable, but introduces other issues, around the validity of the case.
Another ethical problem arises as soon as a therapist starts to think
that she might use a case for research purposes. Might she not
then unconsciously steer the case in the direction of a desired set
of conclusions? It is important not to overstate these ethical issues.
With personal integrity and use of consultation and supervision
they can, in principle, be addressed. The point is that ethical
questions, along with the issue of data 'smoothing', mean that
many people are sceptical about the contribution that clinical case
studies can make to research, other than to describe phenomena
that may then be explored further by other methods. Examples
of clinical case studies can be found in the *British Journal of
Psychotherapy* and *Psychodynamic Counselling* as well as in
psychoanalytic journals.

'n = 1' single case studies

A different way of carrying out research on single cases is to
adopt what has been called the 'n = 1' method (where 'n' refers
to the number of 'subjects'). This is a method that was originally
developed in behavioural, or cognitive-behavioural clinical
psychology, and involves regularly collecting data on some
aspect of the client's behaviour. The aim is to be able to show
how the principal indicators of progress, or therapeutic target
behaviours, change over time. For example, if a client presents
with a problem of over-eating, he might be asked to keep a diary
recording how often he snacked each day, or how much his fat
intake was. A client who had problems in studying might keep a
record of how many minutes each day he spent at his desk. A
counsellor working with a person who needed to comply with a
drug regime might phone every evening to check that pills had
been taken on time. These are all examples of behavioural
change indicators, but the same principle could be applied to
other counselling issues. For example, a depressed client might

---

Box 2.3

Landmark studies on practitioner experiences

Burton, M.V. and Topham, D. (1997) 'Early loss experiences in psychotherapists, Church of England clergy, patients assessed for psychotherapy, and scientists and engineers', *Psychotherapy Research*, 7: 275–300.
Guy, J.D. (1987) *The Personal Life of the Psychotherapist.* New York: Wiley.
Skovholt, T.M. and Ronnestad, M.H. (1992) *The Evolving Professional Self: Stages and Themes in Therapist and Counselor Development.* New York: Wiley.

---

make regular ratings on a mood check list. Further information on this approach can be found in Chapter 9.

Research on practitioners

An important genre of practitioner research comprises studies on the characteristics of practitioners themselves. Among the topics that have been studied are the effectiveness of different types of training experience, the experience of supervision, early childhood experience of therapists, the value of personal therapy, stress and burnout, and adherence to ethical standards. Research into these issues can make an important contribution to improving professional standards. Some of the most influential studies of the role of the therapist are listed in Box 2.3.

Cultural/historical studies

There has been some very useful research into counselling and psychotherapy which has used historical sources to explore the social and cultural background of therapy. The classic early study in this domain was Ellenberger's (1970) massive review of the precursors to Freud. The classic contemporary study in this vein has been Cushman's (1995) analysis of the social, political and economic factors responsible for the growth of psychotherapy in the USA. Another important piece of historical research, in a British context, has been the account of the development of Marriage Guidance by Lewis, Clark and Morgan (1992). Historical studies help to place practice in perspective, and to clarify the links between counselling and other forms of 'identity work' and social care that exist within society. It is perhaps worth noting that the best of these studies, by Cushman (1995), is very much a piece of practitioner research; Phillip Cushman makes his living as a psychotherapist in San Francisco. The final chapters of his book give a clear account of how his historical research has had an impact on his practice.

Economic/cost-effectiveness research

A research genre which is gaining in importance is research which examines the economic costs and benefits of counselling and psychotherapy. The technical complexities of economic cost-benefit analysis means that it is unlikely that any practitioner would be able to embark on this type of study, unless he or she were a member of a research team which included a health economist. Nevertheless, it is vital to know about economic research, because in the future it is probable that it will be increasingly used by governments and other service purchasers to determine whether or not counselling will be made available to particular groups. The book which explains this approach most lucidly is Tolley and Rowland (1995).

Treatment manual research

One of the significant developments in counselling and psycho-therapy research over the last decade has been the advent of the *treatment manual*. Researchers conducting outcome studies have been aware for many years that different counsellors or psychotherapists included in a study as exponents of particular approaches to therapy might not in fact be working in the same way. For example, two therapists who labelled themselves as 'psychodynamic' might in reality be employing quite different types of interventions. One of the most dramatic demonstrations of this phenomenon is in the classic Lieberman, Yalom and Miles (1973) study of the effectiveness of encounter groups, where it was found that encounter group leaders who considered them-selves as applying the same approach were doing very different things. This phenomenon of therapist individuality in styles creates a major problem for outcome researchers: how can a study be assessing the effectiveness of psychodynamic counselling if the counsellors in the study behave in different ways? The solu-tion to this methodological problem has been through the use of treatment manuals. These are workbooks which explain the principles of an approach, give examples of how it is applied, and provide ways of monitoring whether it is being followed. In most contemporary outcome studies, it is usual to take steps to ensure that therapists are following a single approach as specified by a manual.

The concept of the *treatment manual* has a great deal of potential for practitioner research, but perhaps not in the way that the originators of this idea intended. Given that the majority of counsellors describe themselves as 'eclectic' or 'integrative' in their orientation, the notion that outcomes should be assessed in the context of 'purist' manual-driven approaches does not seem all that relevant for practice. But what is much more relevant is the use of manuals in training and as a means of defining agency or clinic protocols and procedures. It is important that people who work together in a counselling agency should have a shared collective understanding of the service they intend to offer clients. The construction of a manual is one way of achieving this shared understanding. Once in existence, a manual can be used to help everyone to understand the function of supervision, and can be used as a way of organising training. If an agency finds itself taking in new types of clients, then the manual will need to be adapted. For example, a counselling agency which specialises in work with bereaved people but secures a contract to provide a service for refugees can use the manual as a basis for deciding how its style of counselling needs to change to accommodate these new clients. Once a manual is in place, it can serve as a focus for on-going research. For example, if the manual or protocol used by an agency specifies a particular type of assessment interview, a study could be done around perceptions of how clients experience that interview. The findings of such a study may suggest alterations to the manual. The manual therefore provides a framework for feeding research results back into practice.

It is usual for health professionals to operate in accordance with clinical protocols or guidelines. Part of the rationale for the development of counselling protocols or manuals is to be able to engage meaningfully in debates over treatment provision that would otherwise be dominated by health service colleagues. Some of the issues associated with the use of therapy practice guidelines in health settings in the USA can be found in Clinton et al. (1994), Schulberg and Rush (1994) and Munoz et al. (1994).

Box 2.4

Designing and using treatment manuals

Some examples of treatment manuals are:

Greenberg, L.S., Rice, L.N. and Elliott, R. (1993) *Facilitating Emotional Change: The Moment-by-Moment Process*. New York: Guilford Press. (This is the manual of how to do process-experiential psychotherapy.)

Mearns, D. and Thorne, B. (1988) *Person-centred Counselling in Action*. London: Sage. (Not normally regarded as a treatment manual, but in fact a principle-driven proto-manual of how to do person-centred counselling.)

Strupp, H.H. and Binder, J.L. (1984) *Psychotherapy in a New Key: A Guide to Time-Limited Dynamic Psychotherapy*. New York: Basic Books. (The manual of how to do therapy like Hans Strupp and his colleagues.)

Van Hasselt, V.B. and Hersen, M. (eds) (1996) *Sourcebook of Psychological Treatment Manuals for Adult Disorders*. New York: Plenum Press. (A collection of treatment manuals, along with a discussion of how to apply them.)

Articles on some of the issues involved in devising and using manuals are:

Gaston, L. and Gagnon, R. (1996) 'The role of process research in manual development', *Clinical Psychology: Science and Practice*, 3: 13–24.

Lambert, M.J. and Ogles, B.M. (1988) 'Treatment manuals: problems and promise', *Journal of Integrative and Eclectic Psychotherapy*, 7 (2): 187–204.

Luborsky, L. (1993) 'Recommendations for training therapists based on manuals for psychotherapy research', *Psychotherapy*, 30 (4): 578–80.

Luborsky, L. and DeRubeis, R.J. (1984) 'The use of psychotherapy treatment manuals: a small revolution in psychotherapy research style', *Clinical Psychology Review*, 4: 5–14.

There is a lively literature on the use of treatment manuals in counselling and psychotherapy (see Box 2.4), for example around whether manuals should be written in terms of broad principles or based on more prescriptive rules. From a practitioner perspective, it is perhaps useful to see a manual as never being a finished piece of work but as a document that brings together current thinking in an agency or clinic on 'the way we do things here', thus facilitating research and reflection on practice.

Conclusion: practitioner research as a new genre

The survey of research genres offered in this chapter is not comprehensive, and never could be. Within qualitative process research, for example, there is a myriad of sub-genres: phenomenological research, co-operative inquiry, feminist research, etc. Some of these approaches are discussed in later chapters. The point of thinking about genres is that, for beginning researchers, it is helpful to know what to aim for. It is not sensible to attempt to re-invent research methods. Almost certainly, any research topic or question can be addressed through one or more of these genres. By looking at published studies carried out within that genre it is possible to learn about the design constraints of that approach.

But there is another aspect to all this. Although all of these existing styles of doing research can claim some relevance to practice, none of them can be clearly identified as specifically attuned to practitioner interests and priorities. Practitioner research can be seen as representing an emergent genre of counselling and psychotherapy research, which requires creative adaptation of existing methods to meet the goal of generating knowledge-in-context.

3

What's the Question?

One of the crucial tasks at the beginning of a research study is to give careful thought to the research question(s) that will be asked. Good research can be seen as a matter of asking good questions; in many ways, questions can be more important than answers. An interesting question opens up an area of knowledge, it allows different aspects of a topic to be seen. Another respect in which the research question can be a matter of concern at the beginning of a study is that it is essential to create a match or fit between the question and the resources available to answer it. Usually, people start off their research with fairly global questions that can only really be addressed through the efforts of a decade-long international collaborative project. For example, a question such as 'Is psychodynamic counselling effective?' is undoubtedly highly important and relevant, but it is of a scope that is far beyond what could be achieved by a single piece of practitioner research. The question that might be more realistic could be: 'How effective is this particular style of psychodynamic counselling with this particular group of clients in this setting, as measured on these two outcome variables?' The alternative question is less bold and dramatic, but the big ambitious questions such as 'Is psychodynamic counselling effective?' can only be answered, or even begin to be answered, by accumulating evidence from a multitude of smaller-scale studies.

When planning a research study, it is necessary to move from a broad area of interest (for example, the effectiveness of psychodynamic counselling) to a focused research question. This is not at all an easy matter, which is why there is a whole chapter of this book devoted to the issue. Basically, areas of interest can generate an almost infinite variety of alternative questions. It can be very hard for researchers, particularly at the start of their research careers, to decide on the precise question they intend to pursue. Once a piece of research has been completed it can sometimes be fairly obvious which are the next questions that need to be addressed. But at the beginning of working on a research topic it can seem almost like betting on the question. Will this turn out to be a relevant or fertile question? What if this question leads nowhere? Is this way of looking at the topic too simplistic, or, on the other hand, might it produce overwhelmingly complex and confusing results?

It can be useful to make sense of research as a *cyclical* process. Just as with any other form of experiential learning, research moves through stages of planning, action and reflection. As has been already suggested, the surest way of developing a focused research question is through actually doing research and learning experientially what works, and what questions are worth asking. Another way of looking at this is that questions arise from *dialogue*. Doing research, even a small-scale pilot study, is a means of entering into a kind of dialogue with the topic. It can be helpful to engage in dialogue with other people over the research question. Try out your questions on colleagues, supervisors and clients.

In the end, though, arriving at a research question that is both practically relevant and personally meaningful requires a substantial amount of individual thought and working-through. The remainder of this chapter is organised around a series of exercises that have been designed to facilitate the process of constructing a research question. These exercises can be approached as a worksheet (see Box 3.1). If you are at the stage of actually planning a research study it could be valuable to take the list of questions in Box 3.1 and respond to them before reading the commentary which follows. In Chapter 5 there is a discussion of the usefulness of keeping a Research Journal. Your responses to the 'Finding a Research Question' worksheet could be incorporated into this journal.

Box 3.1

Finding a Research Question worksheet

The list of questions below is intended to help you to open up different facets of your research question. You might find that it is useful to employ brainstorming techniques such as mindmaps, pictures/images and colour.

1   What is your research question? Write down, quickly, whatever comes into your head. Free associate. Don't censor what you write.

2   What is your *personal* interest in this question or topic area? What drives your interest? How does it fit into the story you tell about yourself and your life? What do you really need to know? What would your therapist say about this question? Or your mother?

3   Returning to what you wrote at step 1, does this look like an open-ended, exploratory, qualitative question, or a precise, hypothesis-testing quantitative question?

4   What are the *key words* in the question? What alternative key words might you use?

5   What happens to the question when you make the question *more specific*, for example specifying more explicitly the client group, key variables, conditions/circumstances, etc.?

6   What *audience* do you have in mind for your research? What question(s) would they ask? How might the question be slanted differently to appeal to different audiences?

7   Make a model or flow-diagram of the question, showing how the different variables/factors/processes you are interested in are all connected up. Does this model help you to focus your question? Which part or parts of the model can you include in the research? What are the most important or interesting sections of the model?

8   Re-ask the question from different theoretical perspectives. For example, how might the question be asked from a psychoanalytic perspective, or a behavioural one?

9   Do you have any images or fantasies about this research topic? Have you had any dreams about it? Where are these images taking you, where do they lead?

10 Imagine that you have completed your study and are being interviewed on the radio about what you have found. You have two minutes to summarise your results and their implications. What does this summary statement imply about which aspects of the question are of central importance to you?

11 What do you need to know in order to focus the question? Imagine that you have given yourself two hours to wander around the library looking at research articles. Which articles capture your interest and excitement? What do these articles have to teach you about how to ask an appropriate research question, or about *your* question?

12 What do you need to do to take this further? Who could you talk to, what could you read, to enable you to finalise your research question? What kind of information do you need about methods, techniques, previous research?

What is the topic?

If you are doing research, people will ask you what you are doing research *on*. They may ask what you are *looking at*. These images imply the existence of a research topic 'out there' in the external world, like a laboratory specimen. A research *topic* usually refers to a broad area of interest, within which many questions can be asked. A research question is like a searchlight that illuminates parts of this area of interest, or like a tool for dissecting it or digging into it. Areas of interest are expressed in book titles and chapter titles. The titles of research studies are quite different. If you have a research question that reads like the title of a book or a chapter in a book, chances are that it is not yet sufficiently focused, concrete and specific to operate success-fully as a research question.

What does the question mean to you personally?

Practitioner research is usually motivated by a burning interest, a need to know more about some area of experience. In big, programmatic research studies, the research question may have been laid down by someone else (a principal investigator, a government committee), with the result that it may possess only limited personal meaning for the person or people actually carrying out the research. But practitioner research tends not to be like this. Practitioner research is much more integrated with the life of the researcher, and so it is important to be aware of the conscious and implicit meanings that the investigation may hold. Some of the reasons for examining the personal meaning of research include:

- avoiding potential sources of bias, for example through collecting data that 'confirms' what the researcher needs to believe;
- making the research more alive and interesting, and not getting trapped into a sense that the topic is alienating and distant;
- creating the possibility of drawing on emotional and spiritual sources of understanding, to augment cognitive/intellectual analysis of the topic;

- from a counselling perspective, creating the conditions for using 'countertransference' reactions to the research in a positive or constructive way. All researchers have feelings about the work they do; counselling researchers possess the skills and awareness to begin to understand what these feelings might mean;
- acting in accordance with a view of scientific inquiry which questions the role of the detached scientific 'observer' and holds instead that knowledge is intrinsically linked to personal interests and values;
- working within a research genre that requires a reflexive stance, and using exploration of the meaning of the research to establish a kind of reflexive 'baseline' for writing a research journal.

Becoming aware of the personal meaning of research can be a painful process. In my own work, for example, I know that the research I have done into experiential groups, and into story-telling in therapy, are closely tied to areas in which I have a strong personal need to learn. It is as if there has been a personal gap that research has helped to fill. The research has been personally enabling but also disturbing. In carrying out this research, I have been sensitive to the danger that exploring personally meaningful issues solely through research could lead in the direction of an over-intellectualised kind of pseudo-resolution that could cut off what are much more important emotional and interpersonal dimensions of who I am, or can be, in relation to these areas of my life. Research as a way of knowing needs to operate alongside other ways of knowing, such as practical action or therapy. Other dangers include inarticulacy (learning about the research topic at a feeling level, but having difficulty putting it into words), and being personally 'thrown' by what the research uncovers.

One of the consequences of examining the personal meaning of a research topic may be a decision *not* to pursue that topic. It may turn out that opening up a set of issues by subjecting them to research inquiry could lead to so much personal material being generated that it might be difficult to complete the project in the time allocated to it. For example, this can happen when someone researches an issue that is linked to a problematic life episode. One student was drawn to studying the experience of people who had been hospitalised during psychological break-down. His interest in this question was derived from a similar experience he had undergone in his adolescence. As the research progressed, he found that more and more memories of this painful episode in his life were intruding into the research process. He decided to change topics and carry out his research on a different question.

The personal meaning of a research topic may be bound up with the meaning of doing research itself. For some people, carrying out a research study for a Masters degree or Doctorate may have great personal significance, in defiantly demonstrating their intellectual abilities: 'at last I'll show them that I am just as good/clever as my brother/sister, etc.' Other researchers may have a strong sense of responsibility toward the subjects of the research, a desire to use the research to help people in need, perhaps by using the findings to justify services and resources for these clients. Still others may be driven by a wish to be a heroic innovator, to make new discoveries (Freud was one of these). All of these factors can have an effect on the ultimate form that the research question takes.

Is the question open-ended, exploratory and qualitative, or precise, hypothesis-testing and quantitative?

The qualitative and quantitative research traditions are associated with different types of research question. Qualitative research tends to be based around open-ended, 'discovery-oriented' questions. Some of the key aims of qualitative research are to describe what people feel, experience or believe, and to build up a framework for understanding that is inductively grounded in informants' accounts or stories of their experience. The general sense of a qualitative research question can be summed up as 'tell me about . . .'. On the whole, the concepts used to explain qualitative findings emerge from the data. A quantitative research study, by contrast, needs to be much more precisely defined. In quantitative research, the concepts used to explain the data are already present in the initial research question, which may often take the form of a *hypothesis* that is being tested. Indeed, the statistical techniques that are usually employed in social and psychological research can only be applied if there is a hypothesis to be tested.

An example of a qualitative research question might be: 'How do clients experience interpretations made by psychodynamic counsellors?' This question might be pursued by interviewing clients following a counselling session, using the *qualitative process research* genre or model described in the previous chapter. A parallel quantitative question might be: 'What are the differences in helpfulness ratings made by clients following accurate and inaccurate counsellor interpretations?' Note that this question contains an implicit hypothesis (that is, that accurate interpretations will be rated as more helpful than inaccurate ones). The quantitative question clearly specifies the variables that are to be measured: helpfulness as perceived by the client, and accuracy as rated by an external observer. This is an example of the *quantitative process research* genre described earlier. Both types of questions could conceivably converge on the same result. The clients in the qualitative study might well report that the most important thing about counsellor interpretations was that if they were accurate they were helpful. On the other hand, informants in a qualitative study might not mention accuracy at all.

What are the key words in the question?

Trying to deconstruct the question, by finding different meanings and implications within it, is not only a way of working with the topic to arrive at the most effective formulation of the question, but is also a means of achieving a suitably focused question. It can also lead to an increased appreciation of theoretical aspects of the question. A good way to deconstruct a topic or question is to begin by looking at the *key words* within it, and to consider what these words mean. This process can be illustrated through two examples.

Example 1 'How effective is an information leaflet in changing attitudes towards stress counselling in police officers?'
This is a research question that might be asked by a counsellor working in a police force who was finding that the uptake of services was low. The key words in this question are: 'effective', 'information leaflet', 'change', 'attitudes' and 'police officers'. All of these words or concepts can be opened up to further

reflection. For example, what is meant here by 'effective'? 'Influential', 'persuasive', 'useful' or 'cost-effective' are other terms that might replace 'effective', and introduce slightly different meanings and research possibilities. Another angle on effectiveness is to think about who *defines* effectiveness. Is effectiveness to be estimated by clients, other officers, senior officers or counsellors? The term 'attitude' can also carry many meanings. It could be interpreted in terms of image, fantasy, expectation, behaviour (e.g. attendance at counselling), or beliefs (e.g. accurate knowledge about what a stress counsellor does). Even the term 'police officers' can be opened up. Does this mean *all* police officers, or only stressed officers, or particular ranks or age groups? Each of these alternative readings of key words would lead in the direction of different types of research study. A definition of 'attitude' in terms of what can be measured by an attitude questionnaire might result in a study in which 100 officers complete the questionnaire before reading the information leaflet, and then one month later. A definition of attitude in terms of behaviour might involve looking at take-up rates for counselling for the year before and year following distribution of a leaflet across the entire force. A more psychodynamic approach to attitude might define in terms of unconscious fantasy, and lead to a research design in which a small number of officers were interviewed in depth around their responses to a leaflet.

Example 2   'What is the impact of counsellor self-disclosure on the therapeutic relationship?'

There are three key concepts here: 'counsellor self-disclosure', 'impact' and 'therapeutic relationship'. All three would repay close inspection, but for reasons of space only 'counsellor self-disclosure' will be examined in detail. The concept of self-disclosure has been interpreted very differently by researchers in this field. For some, it has been understood to refer to communication of factual biographical information (e.g. where the counsellor lives, whether he/she is married, etc.). It can also be interpreted in terms of the communication of here-and-now feelings (e.g. 'I feel disappointed about our progress together') or intentions (e.g. 'my belief is that it would be more helpful to spend this session talking about the loss, without looking at your work situation'). Some researchers have also explored self-disclosure through its opposite ('things not said') and have assessed the impact of what the counsellor holds back. Self-disclosure can also be planned versus spontaneous, can vary in timing (early versus late in a session), and can refer to different domains of information about self (emotional, autobiographical, sexual, religious). Self-disclosure can follow the client (e.g. the client mentions their religious affiliation, and then the counsellor follows) or can be initiatory. Many more facets of self-disclosure can be imagined. The effect of this kind of close attention to the meaning of a key term has the result that a researcher who begins with an intention to study an experience such as counsellor self-disclosure finds that he or she is faced with choices about which aspect of the topic to follow up. Some of these aspects are not interesting or relevant and some are, and in this way the researcher converges (eventually) on the precise question that is right for them.

Make the question more specific

Most of the time, new researchers start off with questions that are too broad. The act of looking closely at key words can be one way of achieving a clearer focus for a study. Another way can be merely to think about how the question can be made more specific. This involves narrowing down time, place, person and method. This process can be illustrated through the use of an example. *'How effective is counselling for patients referred by their GP in a Primary Health Care setting?'* This question has in fact been the focus of a number of recent studies, and one of the criticisms that has been made of these studies is that, on the whole, they have not been specific enough. Studies of the effectiveness of vaguely defined 'counselling' with heterogeneous groups of primary care patients inevitably lead to results that are difficult to interpret, since the outcome of the counselling will in all probability be highly influenced by such factors as the mix of patients referred (e.g. how seriously disturbed or needy they are), the experience of the counsellor, the quality of the GP–counsellor collaboration, and so on. It is easy to see that this is an area where the more specific the research is, the more likely that it will produce useful results. There are several strategies that can be used to increase specificity. Narrowing *time* parameters might involve such decisions as: looking only at clients seen over a six-month period; using only clients that have received at least three sessions; using only counsellors who have received two years of training and have been in post for at least one year. Narrowing *place* parameters could be achieved by selecting the clinics to be used (e.g. urban, rural, group practices, single-handed practices) or choosing areas in which there were either a range of other counselling services available or where the GP counsellor represented the only therapy service on offer. Making *person* more specific entails considering the various central participants in the study: clients, counsellors, GPs. The study could be restricted to clients from particular diagnostic groups, such as anxious, bereaved, depressed, relationship problems. Alternatively, clients could be included on the basis of other factors such as age, gender, previous use of psychiatric services or psychotropic drugs, or attitude to counselling. Counsellors could be chosen on the basis of theoretical orientation, training in time-limited counselling, or knowledge of medical procedures. GPs might be used to represent those who are positive about counselling versus those who are critical, or on the basis of previous training in psychiatry. Making the study more specific in terms of *method* could involve general methodological choices (for example designing the study as a randomised controlled trial, a naturalistic outcome study, a survey of GP attitudes, an ethnographic inquiry, etc.). Also, method specificity includes making choices about the actual technique or techniques used for gathering data. For instance, if the client group comprised depressed people, it would be appropriate to assess outcomes using an instrument such as the Beck Depression Inventory.

The point here is that it can be helpful to think creatively about how your piece of research could be made more specific. Some of the ideas you come up with will certainly be off-beam, but the process of opening up your set of options should make it possible to be more confident about the final version of the question that you decide to adopt. Thinking about how to make the question more specific may well stimulate you to search the literature. For instance, in the counselling in General Practice example discussed above, if it made sense to focus the study on depressed patients, it would be useful to review some of the literature on the advantages and disadvantages of alternative questionnaire measures of depression, to see which one would be most appropriate for counselling clients in a General Practice setting.

What is the intended audience for the research?

In this book, research is understood as an activity that contributes to the development of a *collective* awareness, capacity for understanding or knowledge base. Although research may be based in experiential knowing, ultimately it is necessary to translate this personal or tacit understanding into propositional (usually written) knowledge that then in some sense becomes the property of the group. In the field of counselling, the potential consumers of research encompass counsellors, counsellor educators and trainers, managers and administrators of counselling agencies, clients, potential clients, policy-makers, the general public, and academic theorists and researchers both within counselling and also in cognate disciplines such as psychology, sociology, management studies, nursing or social work. Each of these audiences has different interests, and looks for different things in what it reads (and in fact reads quite different kinds of publications). For example, an academic audience will be interested in the methodological rigour of a piece of work, and in how adequately it addresses issues raised by previous research. Managers of counselling agencies, by contrast, are likely to be primarily interested in what the research tells them that will make a difference to the running of the organisation. And counsellors will be interested in what makes a difference to their direct work with clients. A research question that exemplifies some of these contrasting perspectives is: *'How best can counsellors establish a productive therapeutic alliance with their clients?'* An academic reader of a research paper on this topic would be aware of the huge amount of previous research on the issue, and would want to see how this new study helped to advance that research, in terms of innovations in theory or methodology. A manager of a counselling agency, on the other hand, might want to know about how to assess or detect therapeutic alliance competencies in counsellors, for example in counsellors applying for jobs in the organisation. Finally, counsellors reading such a paper would be only minimally interested in the academic or administrative aspects of the topic, and would want to read something that perhaps laid down the skills or strategies necessary for a good therapeutic relationship, or was structured around interesting case descriptions.

There is a practical side to these issues. At some point, as a researcher, it may well happen that you do present the results of the study to a live audience. This may be a panel who are interviewing you for a job, the executive committee of the counselling agency which sponsored the research, or a group of academic researchers at a conference. It can be useful to imagine being in that situation, and anticipating what these people might find convincing and plausible, and what you would want to be in a position to say to them.

Building a model of the question: how different variables/factors/processes might be connected up

One of the fundamental aspects of any research topic in counselling is that understanding will inevitably involve making sense of how a variety of different factors inter-relate. Cause-and-effect linkages are not easy to identify in counselling, because events tend to have multiple causes or antecedents and in turn produce multiple effects. A valuable means of making sense of the complexity of a topic or phenomenon can be to construct a model. Building a model is a good way of becoming sensitised to the different dimensions of a question, and as a result becoming better able to focus in on the facets of the question that are most important, are most open to research, or have/have not been studied before. Box 3.2 gives an example of a tentative model that was constructed in order to tease out some of the factors that might be relevant to exploring the question: 'How effective is time-limited counselling in the workplace?' Using a model-building approach, it is possible to see very quickly that there are far too many factors to be included in a single piece of practitioner research. Indeed, there are probably too many factors to even be taken on board in a government-funded major research initiative on the issue (in the highly unlikely event of such an initiative being set up). Anyone researching this topic therefore needs to make a choice about which factors are most important or relevant to them, or which can realistically be included, given the time and resources available. Finally, building a model should ideally be seen as a kind of 'thought experiment' which can in itself lead to new discoveries. As the model of workplace counselling in Box 3.2 expanded and became more differentiated, it became possible to *see* new questions. For instance, the model points toward a sub-set of questions related to gender:

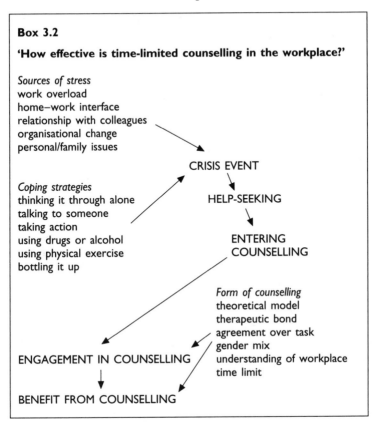

Box 3.2

'How effective is time-limited counselling in the workplace?'

Sources of stress
work overload
home–work interface
relationship with colleagues
organisational change
personal/family issues

CRISIS EVENT

Coping strategies
thinking it through alone
talking to someone
taking action
using drugs or alcohol
using physical exercise
bottling it up

HELP-SEEKING

ENTERING
COUNSELLING

Form of counselling
theoretical model
therapeutic bond
agreement over task
gender mix
understanding of workplace
time limit

ENGAGEMENT IN COUNSELLING

BENEFIT FROM COUNSELLING

Do men and women differ in their use of counselling, just as they differ in their use of other coping strategies? Are there gender differences in outcome – do men and women have different criteria for what counts as 'successful' counselling? To what extent do these differences depend on the 'gendered' nature of the work (e.g. nursing versus the fire service), or on the organisational culture? Do men and women have different perceptions of in-house and external counselling services? Does the provision of male or female counsellors make a difference? Once the model is 'externalised' through being pictured on a piece of paper, it becomes possible to look at each element of the model and ask further questions about it. In this instance, it became apparent that virtually all the 'building blocks' of the model concealed interesting questions about potential gender differences. There are, of course, many other sub-questions implicit in the model. The point is that model-building is a way of generating more specific questions.

Consider alternative theoretical perspectives

It may well be the case that, if you are beginning research for the first time, your questions may be highly practical ones, inspired by your experience as a practitioner. However, it can be very useful to think about the relevance of alternative theoretical approaches to your question. Theoretical constructs can be seen as having a *sensitising* function: they tell you where to look but not what to find. Theoretical ideas may also help you to reflect more deeply on a topic, to go beyond your immediate assumptions. Finally, an awareness of alternative theoretical perspectives may enable you to take a more questioning and critical, and ultimately more profitable, use of your review of the literature. Quite often, when reviewing previous studies, there may seem to be 'something not quite right' about the way that the researcher has approached the topic. The temptation can be to attribute this unease to methodological weaknesses in the study (was the sample representative? was the data analysed properly?). More often, however, the difficulty lies in the way that the researcher has *conceptualised* the topic of inquiry. By gaining proficiency in considering alternative theoretical perspectives it becomes possible to uncover conceptual contradictions in published research.

An example of what is involved in looking theoretically at a topic is a study of the experiences of counsellors who specialise in working with survivors of sexual abuse. This area of therapeutic work is frequently harrowing and frustrating, and has a profound effect on practitioners. It is therefore an important topic for research. Box 3.3 presents some of the different theoretical approaches that can, and have, been taken to this research question. These alternative approaches lead in quite different directions. They produce radically different kinds of knowledge. But also, each theoretical construct brings with it an associated set of debates and controversies. To use a psychoanalytic theoretical perspective in relation to this research question would require giving some attention to the many different ways of

---

Box 3.3

Exploring alternative theoretical perspectives

Basic research question: *What is the impact on counsellors of working with survivors of child sexual abuse?*

Alternative theoretical perspectives

1   *Stress theory.* Key concepts: *sources and symptoms of stressors, coping strategies.* Preferred method: *stress questionnaire.*
2   *Burnout theory.* Key concepts: *emotional exhaustion, depersonalisation, lack of personal accomplishment, stages of burnout.* Preferred method: *Maslach burnout questionnaire.*
3   *Psychoanalytic theory.* Key concepts: *countertransference, the unconscious, defence mechanisms, fantasy.* Preferred methods: *clinical interviews with therapists, projective techniques.*
4   *Humanistic psychology.* Key concepts: *empathic strain, self-fulfilment, authenticity.* Preferred methods: *open-ended interviews, diaries.*
5   *Phenomenology.* Key concepts: *horizon of meaning.* Preferred methods: *open-ended interviews, therapist written accounts of experience.*
6   *Social constructionist.* Key concepts: *narrative, co-construction of social reality.* Preferred methods: *dialogue, analysis of discourse.*
7   *Feminist.* Key concepts: *power, relatedness.* Preferred method: *collaborative action research.*

---

defining and understanding the concept of 'transference' that exist within the psychoanalytic literature. Similarly, adopting a humanistic perspective would require taking a position on the meaning and definition of 'empathy' and the processes by which it can be achieved or threatened.

Is the question researchable?

The final consideration that needs to be taken into account concerns the feasibility of the question. Very often, people new to research generate questions that would happily supply a lifetime of endeavour for a lavishly funded research unit. The trick in finding a good research question is to narrow and sharpen the focus of inquiry so that it becomes a question that can be answered within the resources that are available, but without ending up with a study that is so dry and technical that the original meaning and value of the study, the big issues that inform the question, are lost. There are certainly questions which I personally have laid aside because I could not figure out *how* to research them. There are other questions which just take a very long time. Sometimes it can be years before one feels able to say something on a topic, or even to know what are the meaningful questions that might be asked about it. As Flick (1998: 53) has written, 'research questions are like a door to the research field under study'. The image of the door is of course an important metaphor in therapy. Opening the door is good, but so is finding the handle, or even believing that the door exists.

4

Using the Literature

For counsellors, one of the benefits of an interest in research is that it inevitably leads to engagement with the literature. Actually doing research that is relevant to practice is useful, but so is reading the literature that informs that research. Without a research focus, reading articles in journals can be unrewarding. On the whole, theoretical and research papers and books are written in a fairly dry style. It is when these publications are read from a position of *looking for* something, when the reader is guided by a passion to expand or check out his or her own ideas, that this kind of reading material comes alive (further discussion of the functions of reading for counsellors can be found in McLeod, 1997). The aim of this chapter is to discuss some of the ways in which practitioner-researchers can gain access to, and make use of, previously published research that is relevant to their interests.

Exploring the literature

The literature on counselling and psychotherapy is highly fragmented and complex. There exists a very long list of academic journals which publish research into counselling and psychotherapy (see Box 4.1, which is not exhaustive). No single university library could ever carry all these journals, so in many instances access to copies of articles may require the use of inter-library loan facilities. Unlike other disciplines, as yet there is no specialised abstracting service which will provide summaries of recent research in therapy. It can therefore be difficult to keep track of what has been published.

Box 4.1

Journals which publish research in counselling and psychotherapy

American Journal of Orthopsychiatry
American Journal of Psychiatry
American Journal of Psychotherapy
American Psychologist
Archives of General Psychiatry
Arts in Psychotherapy
Behavior Therapy
Behaviour Research and Therapy
British Journal of Clinical Psychology
British Journal of Guidance and Counselling
British Journal of Medical Psychology
British Journal of Psychiatry
British Journal of Psychotherapy
Canadian Counsellor
Changes
Clinical Psychology and Psychotherapy
Clinical Psychology Review
Cognitive Therapy and Research
Counseling Psychologist
Counselling
Counselling Psychology Quarterly
Counselling Psychology Review
Counselor Education and Supervision
European Journal of Psychotherapy, Counselling and Health
International Journal for the Advancement of Counselling
International Journal of Group Psychotherapy
International Journal of Short-Term Psychotherapy
Journal for Specialists in Groupwork
Journal of the American Academy of Child and Adolescent Psychiatry
Journal of Behavior Therapy and Experimental Psychiatry
Journal of Child Psychology and Psychiatry
Journal of College Student Development
Journal of College Student Personnel
Journal of Consulting and Clinical Psychology
Journal of Counseling and Development
Journal of Counseling Psychology
Journal of Eclectic and Integrative Psychotherapy
Journal of Humanistic Psychology
Journal of Mental Health Counselling
Journal of Sexual and Marital Therapy
Patient Education and Counseling
Professional Psychology: Research and Practice
Psychiatry
Psychological Medicine
Psychotherapy
Psychotherapy Research
Small Group Research

The counselling and psychotherapy literature is organised around a number of different types of publication. Most research reports are published in the academic journals listed in Box 4.1. Typically, these journals each publish four issues in a year. These issues will mainly contain a mixed collection of papers which are included in sequence of their final approval for publication (see Chapter 12 on 'Getting into print'). Some of these journals will occasionally devote a whole issue to a single-topic symposium. *Counseling Psychologist*, *Psychological Inquiry* and *Psychoanalytic Dialogues* are structured around a keynote paper (usually a theoretical article or review of the literature) followed by a series of commentaries. Alongside these academic journals are professional journals (such as *Counselling*) which publish some research and theory but are mainly devoted to professional issues and business. Also somewhere alongside these academic counselling and psychotherapy journals are journals from other disciplines which will nevertheless from time to time publish papers that would be of interest to psychotherapists and counsellors. Such journals would include those in adjacent fields such as nursing and social work, but also such diverse titles as *British Journal of General Practice*, *British Medical Journal*, *Social Science and Medicine* and *Sociological Review*.

It is useful to think about academic and professional journals as belonging together because they can usually be found together in the same location in a library (the *periodicals* collection). Also, most journal articles are listed in on-line computer databases (see below) and can be searched without ever visiting a library.

Books represent a second category of published literature. It is probably sensible to think about books in terms of those that are teaching texts, and those which contain new theoretical or research material. Teaching texts may be very useful in providing a 'map' or overview of an area of interest, and in supplying references. For most research purposes, however, it is necessary to use primary source material.

A third category of the literature comprises what might be called semi-published items. These are reports or monographs which are in the public domain but are difficult to get hold of because they have been published in small numbers or only distributed locally. A potentially important resource for researchers can be unpublished Masters and Doctoral dissertations, which are normally held in the library of the university at which the person did their degree. In Britain most PhD theses can be borrowed through inter-library loans (under very strictly controlled access arrangements). Copies of PhD theses from the USA are available, for a price. MA or MSc dissertations can be more difficult to get hold of, because they may be stored in departmental rather than university libraries and as a result may not be catalogued. There are many interesting and valuable research reports produced by counselling agencies and government or local authority departments. Often, these reports may be quite widely publicised at the time of publication, but thereafter can be hard to trace. Access to this kind of material is usually through writing directly to the organisation concerned. Libraries may be reluctant to stock what they regard as ephemeral material of this kind.

There exist, therefore, a number of different means of gaining access to theoretical and research papers and books. These include:

- personal 'handsearching' in a library
- on-line databases (e.g. BIDS, Psych-Lit, Medline, etc.)
- reference lists of books and articles
- consulting the index of Bergin and Garfield (1994)
- asking tutors and colleagues
- writing to authors of articles
- website discussion pages and other Internet resources

If you find that one particular person has published useful research in your area of interest, it can be fruitful to write, asking if they could send you off-prints of specific articles, and any additional published or unpublished papers they might have available on that topic. When a paper is published in a journal, the author gets a set of free off-prints, and most researchers are quite keen to pass these on to anyone who might be studying the same area. Research can be a lonely business and it can be reinforcing to receive letters asking for off-prints, so there is a good chance that a reply will be forthcoming. If you write to a fellow researcher, it is best to be clear about what you want, and not to request general advice that may demand a lengthy written response and therefore deter them from getting back to you at all.

Librarians are usually very willing to help you in developing literature searching skills, but will not have the time to carry out an actual literature search on your behalf. It is not realistic to give a librarian a piece of paper with 'the effectiveness of time-limited counselling' on it and expect them to produce a list of references for you. What is more realistic is to ask a librarian about the on-line facilities that are available. Often, libraries can offer leaflets or computer self-tutorial sessions that will teach you how to use on-line databases or the Internet. It will be helpful for a librarian if you can show them a few examples of the kind of thing you are looking for, such as specific references from journals. The librarian can then help you to find that journal, or similar journals. Remember, it is very unlikely that a librarian would be familiar with the counselling or therapy literature – they need some clues from you as to where to start. Apart from hand-searching, which depends on your capacity to skim-read journal contents pages and abstracts and pick out relevant items, all the 'quick' methods such as on-line searches depend on *keywords*. To get the best yield from these searches it is important to be creative in your thinking about keywords. For example a search for articles on 'time-limited counselling' may involve trying out a variety of alternative keywords: time-limited, time-conscious, counselling/counseling, psychotherapy, intervention, brief, dose, treatment planning, workplace counselling, EAPs, single-session, solution-focused, and so on. On-line searches *always* miss some articles, either because these articles have been published in obscure places, or because they have been filed under odd keywords. An exhaustive handsearch (if you have time) will always produce some items that do not show up on computerised searches. Conversely, handsearching alone will miss a vast amount, because it is physically impossible for an individual researcher to get hold of all the journals that might potentially include relevant papers.

It can take a substantial amount of time collecting research books and articles to arrive at the point of feeling that one has a secure overview of the work that has been done in that area. To some extent the time spent on literature reviewing is time spent waiting for items to be delivered by inter-library loans. Once a useful article or two is found, the references in that paper will lead to other sources, which in turn need to be located and again may lead to yet new sources. In planning a research study it is important to include enough time for literature searching. Another factor which may eat up time arises from the incomplete and fragmented nature of much counselling knowledge: in many areas the research just does not exist. If, for example, you are interested in carrying out research into the effectiveness of therapy for depression, or the effectiveness of counselling in primary care, your file of research articles will grow fairly rapidly. There are many papers on these topics. However, there are other topics which are very important but which have not generated a research literature. For example, it is difficult to review the *research* literature on commonplace counselling concepts such as 'respect', 'acceptance', or 'boundaries', simply because little or no research has been done. In carrying out research into these latter topics, it may be necessary to create a platform for the research by looking at studies on similar issues. For instance, an understanding of how to approach 'boundaries' from a research perspective might be pieced together by looking at work on contracts, missed appointments or therapist techniques.

When collecting research literature, it is of course essential to know when to stop. No-one can know everything. To design a piece of research, or to use research to inform practice, what is important is to have a *sufficient* grasp of the literature. It is perhaps worth bearing in mind that when the NHS wishes to establish a *definitive* review of knowledge in a particular area it sets up what is known as a 'Cochrane Review', which is a team of five or six people who work for one or two years on the project.

What to do with research articles

Having collected some research articles, books or chapters in books, it is important to work through them in a systematic manner. Many people, myself included, take the attitude that the knowledge contained in books will be transferred by some kind of osmosis if only the books are on a nearby shelf, or, even better, carried around in a briefcase. Unfortunately this is not the case. What is crucial is to learn how to read articles critically, so that the information and ideas contained within them can be retained for later use. This can only be done if articles are read *purposefully*, which depends on having a clear sense of purpose. Working on refining the research question (see Chapter 3) and keeping a research diary (Chapter 5) can be useful in helping to keep the purpose(s) of the research in focus.

Some of the key skills involved in critically reading a research paper include:

Note down the publication details: author, date, title, journal, volume, pages, keywords, etc. This information can be kept on index cards, in a word processing file, or catalogued in a specialist software bibliography file such as *Papyrus* (see Appendix).

Read the abstract   of the paper (a 300-word summary that appears at the beginning or end of the paper). If this seems relevant, read on. If it does not seem relevant (fairly often, the title of a paper may bear little relation to what it contains), then skim it to check whether there might be little nuggets of useful information or new references. Do not waste time reading stuff that you will not use later. If a paper subsequently turns out to be more important than it originally appeared, you can go back to it because you have kept the reference details.

Identify the plot   Any research paper is organised around a plot structure which tends to follow a pattern such as:

- this topic is important (theoretically or practically) because . . .
- previous research has shown that . . .
- what still remains unclear, or what is wrong with this previous research, is . . .
- what we were aiming to do was . . .
- this is how we did it . . .
- this is what we found . . .
- we think these findings add to previous knowledge because . . .
- the implications of what we did for future research and practice are . . .

It is useful to think about a research paper as telling a story because this perspective opens up an awareness that there might be sub-plots (we really did this study because we hate behaviour therapy and wanted to show that it is misguided and wrong . . .). As in any story, there are portions of the narrative that are glossed over (major parts of the questionnaire didn't work out

but we don't want to go into that in any detail if you don't mind
. . .). Finally, a narrative perspective gives permission to recognise that there are *other* stories that could be told about the same
set of events. And this is a key point. Critical analysis of a paper
means thinking about whether the results could plausibly be
accounted for in other ways.

Examine the methodology When most people begin research,
and start to read research papers, they pay too much attention to
the findings or results of published studies, and end up assembling literature reviews that focus solely on 'facts' (e.g., 'Smith
[1996] demonstrated that client-centred therapy was not effective
with test-anxious college student clients.' This is a fictitious
example). Treating studies as if they were little 'fact modules'
leads to a rather superficial approach to the literature. It assumes
that we are just piling up knowledge in an inexorable fashion. It
is more useful to recognise that, although each study indeed may
contribute to some great heap of knowledge, there are limitations
to any study, and that debates and disagreements exist over how
to interpret data. It is essential therefore, to pay attention not
only to *what* was found, but at *how* it was found. Some of the
questions that can be usefully asked about the methods used in a
study are:

Who carried out the study? What might their allegiance be? What
were they trying to prove?
What was the sample? How was it selected? Does it reflect the
wider population? Might the sample have biased or skewed
the results, and in what directions?
What questions were being asked, or what hypotheses were
being tested? Did the methods of data collection produce
information that was relevant to the questions/hypotheses?
For example, did Smith's definition of 'test anxiety' and
questionnaire measure of 'test anxiety' mirror the anxious
students I have seen in my own practice?
Would I want to use these methods in my own research? If I
wanted to evaluate test anxiety in my own research on my
college student clients, would the Smith questionnaire be the
best technique to use? How do I know whether or not it is a
good technique?

These are the kinds of questions that allow a reader to begin to open up the methodological assumptions and choices implicit in any piece of published research. There are at least three reasons for paying close attention to methodological aspects of research papers. First, the methods used may be so flawed (in your eyes at least) that you cannot place any credence in the results of the study. Second, different findings in the literature may reflect the use of different methods. For example, the reason why an imaginary Brown (1997) may be able to report positive results for client-centred counselling with test-anxious college students is that she used a different questionnaire from Smith. Third, in preparing yourself to carry out some personal research, it is necessary to decide on which methods to use. This involves considering alternative methods, and perhaps acquiring further information on them (such as writing to Smith and Brown asking for copies of their questionnaires).

Plunder the paper for useful detail   In reading a paper or chapter it may strike you that the author(s) have used vivid and memorable imagery or writing that would be worth quoting in your own work. There may also be some quite specific or off-beat aspects of their results that may be worth retaining for future use (perhaps Smith found that it was mainly humanities students who reported with high test anxiety).

Consider the big picture   Having read a research paper carefully, drawing on the strategies described above, it is useful to reflect on the implications of the paper, on where it fits in to the wider context. Some of the key questions here are: What does the paper add to previous knowledge on the topic? Where does the paper lead, in terms of further research? What are the implications of the paper for training, supervision or practice?

Writing a review of the literature

When the time comes to assemble a literature review in a form that will be read by other people, in an article or dissertation, there are several issues which need to be faced. These concern the length of the review and the way that the material will be organised. It is no easy matter to condense detailed notes on a set of papers into a well-rounded review. In a Doctoral thesis a literature review chapter may be as long as 8,000 to 10,000 words. A theoretical or literature review paper in a journal would normally be around 5,000 words. However, a literature review at the start of an empirical research paper may need to be as short as 1,000 words.

One means of learning how to write a satisfying literature review is to look at how other authors have accomplished this task. For example, if you are planning to submit a research article to a particular journal, it is invaluable to spend some time analysing how past contributors to that journal have tackled the problem of constructing a brief review of the literature in the introductory sections of their papers. Longer literature review papers or chapters can often take a *thematic* approach, in which the literature is broken down into sub-topics and then summed up at the end. Alternatively, some literatures can lend themselves to a *narrative* or *historical* approach, where previous research is unfolded in chronological order. This is a good strategy where it is appropriate because it neatly leads up to the present time and the present conclusions or research study. However, if a body of work is fragmented or does not proceed in a reasonably neat chronological pathway a narrative approach can read as though an artificial structure has been imposed on the material. Finally, where there is a lot of material to be covered in a review, some kind of *meta-analysis* can be helpful as a means of summarising the main points from many studies. The papers in the *Counseling Psychologist* or *Psychological Inquiry* journals represent excellent examples of carefully constructed long reviews. The *Counseling Psychologist* reviews are particularly interesting because many of them explicitly conclude with recommendations for practice. Good examples of more technical meta-analytic reviews, which seek to summarise in a systematic fashion all the knowledge on a particular question, can be found in Parts 2, 3 and 4 of Bergin and Garfield (1994). Other journals, such as the *British Journal of Guidance and Counselling*, or *Psychotherapy* are good sources for learning about how to structure well-crafted review essays.

Conclusion: using the literature

One of the traps in which I believe some counsellors can become caught up when beginning research is the illusion that the research literature represents a source of authoritative wisdom. If this relationship with the literature is adopted, then reviewing the literature becomes almost like an act of ritual obeisance to an idol. Reviewing the literature is a way of demonstrating that one is well-read and that one respects one's elders. I would argue that any such approach is a recipe for paralysis, and for bringing to a halt any possible dialogue between research and practice. This is because it is apparent to most practitioners that the vast bulk of the published literature holds little or no relevance to their practice. This realisation can sometimes lead to a sense of 'my practice is inadequate' or 'I am not clever enough to understand this research stuff.' Or it can lead to a process of going through the motions of reviewing literature (and doing research) but treating it as an empty exercise that must be endured in order to gain a professional qualification.

It is more helpful to regard the literature as consisting of a multiplicity of voices. Many of these voices are saying things that, for any one of us, we would never be in a position to learn otherwise. The literature is full of tales of strange therapeutic practices, and accounts of clients who might never appear in our own counselling room, no matter how long we were to practice. In the literature are the voices of people who have spent 10 or 20 years studying one thing. In the literature there are people who argue quite opposite conclusions. The literature is a dialogue, or a conversation, and reviewing the literature is a prelude to joining in that conversation.

From a practitioner-researcher perspective, there are probably two main uses to which the literature can be put. First, research and theory provide a framework for deciding how to practice. I do not believe that, so far at any rate, counselling and psychotherapy research has arrived at a stage where it is possible to make statements about which intervention might be best for any specific client. But research *can* provide background awareness of the factors which need to be taken into consideration in these practical situations. Second, previous research also serves as the platform from which further research can be carried out. In initiating a process of inquiry into a topic, it is extremely unlikely that any practitioner or researcher will come up with a method or model that has not been tried before by someone, somewhere. It makes sense to learn from previous research, to make up one's own mind about what worked or did not work in previous attempts to study a particular phenomenon.

There is more research into counselling and psychotherapy being published now, in comparison with previous eras. CD-ROM bibliographic databases and the Internet make it easier than ever to gain access to these materials. In all probability, the development of Internet books and journals will make access even easier within the next 20 years. At the same time, the professionalisation of counselling within the context of university-based training, and the demands for accountability being made by purchasers of counselling services, increase the pressure to move in the direction of research-informed practice. And in all this, clients and service users are becoming more able to tap into information about research effectiveness. Developing a good relationship with the research literature is therefore becoming a competency which professional counsellors need to nurture.

5

Setting up a Research Study

The purpose of this chapter is to review some of the main issues that need to be considered when beginning a practice-focused research project. In thinking about doing research, it is useful to have a model of the research process as a whole. It can be particularly valuable to think about research in terms of a cycle of inquiry (see Box 5.1). Any research begins with a period of reflection, reading, discussion and general question-finding. This leads to the formulation of a research plan (what is sometimes called the *research design*), leading to data collection and analysis, and then concluding with a written report which is seen by other people. This is a cycle which may be repeated several times in the lifetime of a project. For example, there may be a very preliminary cycle based on testing out some vague ideas against what is available in the published literature, and then writing a paper for agency or clinic management, or for a research supervisor, that floats a general proposal for research into a particular topic. There may then follow another cycle of inquiry in the form of a pilot study in which an interview schedule or questionnaire is tried out with two or three selected participants. Having reflected on the results of the pilot study, the researcher will be ready to enter into the cycle that represents the 'proper' study. But even this will almost always generate loose ends or new ideas that demand further cycles of inquiry. For instance, presenting the results of the study at a conference or professional meeting may trigger questions that call for further research. It is important to realise that the model of the research cycle presented here describes

---

Box 5.1

The research cycle

Stage 1   Immersion and gestation. Reflecting on personal experience on the topic. General reading. Discussion with others. Question-finding.

Stage 2   Planning. Being explicit about the research question and how it will be answered. Addressing ethical issues. Formulating a timetable and plan of action.

Stage 3   Data collection. Gathering relevant information. Storing and cataloguing data.

Stage 4   Data analysis. Making sense of the data, drawing conclusions.

Stage 5   Writing up. Bringing the findings of the project into a written report.

Stage 6   Dissemination of results. Publicising the findings of the study through publications, conference papers and workshops.

Stage 7   Reflecting on what has been learned, and starting again.

---

stages in the research process which may in reality overlap and run into each other. In some research, for example when carrying out qualitative interviews, some of the most useful analytic ideas may occur when actually doing the interview (data collection). Similarly, reflecting on the meaning and implications of the research may, and should, take place at all stages.

The image of the *designer* can be both helpful and unhelpful in making sense of the research process. It is helpful because it evokes a sense of being like an architect creating a blueprint for a building which will meet the specifications of various groups of people – the property owner, the builders, the neighbourhood, the building inspectors. But once the building work actually commences, unforeseen problems may arise and the design may need to be modified. The notion of the researcher as designer captures well the need for careful planning, consideration of the interests of different groups of people, working to a budget and timescale, and anticipating problems. Where the image of the researcher as designer is less satisfactory, for me at any rate, is that many psychology or psychology-oriented research methods text-books include chapters on research design that are highly prescriptive in specifying a limited set of designs that (in their view) meet the requirements of scientific rigour (the equivalent of the building inspectors). This approach to research design is, I would argue, derived far too much from a tradition of laboratory experimentation, where the researcher can aspire to some sort of absolute control over his or her 'subjects'. In practitioner research, it is important to be creative and flexible in planning and conducting research and to recognise that conventionally defined 'rigour' is only one among several sources of value. Another important factor in practitioner research is that collecting data normally requires co-operation and approval from other people. For example, if a study is carried out in a counselling agency or clinic then there will almost certainly need to be quite lengthy negotiations with managers, administrators and clinicians. Some of the organisational and political issues involved in setting up research are discussed by Hardy (1995). McLeod (1998, ch. 15) offers a framework for beginning to understand some of the organisational dynamics of counselling agencies. Resistance to research is not uncommon in counsellors and counselling organisations (Shipton, 1994; Vachon et al., 1995).

One thing that professional designers tend to do is to show a great interest in how other designers operate. For example, design teams in motor companies will buy cars from rival firms and then systematically dismantle them in their workshop, in order to work out how they were put together in the first place. In designing a piece of research, it is useful to pay a similar interest in the activities of previous designers. Specifically, what can be helpful is to identify a research paper which comes closest to the research that you would want to do, and then analyse closely how it was put together. By the end of this exercise you should have a clear idea of which design features from that paper you wish to include in your own study, and also where your 'blueprint' diverges from their plan, and why.

The following sections of this chapter focus on the three key tasks associated with getting started in research: keeping a research diary, constructing a research plan, and taking account of ethical issues. Further recommended reading on the planning and design stage of practitioner research in counselling can be found in any of the research textbooks mentioned in the list provided in the Appendix.

Keeping a research diary

I would always strongly advise anyone embarking on a research study to begin keeping a research diary or journal at the earliest

---

Box 5.2

The role of the research diary

Keeps the emphasis on the personal nature of research.
Enables the identification of pre-understandings and assumptions.
Builds up a record of the experience of doing the study, which can later be used in reflexive writing.
Facilitates exploration of the personal meaning of the research.
Provides a place to keep a note of emerging insights into the material.
Allows exploration of the links between research and current practice.
Keeps a record of ideas that can feed into later studies.
Builds up a body of writing that can be 'raided' when compiling reports and writing papers.

---

possible opportunity. Some of the functions of a research diary are listed in Box 5.2. Very often, counsellors and psychotherapists who carry out research are vaguely aware of the personal meaning of the investigation, but have no means of tying together the various personal strands of significance which arise, or of building these into their written research reports. In Chapter 1, I have suggested that one of the distinctive features of practitioner research in counselling is that it both makes use of, and contributes to, the developed self-awareness of the practitioner. A research diary is a vehicle for promoting critical reflexivity and also for doing research that will be relevant for practice.

There are many alternative ways of keeping reflective diaries (see, for example, Lukinsky, 1990; MacMillan and Clark, 1998; Rainer, 1980). It is essential that anyone who keeps a diary develops their own style of diary writing. However, apart from general 'rules' of diary writing such as dating entries and writing quickly without self-censorship, it may be useful to think in terms of a series of diary sections.

Pre-understandings and expectations
Before beginning work on a study, it can be useful to write about what you expect to find. Before collecting data, or even before doing any preliminary reading, it can be helpful to take a blank page and write out what results you expect to get. This exercise can be useful in identifying those aspects of the topic that you already understand, and those that require further exploration. It

can also put you in a position at the end of the study to tell your readers or audience what you had expected, and how what you discovered differed from these expectations. Writing about pre-understandings can aid communication between co-researchers, or between a researcher and his or her supervisor. Finally, being explicit about expectations can allow you to check during the process of the research that you are not just engaging in an exercise in self-fulfilling prophecy.

The experience of doing the research

This section refers to what sociologists and social anthropologists call 'fieldwork notes', and includes any events or feelings associated with being in a research role. For example, you may find that you are writing about strong feelings of liking or antipathy toward certain research participants. Alternatively, there may be critical incidents that sum up the type of relationship you have with research informants. If these are not written down at the time, they are usually lost. Writing them makes it possible, at the end, to reflect more systematically on processes of transference and countertransference, or on the degree of your involvement and investment in the research process. Writing may be helpful in working through personal conflicts, hassles or avoidances that can arise during a study.

Personal and professional implications

What does it mean to you to have chosen a particular research topic? What do you learn about yourself from your involvement in the research process? In what ways does the research generate new ideas or understandings that can be applied in work with clients? Keeping a diary can help to maximise the personal learning that can occur in research. There may also be some audiences that you would wish to write for who will find the research more meaningful if you can place it in a personal and professional context, who will ask 'What difference did it make to you, and to your work?'

Research memos

There is another category of research diary-writing that is associated with the job of keeping tabs on the flow of good ideas that accompany all the various tasks of researching – reading, collecting data, analysing data. The conclusions of a research study do not emerge freshly minted on the morning when you have decided to sit down at your desk and write your conclusions section. The analytic themes around which you will structure your results section do not occur only when you are actually analysing the data. If you are immersed in a research study, then ideas will come to you all the time. It is good to write these down as they happen, even if they seem strange or confused. It is from this stock of images, metaphors and speculations that your findings and conclusions will emerge. These are the understandings that are on the edge of awareness, that represent the direction in which your investigation is heading.

Finally, there is one last reason for keeping a research diary. There is nothing worse than being faced with the task of writing a report from scratch, particularly when there is a deadline looming. It is always better to have a stock of words that can be edited, moved about, added to. This is of course much easier when the words have been stored on a word-processor. Keeping a diary can be seen as investing in writing through laying down early versions of what will later become part of a formal report, paper or dissertation. It helps to promote a better, friendlier relationship with writing, rather than perceiving writing as a threat best to be avoided.

Constructing a research plan

Before embarking on a piece of research, it is useful to compile a research plan or proposal which covers all the areas specified in Box 5.3. If your research involves access to clients or service users, or work in an NHS or Social Service setting, you will find that you will be required to submit a research plan to an ethics committee before you can begin collecting any data. Ethics committees will have their own proformas to fill in, covering these questions but perhaps asking them in a slightly different way. Medical ethics committee proformas, for example, tend to include questions on drug side-effects, and so on, that are not relevant to counselling research.

There are no fixed right or wrong research plans in relation to specific research questions. For any research topic, there will be many ways of collecting useful data. There are, however, several ways in which research plans can fail to convince ethics com-

---

Box 5.3

Sections in a research proposal

Aims and objectives of the study
Review of the literature on the topic
Implications of any pilot study carried out
Research questions or hypotheses
Design of the study (the type or genre of the study)
Research sample: inclusion and exclusion criteria, arrangements for
  access
Ethical issues and how they will be addressed
Procedures for data collection
Method of data analysis
How results will be disseminated
Practical relevance of the study
Personal significance of the research and pre-understandings
Timetable of work, costings, resources needed
Qualifications and previous research experience of researcher(s)
Arrangements for supervision, support and research training

---

mittee members, research supervisors or other gatekeepers. The main criteria that are used to evaluate research proposals are:

1   Does the proposal give a clear account of what is intended to happen (who, where, when and how), and why?
2   Is the proposal sufficiently informed by knowledge of previous research in this area (including knowledge of alternative methods)?
3   Is the proposal internally consistent? Do the methods and sample enable the research question(s) to be answered?
4   Is the study ethically sound? Has everything possible been done to ensure that no harm comes to participants?

In situations where a proposal is being submitted for funding support in competition with other proposals, two other criteria can be added to this list:

5   To what extent will the study add significantly to previous knowledge of the topic? How creative or innovative is it?
6   Is the study good value for money?

In circumstances where a study is being carried out by an individual as part of his or her own personal development, or has been commissioned by an agency or clinic, these latter criteria are much less important.

One of the aspects of a research plan that perplexes many people embarking on research for the first time concerns the issues around sampling. The research *population* can be defined as the total set of people from whom the sample is drawn (e.g. all the clients who attend a counselling agency in a given year). The research *sample* can be defined as comprising those people who actually participate in the study (e.g. the clients in that year who agree to complete questionnaires). In any research, it is important to be able to make some kind of statement about the representativeness of the research sample (i.e. the extent to which it reflects the range of people in the research population). In quantitative research, there are well-defined procedures for obtaining representative samples. These include *random* sampling (e.g. every third person on a list) and *stratified* sampling (the population is divided into sub-groups or strata, and a random sample selected from each stratum). Another way of checking the representativeness of a sample is to compare the characteristics of the sample with known characteristics of the population as a whole. For example, in a study of the effectiveness of counselling in a voluntary agency, perhaps only 40 per cent of clients complete a questionnaire. Nevertheless, information about the age, gender and number of sessions attended may be available for *all* clients. If the age, gender and sessions attended for those who completed questionnaires is similar to the range found in the client population as a whole, it would be possible to argue that a reasonably representative sample has been achieved, despite the 60 per cent attrition from the study.

In quantitative research, another issue that is related to sample size is statistical *power*. If statistical comparisons are to be made between groups, then there need to be sufficient cases or subjects in each group. If the numbers in any one group are too small, then the statistical tests used will not be able reliably to detect differences. The 'power' of a statistical test depends on a number of factors, among which sample size plays a major role. On the whole, the bigger the sample, the easier it is to obtain statistically significant results. When making sampling decisions, it is therefore important to ensure that there are sufficient numbers of people in the *smallest* category that is being examined. Here, a 'sufficient' number probably means at least 12 (although 20 is better). In a hypothetical study of the effectiveness of a voluntary counselling agency, it would almost certainly be of interest to know if men benefited more/less than women clients. It is not unusual for women clients to outnumber men in a 4:1 ratio. So, while it might be quite easy to gather data on 12–20 female clients, it might be difficult to get data on a similar number of male clients.

In qualitative research, there is a quite different set of considerations that influence sampling decisions. A lot of the time in qualitative research a large sample is undesirable. If there are too many cases, it becomes impossible to carry out the kind of sensitive, intensive analysis of each case that is the hallmark of good qualitative inquiry. Many published qualitative studies are based on sample sizes of between 10 and 20. The challenge in qualitative research is to ensure that each person interviewed or included is 'theoretically interesting' in that they represent as far as possible a different aspect of the phenomenon being studied. In qualitative research, the decision that enough cases have been included is based not on statistical criteria but on the researcher's feel for the material. Does he or she feel they have learned all they can about the phenomenon? Have the last in the series of interviews failed to generate new insights? Have the researcher's categories of analysis become 'saturated'?

In practitioner research, there may be little or no control over the sample size. There may only be one, two or three clients or colleagues willing to participate in a study. Alternatively, agency politics may mean that *every* client be asked to complete a questionnaire. *This does not matter.* There are many alternative models or genres of research (see Chapter 2). For example, there are $n = 1$, case study or discourse analysis designs that only require one participant. What is important is that the sampling decision is consistent with the overall research approach or genre. It does not make sense to carry out a questionnaire survey on six people. Equally, it does not make sense to attempt intensive qualitative interviews with 100 people.

Ethical issues

In a sense, all aspects of a research plan or proposal reflect ethical or moral issues. There are specific ethical issues that relate to maintaining the well-being of participants (these are discussed below). However, the basic coherence of the study is also a moral issue, in that a study which produces no new knowledge or understanding is basically wasting people's time. The moral dimension of practitioner research represents an important set of issues which have not been sufficiently discussed within the field. Most codes of research ethics implicitly assume that the roles of researcher and clinician are quite separate. This separation introduces certain safeguards, by making it clear to everyone that the interests of the researcher and those of the therapist are quite distinct. It is therefore necessary to look closely at the ethical dilemmas associated with practitioner research. The aim here is not to attempt to produce a set of ethical guidelines, since most practitioners will be covered by ethical codes published by professional associations such as the BAC, BPS, or UKCP and will need to familiarise themselves with these documents. The aim is rather to open out for discussion some of the questions that must be considered by any practitioner planning a research study that involves clients or service users.

Within the general professional ethics literature, a set of core ethical principles have been identified. These are: *beneficence* (acting to enhance client well-being), *nonmaleficence* (avoiding doing harm to clients), *autonomy* (respecting the right of the person to take responsibility for himself or herself), and *fidelity* (treating everyone in a fair and just manner). Taken separately, each of these moral principles can be seen to embody values with which most people would agree. However, in practice there are situations where two or more of these principles can come into conflict. There are also other situations where it is difficult to live up to these ethical ideals.

Many of the ethical questions faced by practitioner-researchers are the same as those encountered by anyone carrying out psychological or social science research. However, there are two distinctive ethical dilemmas which arise for practitioners who carry out studies of their own clients, or of clients within the agency or clinic in which they work. First, for the most part researchers have restricted their moral responsibility to that of avoiding harm, whereas counsellors seek to go beyond nonmaleficence in striving to enhance client well-being (beneficence). It is surely morally wrong for a counsellor or counselling agency to compromise beneficence in the interests of research.

An example here is that of a randomised controlled trial (see Chapter 2) in which clients are evenly allocated to each of two types of therapy. From a research perspective there are various safeguards that can be built in to prevent harm to the client during this process. From a clinical perspective, on the other hand, it would be normal practice in any clinic where there were two alternative therapies on offer to explore fully with the client their feelings about what was available, and to let the client make the choice.

The example of the randomised controlled trial represents an extreme instance of the tension between research ethics and therapy ethics. In a more general sense, many counsellors believe that, if their responsibility is to the well-being and development of the client, then *any* activity which distracts either client or counsellor from this goal should be avoided. No matter how well-intentioned the study, introducing research into counselling runs the risk of bringing another factor into an already complex task. Even if it could be argued that a research study might benefit clients in the future, it might well be that participating in it would not actually *help* this client, today. From this standpoint, even asking the client whether he or she wished to take part in research could potentially endanger the therapeutic frame.

A second distinctive ethical dilemma in practitioner research in counselling is associated with the creation of *dual roles*, for instance when the person who is the counsellor to a client also becomes a researcher and asks permission to use a session tape-recording for research purposes. Many people have written about the problems thrown up by dual roles in counselling (Bond, 1993; Pope, 1991). There are some dual roles (for example when a counsellor also provides nursing care to a person) where both roles involve the 'counsellor' acting solely in the interests of the client. The problem here is that the counselling process may become diluted and lose its focus, or that the therapeutic contract may be unclear. There are other dual relationships where one of the roles requires the client acting in the interests of the counsellor. For example, a client who is a lawyer may then give free legal advice to the counsellor. The risk here is that the acceptance of personal benefits may induce the counsellor to step outside their duty of care to the client. The counsellor may start to ask legal questions at the end of therapy sessions, thus preventing the client from engaging in the normal process of reflecting on the impact of the session. A counsellor who is also researcher to his or her own clients is in this kind of situation; the research data is a benefit to the counsellor, not to the client. The counsellor gains from getting a PhD or a publication. The client only gains from getting good counselling.

In counselling research, as in other types of research on people, the main procedures that are used to ensure ethical standards are *informed consent, confidentiality* and *avoidance of harm*. All three of these procedures are harder to implement effectively when a practitioner is researching his or her own clients, or even when a counsellor is collecting data on the clients of colleagues within the same agency or clinic.

Informed consent

Informed consent arises from the principle of autonomy. The person is regarded as having the right to choose whether or not to participate in research, and therefore must be given the information necessary for this choice in a non-coercive manner. If a counsellor asks a client to participate in research, how possible is it for the client to refuse? Clients may seek to please someone who has helped them. They may be afraid of the consequences of refusing. Can the client believe the counsellor when she asserts that withdrawing from the research at any time is perfectly acceptable? Much of this also holds, although perhaps to a lesser extent, when the researcher is known to be a colleague of the counsellor.

Confidentiality

In most counselling agencies, personal information that could identify clients is very carefully controlled and restricted. Any kind of research involves information passing outside this secure loop. An independent researcher can possess client data that can be made thoroughly anonymous, by identifying cases only with code numbers and never allowing the researcher access to names. For a counsellor researching her own clients, however, the identity of the research participant is always known. In talking about research findings to different audiences, the counsellor-researcher can be in many situations where the identity of the client may inadvertently be disclosed. Clearly, any counsellor would take great pains to avoid such a disclosure. Nevertheless, he or she is in a position of knowing much more about the client when in the role of counsellor than in the role of researcher. It can sometimes be quite hard to keep these 'knowledges' separate. For example, when giving a research presentation at a conference an independent researcher would be asked questions based only on the actual data, because it would be obvious that this data comprised the only knowledge that he or she had about research participants. It is quite common for practitioner-researchers to be asked questions along the lines of 'With your counsellor hat on . . .?' or 'From a practitioner perspective . . .?' In attempting to respond to such questions it is difficult to avoid drawing on personal experience rather than sticking to research data.

Avoidance of harm

In most therapy research investigations, the moment of data collection is explicitly separated off from the moment of therapy. For example, at the end of a session a client may leave the counselling room and go into another room where they complete a questionnaire for fifteen minutes. The questionnaire may be given to them to take home. Within this framework, what happens in the counselling room is clearly marked off from what happens in the research study. The research does not actively intrude into the counselling session. Even when a session is taped, the goal is to make this as much of a 'passive intrusion' as possible. The tape is switched on and then forgotten. If the counsellor is the researcher then none of this is possible, because the counsellor is aware of the aims of the research and of how what is happening in the counselling session is relevant to the research. If, for instance, a counsellor is taping sessions because he is interested in the role of metaphor and figurative language in facilitating therapeutic change, surely he will be super-alert for the occurrence of metaphors in his own and the client's language. He may suppress his own metaphors, for fear of over-influencing the study, or exaggerate them, to produce something that can be analysed later. Can this kind of intrusion into the counselling process be harmful for clients? As far as I know, no one has studied this issue, but it is clearly possible that counsellor involvement in research may skew the counselling process in directions that may not be helpful for clients. Again, this is a situation where the same issues arise even when it is not the actual counsellor, but a colleague, who is the primary researcher. It is highly unlikely that a counsellor could be 'blind' to the research interests or hypotheses of one of his or her colleagues.

In passing, it is perhaps worth reflecting on the fact that all three of these ethical problems are highlighted in one of the oldest and most influential of practitioner research methods in the therapy world – psychoanalytic case studies. To the best of my knowledge, psychoanalysts do not seek informed consent (certainly not in advance) around any research intentions they may have in relation to client material. They have no data set apart from their own clinical notes and memories. They are free to pursue their own theoretical/research interests in their interpretations of client material. So, although psychoanalytic case studies have been hugely successful in generating a coherent body of knowledge (see Kvale, 1996: 74), they carry with them some worrying ethical issues.

I have intentionally constructed a rather gloomy picture of the depth of ethical dilemmas faced by counsellors who decide to research their own practice. This is a gloomy picture because I believe that it is indeed possible to harm clients by 'using' them for research. It is bleak too because there are other, non-ethical, issues that also need to be faced here:

- How honest will a client be when interviewed by their counsellor for research purposes? To what extent can a client be critical of the counselling process?
- How valid is a counsellor's understanding of a client, or of their own work with that client? As an involved participant in a relationship with a client, it can be very difficult for a counsellor to take a detached view of what is happening, or has happened. The actual experience of being the counsellor is so powerful that it is hard to go beyond this experience and develop an understanding that actually makes use of research data.

The point at stake is that it can be very difficult to evaluate or interpret the results of practitioner research into their own clients, notwithstanding any ethical issues. The critique of the psycho-analytic case study method by Spence (1989) offers further elaboration of this question for anyone wishing to explore it in greater depth.

Returning to the ethical challenge represented by practitioner research into own clients, there are a number of possible ways forward:

1 Seek informed consent in advance, before counselling has started, and make it absolutely explicit that receiving counselling is not contingent on participating in the research.
2 Ask for consent at various stages in the counselling, and at the end, to make it possible for the client to withdraw from the study if, for instance, they feel that the material they are disclosing is too sensitive.
3 Make sure that the client has the name of an independent arbiter whom they can contact if they feel under pressure to take part in the research, or are unhappy with any aspect of the arrangements.
4 Collect data that can be analysed by others (e.g. recordings rather than process notes) so that your interpretation of the material, and your impact on the research process, can be checked.
5 If possible, employ a collaborative or dialogical research approach which treats the client as a co-researcher.

Finally, it is important to keep in mind the idea that ethical integrity and good research go hand in hand. Research participants are more likely to open up and contribute good quality information if they trust you and feel safe. Also, at a personal level, there is always ambivalence associated with the role of researcher. This ambivalence can be greatly heightened if, in the back of one's mind, there are worries about whether one is being exploitative or may be damaging research participants.

In recent years there have been several excellent books and articles published on the moral dilemmas arising from research that involves close personal contact with informants. At the end of the chapter there is a list of recommended reading in this area.

Conclusions

The planning phase of a research study is always a time of anxiety. As soon as a topic is identified and the literature begins to open out, it becomes apparent that there are always many alternative pathways that can be followed. The act of deciding on which pathway can be difficult. It is perhaps useful to remember that no piece of research can be perfect. Every method and every research design has its limitations. No research study ever proves anything in itself. The best that can be done is to add another fragment to the mosaic of previous research on the topic. The key skill in research design is perhaps *anticipation*, thinking ahead to what the study will look like in a printed report, and what needs to be done to generate and analyse data that will be necessary to make that report do what it is intended to do.

Further reading

How researchers have struggled with ethical and moral dilemmas

Etherington, K. (1996) 'The counsellor as researcher: boundary issues and critical dilemmas', *British Journal of Guidance and Counselling*, 24 (3): 339–46.

Grafanaki, S. (1996) 'How research can change the researcher: the need for sensitivity, flexibility and ethical boundaries in conducting qualitative research in counselling/psychotherapy', *British Journal of Guidance and Counselling*, 24 (3): 329–38.

Josselson, R. (ed.) (1996) *Ethics and Process in the Narrative Study of Lives*. Thousand Oaks, CA: Sage.

Meara, N.M. and Schmidt, L.D. (1991) 'The ethics of researching the counseling/therapy process', in C.E. Watkins, jr, and L.J. Schneider (eds), *Research in Counseling*. Hillsdale, NJ: Lawrence Erlbaum.

Riches, G. and Dawson, P. (1996) 'Making stories and taking stories: reflections on researching grief and marital tension following the death of a child', *British Journal of Guidance and Counselling*, 24 (3): 357–66.

6

Gathering Data

Research involves collecting new information about the phenomenon being investigated. Often, as reflected in the title of this chapter, this information is called *data*, from the Latin *datum* or 'given'. Although widely used, the term 'data' embodies a particular stance in relation to knowledge. If the information we collect is 'given' (i.e. out there in nature waiting to be harvested) then by implication we are making an assumption that there exists an objective reality that is not affected by our attempt to know it. An alternative way of understanding the nature of knowledge is to regard it as *constructed*. From this perspective, any information that we might collect is shaped by the frame of reference of the inquirer and the process of inquiry. In recognition of this perspective, some researchers talk about gathering 'accounts' or 'representations' rather than 'data'. The word 'data' will be generally employed in this chapter, for the sake of simplicity. But it is important to bear in mind the 'constructed' nature of all data, and not to fall into the trap of equating research data with 'facts'.

There are basically six types of data that have been used in counselling research:

- informant self-report
- external observer reports
- dialogical co-constructions
- official records
- projective techniques
- personal experience

The first two of these data sources (self-report and observation) are the ones that have been most widely applied. In many research situations, the choice is between asking informants (e.g. clients, counsellors) to report on their own experience, or using external raters or judges to code transcripts or recordings.

The choice between different data sources may be made on pragmatic grounds (clients may be willing to fill in questionnaires but not to have sessions tape-recorded), may be associated with theoretical considerations (for example from a humanistic perspective, the client's perceptions or self-reports are the most valid form of data), or can be due to methodological factors (for example when a particular questionnaire has been used by previous researchers).

On the other hand, the choice of data source may not be seen as a choice. For many people, research means filling in questionnaires. The bulk of counselling research studies use self-report questionnaires as their main, or sole, source of data. Questionnaire data is easier to code and analyse than other forms of data. It can therefore be all too easy to assume that a questionnaire is a safe and appropriate method to use. However, there are some significant limitations to self-report questionnaires in the context of counselling research:

- The accuracy of responses to questionnaires depends on the level of self-awareness of the respondent. As counsellors, we *know* that self-awareness is always partial, and that it depends on the quality of the relationship with the person who is asking the questions.
- Questionnaires tend to impose the questioner's categories on the person answering. From a person-centred or humanistic perspective, questionnaires (particularly those employing closed questions) are not good methods for gaining access to the frame of reference of the informant.
- From a psychodynamic perspective, not only will the accuracy of questionnaire data be distorted by defensiveness, but the really interesting material (unconscious fantasies) will forever be out of reach.
- From a behavioural perspective, self-report questionnaires may not be the best way of collecting data on the actual behaviour patterns exhibited by clients (and counsellors) – self-reports convey what the person *thinks* that he or she does, rather than how he or she *actually* behaves.

It is a good policy, therefore, to think carefully about the choice of method of data collection. As a practitioner, the necessity is to collect data that is accurate and sensitive, is appropriate to the research question being pursued, and that makes it possible to write reports and papers that connect with practice. It is also essential to collect data in such a manner as to respect the integrity of the therapeutic process, or even to enhance that process.

Self-report questionnaires

There is a variety of different types of questionnaires that have been used in counselling research. There is a lot of work involved in designing a new questionnaire, so it is sensible to use, or to adapt, existing questionnaires whenever these are available.

Standardised psychometric questionnaires
Psychometric, standardised questionnaire instruments or 'tests' are used in many studies of counselling and psychotherapy. The term 'psychometric' refers to 'measuring the mind', and the purpose of these instruments is to enable accurate measurement of variables relating to different aspects of psychological adjustment, mental health or well-being. Some of the psychometric scales that have been used most often in counselling research are the General Health Questionnaire (GHQ), Beck Depression Inventory (BDI) and the Spielberger State-Trait Anxiety Inventory (STAI).

These instruments have been constructed through a lengthy and demanding programme of development, in order to ensure that they are reliable and valid. The stages of test construction encompass: generating a large pool of possible items or questions, administering these items to a large number of people, carrying out item analysis and (if possible) factor analysis to identify sub-scales, administer a second version of the questionnaire to another sample to develop norms and check validity. These procedures can take years of work. Further information about the principles of psychometric test construction can be found in Beech and Harding (1990), Cronbach (1970), Golden et al. (1984) and Rust and Golombek (1989), as well as in the counselling research texts listed in the Appendix.

When assessing how good a test is, it is necessary to take into account three main criteria:

- *validity* Does the test measure what it is supposed to measure? There are different forms of validity: face, content, criterion (concurrent, predictive), construct;
- *reliability* Is the test robust enough to be used under different circumstances? There are different ways of calculating the reliability of a test, such as internal consistency and test re-test reliability;
- *generalisability* For which populations is the test valid and reliable? Are there norms or validation studies relating to different countries, occupational groups, ethnic groups, etc.?

There are practical issues associated with the use of standardised tests. Because they are so expensive to develop, these tests are often marketed by commercial companies, who charge for their use. Sometimes access to standardised tests or questionnaires is restricted to people who can demonstrate that they are competent to administer and interpret them, such as chartered psychologists.

Difficulties over access, and the problem of choosing from among the range of tests of psychological adjustment that are on offer, have been behind the development of the CORE questionnaire by the Psychological Therapies Research Centre at the University of Leeds (address in Appendix). Funded by the Mental Health Foundation, staff at this Centre have co-ordinated a nationwide project which has culminated in the recent publication of a counselling outcome questionnaire which can be used in a wide variety of settings. The questionnaire is not copyrighted, and is easy to use. Further details of features of the test are displayed in Box 6.1.

The main advantages of using standardised tests are that you can be confident that they will 'work' (i.e. will produce interpretable data) and that you can compare your results with other studies or with published norms. Box 6.2 gives a list of sources of information for finding out which tests exist, and their characteristics. In the Appendix are addresses of the main test publishers. Some tests are controlled and published by their authors, and can only be obtained by writing directly to the author and asking for permission to use the test under specific circumstances. Research

Box 6.1

The CORE questionnaire

CORE stands for Clinical Outcomes in Routine Evaluation, and comprises a system for evaluation, audit and outcome research in counselling and psychotherapy. The main element of the CORE system is a 34-item client-completed questionnaire, which is hand scorable, and gives scores in four main clinical domains: subjective well-being, symptoms, functioning, and risk/harm. There are also 18-item short forms of the questionnaire, which can be used weekly during therapy to monitor on-going change. Items are straightforward, easily understood statements, to which the client responds using a five-point scale. The CORE system was created following a thorough review of the strengths and weaknesses of existing outcome measures, and the needs of users, and was launched in 1998. It looks very likely that it will be widely adopted in clinical psychology, counselling in primary care, student counselling and employee counselling services in Britain, and that within a year or two a substantial bank of normative data will be held by the CORE System Group at the Psychological Therapies Research Centre (PTRC), which for the first time will enable meaningful 'bench-marking' where the profiles of clients using different agencies can be compared in terms of types of problem, severity of problem, number of sessions, and outcome. The CORE system has been designed for use by practitioners and is supported by a helpful and informative handbook. Further information can be obtained from PTRC (address in Appendix).

Box 6.2

Where to find out about tests

Beutler, L.E. and Crago, M. (1983) 'Self-report measures of psychotherapy outcome', in M.J. Lambert, E.R. Christensen and S.S. DeJulio (eds), *The Assessment of Psychotherapy Outcome*. New York: Wiley.

Bowling, A. (1991) *Measuring Health: A Review of Quality of Life Scales*. Buckingham: Open University Press.

Bowling, A. (1995) *Measuring Disease: A Review of Disease-Specific Quality of Life Measurement Scales*. Buckingham: Open University Press.

Bridges, K. and Goldberg, D. (1989) 'Self-administered scales of neurotic symptoms', in C. Thompson (ed.), *The Instruments of Psychiatric Research*. Chichester: Wiley.

Freeman, C. and Tyrer, P. (eds) (1989) *Research Methods in Psychiatry: A Beginner's Guide*. London: Gaskell.

Watkins, jr., C.E. and Campbell, V.L. (eds) (1990) *Testing in Counseling Practice*. Hillsdale, NJ: Lawrence Erlbaum.

articles which report on studies which use tests will normally contain information that will allow you to trace the author or publisher of the test. Alternatively, psychology departments in universities and Health Trusts often maintain test libraries and may be willing to help. Lambert (1994) offers an excellent review of the main issues involved in using standardised measures in outcome research. Lambert, Ogles and Masters (1992) and Froyd, Lambert and Froyd (1996) provide useful suggestions around which measures to choose for which purposes. Meier (1997), in an interesting paper, makes some suggestions about using tests in ways that will make them more sensitive to practice-relevant aspects of client change.

Specifically designed questionnaires

You may find that there is no pre-existing questionnaire that can be employed for the research purpose you have in mind. It may be necessary to design a new questionnaire specifically for use in a particular study. Specifically designed questionnaires have the advantage of being flexible, but the weakness of being of unknown reliability and validity. With self-designed question-naires there is always the danger of not measuring what you think you are measuring, or even of not measuring anything at all (for example, when the questions are ambiguously worded).

The best practice when designing a new questionnaire is to stick to statements about which the person can agree or disagree, and then ask for responses on a five-point or seven-point Likert scale, ranging from 'strongly agree' to 'strongly disagree'. It is always necessary to carry out a pilot study of a new ques-tionnaire, to find out whether the questions make sense to people and to check that there is a good spread of responses. If all research participants give the same answers to a questionnaire item then that item is clearly not effective in differentiating between shades of opinion and experience. In designing a new questionnaire for the first time, there are many issues which need to be considered around layout, the composition of a covering letter or instructions, length, the phrasing of questions and response format. It is helpful to consult some of the textbooks listed in the Appendix, and to have a look at questionnaires designed by other researchers.

It can be very frustrating to collect data with a new ques-tionnaire and then to find that the results just do not make sense, because the questions were not clear enough. Questionnaires that are poorly designed and laid out can also undermine the confidence which colleagues and clients have in one's competence, or in the professionalism of a counselling agency or clinic.

Personal questionnaires

One of the drawbacks of the kinds of questionnaires which have been described in previous sections is that they present each research participant with the same set of questions. While this degree of standardisation makes it possible to make comparisons across large samples of people, it has the disadvantage, in counselling research, that the questions being asked may miss the key problem or issue that has brought the person to counselling. For example, many outcome studies use scales to measure psychiatric symptoms, anxiety, self-esteem and depression. But perhaps a client has a specific concern which does not readily map on to any of these constructs. It may well be that such a client gains a great deal from counselling but that the nature of his or her gains does not show up on the particular questionnaire(s) being used in a study. To overcome this difficulty, several researchers have devised questionnaires which ask clients to identify and then rate the specific problem that they wish to change through counselling. These questionnaires can be administered regularly during counselling (as in n = 1 studies – see Chapter 9) or merely at outset, termination and follow-up. Although some clients change their goals or 'presenting problem' mid-way through counselling, this does not seem to happen frequently enough to become a major difficulty when using this technique in research, particularly in research into time-limited brief counselling. Further information on a range of personal questionnaire formats can be found in the sources listed in Box 6.3.

Open-ended questionnaires

So far, the discussion of self-report questionnaires has focused on instruments designed to produce quantitative data. It is also possible to use open-ended questionnaires which invite people to write in response to open questions such as 'What was most helpful about today's counselling session?' or 'What are your suggestions for improving the service provided by this counselling agency?' In some research situations it can be useful to include one or two general open-ended questions at the end of standard 'rating

---

Box 6.3

Where to find out about individualised methods for evaluating outcomes

Battle, C.C. et al. (1966) 'Target complaints as criteria of improvement', *American Journal of Psychotherapy*, 20: 184–92.

Cytrynbaum, S. et al. (1979) 'Goal attainment scaling: a critical review', *Evaluation Quarterly*, 3 (1): 5–40.

Deane, F.P. et al. (1997) 'Validity of a simplified target complaints measure', *Assessment*, 4: 119–30.

Paterson, C. (1996) 'Measuring outcomes in primary care: a patient generated measure, MYMOP, compared with the SF-36 health survey', *British Medical Journal*, 312: 1016–20.

Phillips, J.P.N. (1986) 'Shapiro Personal Questionnaire and generalized personal questionnaire techniques: a repeated measures individualized outcome measurement', in L.S. Greenberg and W.M. Pinsof (eds), *The Psychotherapeutic Process: A Research Handbook*. New York: Guilford Press.

---

scale' questionnaires, to elicit reactions that might otherwise be missed. The inclusion of open-ended questions in this fashion can encourage participants to take the whole questionnaire more seriously, since what is conveyed is an implication that their personal views are important. Open-ended questionnaires are particularly useful where there is a reasonable expectation that all participants are comfortable with writing. For example, in a survey of the experiences of counselling trainers, I found that most respondents to an open-ended questionnaire wrote answers that were detailed and which made sense (McLeod, 1996). With other research populations, some people may write a great deal, others may write virtually nothing, and some may veer off at tangents that are hard to connect with the themes of the study. In these circumstances, analysing data from open-ended questionnaires can be problematic. In an interview, of course, the same questions might be asked but could be followed up by the interviewer by using probes or requests for clarification where necessary. Examples of the effective use of open-ended questionnaires in practitioner-oriented research can be found in Cummings et al. (1994) and Llewelyn et al. (1988).

The Delphi technique

A useful variant on the self-report questionnaire is found in the *Delphi* technique, originally devised by Delbecq, Van de Ven and

Gustafson (1975). The Delphi method relies on informant self-report, but is significantly more participative and creative than other questionnaire-based techniques. Essentially, a Delphi poll consists of a series of questionnaires distributed to the same group of people. In the first questionnaire, participants are asked to respond to a broad, open question. Their answers are analysed and categorised, and this material forms the basis for a second questionnaire which is sent round, asking participants to indicate the extent to which they agree or disagree with statements, whether they would re-word statements, or whether important issues are missing. The responses to the second questionnaire are again analysed and built into a third questionnaire. Usually only three cycles are required to reach a reasonable consensus. Clearly, in comparison with normal one-shot questionnaires the Delphi method needs participants who are motivated, knowledgeable and comfortable with writing tasks. The Delphi technique has been used in practitioner research as a means of surveying therapists' views on a variety of topics. Some Delphi studies have asked practitioners to forecast future trends in their profession (e.g. Heath, Neimeyer and Pedersen, 1988; Neimeyer and Norcross, 1997). White et al. (1997) used this method to identify therapists' views on the core skills involved in effective couples and family therapy. The Delphi method can also be applied in research with clients or service users. For example Jeffery et al. (1995) used this technique to elicit community members' perceptions and preferences regarding the way in which a rural counselling service should be organised in their area. Further information on how to use the Delphi technique can be found in Delbecq, Van de Ven and Gustafson (1975), Jenkins and Smith (1994) and Fish and Busby (1996).

Other types of questionnaire
There are several other ways of collecting research data through questionnaires. Questionnaires can be administered on computer rather than in paper-and-pencil form. Response formats can include rating scales, visual analogue scales, forced choice comparisons, choosing between alternative statements, and rank ordering of preferences. In some questionnaires, respondents may be asked to read a vignette and then answer questions on it. These and other variations on questionnaire methodology are described in most standard research methods textbooks.

Interviewing

Carrying out face-to-face interviews is probably (following questionnaires) the most popular method of data collection in social
science and psychology, and in counselling research. There are a
number of different types of interview technique:

- the *structured interview*, which follows a strictly defined
  series of questions;
- the *focused or semi-structured interview* in which the
  researcher asks a few general questions and encourages the
  informant to respond openly around these topics, perhaps
  using prompts to check that certain aspects of these topics
  have been covered;
- *unstructured or 'free story' interviews*, in which the interviewer outlines the area that he or she wishes to explore, but
  does not otherwise constrain what the informant says;
- *focus group interviews* are semi-structured interviews in
  which a small group (around eight) collectively discuss their
  responses to questions;
- *telephone interviews* are conducted over the phone, rather
  than face-to-face;
- *assisted recall interviews* have been used in therapy process
  research (see Chapter 10). Informants are played back
  recordings of their counselling session to remind them of
  what they were experiencing during these moments of the
  session;
- *think-aloud protocols* are a form of structured interview in
  which a person carrying out a task (e.g. making a diagnostic
  decision) is invited to report on his or her internal thought
  processes. This type of interview can also be regarded as a
  type of observational research (see below).

There are a number of advantages to interviewing as a means of
collecting research data. Most people are likely to co-operate
with a request to be interviewed, partly because they feel in
control of the situation. The interview method can deal effectively with complex and sensitive topics. A skilled interviewer
will maximise the chances that information collected is accurate
and complete. Visual or audio material can be presented to the
informant. Return visits can be more easily made to check

information. The respondent gets a chance to get 'into' the topic, thus facilitating recall of information. Sensitive questions can be introduced at appropriate points in the interview. Finally, counsellors possess good interview skills, and therefore should be capable of gathering good-quality data using this method.

The disadvantages of interviewing as a research method are that it can be expensive in time, person-hours and transport. The personality, sex, or appearance of the interviewer may influence the informant to give certain answers. Anonymity is not possible. Poorly trained or unmotivated interviewers may omit questions, mis-record answers, or even fabricate results. If tape-recording is used, transcription and analysis of material may be very time-consuming.

There is a set of key tasks involved in designing an effective interview schedule (see Box 6.4). Interviews tend to go well when the researcher has thoroughly rehearsed the interview schedule. It can sometimes be helpful to send participants a pre-interview questionnaire, or even a copy of the interview schedule a couple of days in advance, so that they can prepare themselves for the interview. At the end of any interview, it is good practice to ask the person for their reflections on the interview process and what they have felt about it.

Although most interviews are carried out in a face-to-face individual meeting, there are several other ways of structuring interview situations. In some studies, telephone interviews can be an appropriate and cost-effective means of collecting data. The *focus group* interview consists of a group discussion on a topic, facilitated by one or two researchers. This technique has been widely used in management, health and marketing research, and has the advantage of allowing participants to comment on the points of view of other members of the group and generally become energised and involved in the topic. Potentially, a focus group can generate good-quality interview material. There are a number of excellent texts which explain how to conduct focus groups (Vaughn et al., 1996; Greenbaum, 1998). Morgan and Krueger (1997) have produced a six-volume *Focus Group Kit* which covers all aspects of this method. Another group-based interview method is the *Nominal Group Technique* (NGT) (Delbecq, Van de Ven and Gustafson, 1995). Compared to focus group approach, NGT offers a more structured format for organising a group meeting, culminating in the collection of quantitative

Box 6.4

The process of designing an interview schedule/guide

Identify your research question(s).

'Brainstorm' to generate as many different questions on this topic as possible.

Sort these into themes or general areas.

In each area or section of the interview, have a few broad, open questions, and other follow-up or 'probe' questions.

Build up to sensitive questions. It is best to begin and end an interview with 'easy' questions.

Prepare a guide for yourself which includes an introduction (e.g. who you are, the purpose of the interview, etc.), a confidentiality and informed consent protocol, 'face-sheet' questions (e.g. the name, age, sex, occupation of the respondent), the questions you will ask, and closing remarks.

Familiarise yourself with the guide.

Try to work out how long it will take to go through the schedule with an informant (45–60 minutes is usually long enough for most people).

Decide how you will record the informant's replies.

Test the interview schedule out on a friend or 'tame' informant to make sure the questions make sense to someone else.

ratings. The Herman et al. (1996) study is an example of how NGT has been used as a method for generating information about service users' perceptions of a family support programme.

No matter which type of interview format is employed, there are a number of practical issues which need to be taken into consideration when using this method. Common problems in interviewer studies include tape-recorder failure, failure to establish rapport/trust, letting the informant dominate the interview, and collecting more information than can be used. In counselling research, an additional dilemma when interviewing concerns maintaining the boundary between research and therapy, particularly when interviewing clients or service users.

A further dilemma involves the degree of mutuality that may be allowed to develop, or may be intentionally fostered, between interviewer and informant. In recent years, feminist researchers have argued that, certainly in relation to studies of women's experiences, an interview situation in which there is a detached, professional distance between researcher and 'researched' is

artificial and counter-productive. These researchers have proposed that it is essential to return to the original meaning of
interview as a meeting place for the views of two people (Kvale,
1996; Oakley, 1981). This point takes us on to another approach
to data collection, which sees mutual collaboration and dialogue
as methods of data collection.

Dialogical methods

There have been two principal approaches to social science
inquiry that have adopted a dialogical approach. First, the
human inquiry, or *co-operative* inquiry movement, inspired by
John Heron, Peter Reason and Judy Marshall (see Chapter 11),
has asserted that the most powerful understandings are generated by groups of people working together to explore their
experience of a phenomenon. Within this model of research, an
important source of research data comprises the various forms of
dialogue occurring between research co-participants.

The second dialogical perspective has been developed by
social scientists influenced by postmodern thinking. These
researchers question the way that much research is published,
in particular the privileging of the 'voice' of the academic
researcher and the concomitant silencing of the voices of research
informants and participants. For some social scientists, there is a
'crisis of representation' within qualitative research, in which the
traditional academic paper comes to be seen as an inadequate
vehicle for representing the experiences of people contributing to
a study. Some of these researchers have begun to experiment with
the creation of 'multi-voiced' texts which convey a dialogical
understanding of a topic of inquiry. Examples of this kind of work
can be found in the study of communal living in Israel by
Josselson, Lieblich, Sharabany and Wiseman (1997) and the study
of the experience of emotional difficulties around eating
conducted by Ellis, Kiesinger and Tillmann-Healy (1997). Neither
of these studies directly investigates therapy, but they are nevertheless pieces of research that are of great relevance to therapists.
It is no coincidence that all of these authors are women.

There are many ways in which dialogical research is highly
appropriate for counsellors. The notion of reality being constructed through a dialogue between different voices is consistent
with the experiences of many counsellors, and with several

theoretical models of counselling. But, more than that, just as many counsellors understand that their reaction to the client is a powerful source of data, dialogical inquiry gives researchers permission to use their reactions to research participants as data.

Observation

It is important to make a distinction between self-report and observation. In any of the self-report methods introduced earlier in the chapter, data arises from the informant's ability to perceive, remember and reflect on the events of his or her life. Whatever form of self-report is used, this approach involves entering the person's awareness and asking them questions. These questions in themselves partially shape and determine the replies that can be given. Observational methods attempt to get round some of these limitations of self-report by collecting information about what a person *does* rather than what they *say they do.* There are basically two types of observational research: participant and non-participant.

Non-participant observation
Non-participant observation refers to studies in which the researcher attempts to make an objective record of the behaviour of a person or group. There have been many studies in the field of counselling and psychotherapy which have employed this approach, particularly in the area of process research (see Chapter 10). In the early years of this kind of research, observers would, for instance watch group therapy sessions from behind a two-way mirror and make a mark on a coding sheet whenever a group member engaged in a particular type of behaviour. This is clearly arduous, potentially intrusive and extremely time-consuming and expensive, as well as being prone to error. In recent years, virtually all observational research has depended on video or audio recording of behaviour.

The difficulty with observational data recorded on video or audio recordings lies in what to do with it once the recording has been obtained. A video tape in itself is not research data, at least for most purposes. It must be transformed into numerical data (usually) so that patterns of behaviour can be analysed and compared. To do this requires the creation of a coding scheme, which observers use to rate segments of the tape. It is necessary to use two or three raters, and to evaluate the level of their inter-rater reliability, to overcome any biases in the way that individual raters might be applying the coding scheme.

Although much valuable research has been carried out using non-participant methods, there are significant methodological issues raised in the context of their use in counselling research. One issue concerns the selection of segments of a tape for analysis. It is usually far too time-consuming to ask observers to rate every minute of a one-hour counselling session. However, choosing a ten-minute segment may mean that the most import-ant passage of the session is missed. Also, raters may find it difficult to rate, for example, empathy levels or accuracy of interpretation within a ten-minute segment if they do not know what has happened before and after the segment. This leads to the issue of meaning. Strictly speaking, non-participant observa-tional data only reflects patterns of behaviour, and cannot give any insight into what this behaviour *means* to the counsellor and client being recorded. Given that counselling is an activity that centres around the negotiation of meaning, this can be a serious drawback, which many researchers have attempted to overcome by combining observational data with at least some self-report information.

There is another category of non-participant observation which may be of value in some counselling projects. Direct observa-tions can be made of physiological variables around health status indicators, using monitoring of heart rate, blood alcohol levels and so on. Clearly, these methods require collaboration with colleagues from other disciplines.

Participant observation
Participant observation involves spending time with people, taking part in their lives, and building up a personal under-standing of how they act and how they view the world. So, although participant observation data is mainly observational, in the form of field notes, it also includes engaging in conversations and informal interviews that introduce an element of self-report. Participant observation is a method that has been widely used in sociology and social anthropology, where it is often described as *ethnography*. The aim of this type of study is to generate a comprehensive account of the 'way of life' of a group of people, including their patterns of relationship, beliefs, rituals, etc.

There are some fairly severe practical issues associated with participant observation research. It takes a long time. It can be difficult to get permission to join a group as a semi-stranger. The data that is collected is complex and not easy to analyse. Ethical difficulties can arise from being so close to informants over a period of time – what if one of them does something illegal? It is a challenge to maintain an appropriate balance between involvement and distance. Adler and Adler (1994) and Atkinson and Hammersley (1994) review various issues associated with the use of participant observation.

Participant observation has not been used to any great extent in counselling research, even though it is a key method in social science as a whole. One of the reasons for this may be that most counselling research is done by counsellors, whereas one of the requirements in ethnographic research is to be a 'stranger', to know nothing about a group and thereby to be in a position to learn without imposing too many assumptions. One of the few ethnographic studies of therapy has been Gubrium's (1992) research into two family therapy centres. This study illustrates the demanding nature of participant observation and also its unique value. The picture of family therapy created by Gubrium (1992) is recognisable to any therapist (or client), but is also disturbingly subversive of our taken-for-granted ways of making sense of our work.

It would be quite possible for counsellors to carry out participant observation research in agencies or clinics other than the one in which they themselves work. It could be quite useful for everyone involved to have a colleague from another agency come in as a 'visitor-consultant' and conduct a participant observation study. I think it is much harder to pull off a participant observation study as an insider, for example as a member or employee of an agency or as a client. In this situation, the tension between the roles of, for example, counsellor, colleague and researcher would be immense. There might also be severe ethical and moral dilemmas involved in writing later about colleagues who, at the time, regarded you as one of them. On the other hand, there are aspects of therapy that may *only* be discoverable through insider participant observation research. The work of Jeffrey Masson, particularly his account of undergoing psychoanalytic training (Masson, 1991), can be seen as a piece of insider participant observation. This data could not have been collected in any other way. The personal cost of collecting it, for Masson, was substantial.

Other approaches to observational research
Any kind of observational research is likely to take up a great deal of research time, and for that reason alone may not represent a realistic choice for many practitioner-researchers. However, there are many research questions where self-reports are not sufficient, and where it is highly desirable to be able to collect observational data of some kind. In these circumstances, it may be useful to consider data collection methods that combine some of the features of self-report, but with an observational focus.

It is possible to ask people to monitor or observe their own behaviour. For example, in a study on the way in which counselling training influences the role of community nurses, participants could be asked to keep daily work diaries for a period of time before and after the training, in which they record the proportion of time spent each day using counselling skills, direct treatment of patients, administration, etc. Other examples of self-observation can be found in the genre of 'n = 1' single case studies described in Chapter 2. In these studies, clients are typically asked to keep a log of the frequency of target behaviours such as eating, smoking or compulsive thoughts. A final example of self-recording of behaviour is the work of Mihalyi Csikzentmihalyi on measuring the proportion of 'flow' experiences in everyday life. In some of these studies, participants are provided with an electronic pager and booklet of self-report forms. Several times each day for one week they will be sent signals asking them to record on a form what they are doing, where they are doing it, and how they feel about it (Csikzentmihalyi and Rathunde, 1993). DeVries (1992) includes examples of the application of this approach in studies of psychotherapy.

Quasi-observational data can also be collected through think-aloud interviews and recall interviews, described earlier in this chapter. Another quasi-observational method is the *critical incident report* (Flanagan, 1954). Instead of asking the person to give their general impressions of some area of experience, they are invited to give a detailed account of a significant incident. The person is encouraged to go into enough detail to get beyond an impressionistic account of an event and get closer to what actually happened.

Projective techniques

Projective techniques represent a method that falls somewhere between self-report and observation. The person is presented with an ambiguous stimulus of some kind. Their response to this stimulus is regarded as expressing the typical way in which they deal with situations. It is as though the person 'projects' himself or herself into the stimulus. This data is partly self-report, in that the informant is personally conveying information about self. On the other hand, they are not aware of what they are saying or writing (supposedly) and the task of the researcher is to observe the way that the participant responds to the task.

The earliest projective techniques were the word-association test and the Rorschach inkblot test. In the 1930s Henry Murray and Christiana Morgan devised what has become perhaps the most useful projective method, the Thematic Apperception Technique (TAT). In the TAT, the person is presented with a series of pictures, and asked to write an imaginative story about what is happening in the story. It is assumed that the writer will project his or her own wishes, needs and attitudes into the hero of the story, and that the other characters in the story, and its general ambience, will convey information about the environment or world in which the person sees himself or herself as living.

Projective techniques are currently unfashionable within counselling and psychotherapy research circles, because they are associated with psychoanalytic ideas and are seen as being very difficult to interpret reliably. Nevertheless, there are some research questions around which it is very difficult to get people to talk freely. Some topics are highly sensitive, or embedded in political correctness, and it may be more effective to give people an opportunity to express their experiences through imagery and metaphor by using projective methods than it would be to ask 'straight' questions. Useful sources of further information about projective techniques are Branthwaite and Lunn (1983), Cornelius (1983), McClelland (1980) and Semeonoff (1976). Hingley (1995) represents an example of the use of projective techniques in a practitioner research study.

Official documents and historical data

Documentary data represents a resource which is under-utilised in counselling research. There is a powerful expectation in counselling research that doing research always involves going out and collecting new primary data. This is a pity, because there is a great deal of data that already exists and is not being exploited. Some of these sources are:

■ Historical documents such as books and articles written by therapists or about therapy. There is much that needs to be understood about the historical development of counselling and psychotherapy. The research by Cushman (1995) represents the kinds of insights that can be generated by analysing historical accounts.

■ Personal accounts written by clients. There are many novels, poems, letters and diaries that have been written by clients and service users. These provide a unique perspective on counselling process and outcome, in so far as they have not been written in response to researcher demands.

■ Case material that is stored in archives. Any attempt to record, transcribe and write about counselling with current clients faces formidable practical and ethical difficulties. There exist, however, several archives containing transcripts of cases (often conducted by eminent and presumably expert therapists) that can be made available to *bona fide* researchers.

■ Information in agency or clinic files. It is difficult to do much research on counsellor notes, because these are not standardised, may be written in a hurry, and may not make sense to anyone else (quite apart from being confidential). Nevertheless, in most agencies and clinics there is a wealth of data that can be used appropriately for research purposes: age, gender, occupation and postcode of clients; identity, age, gender and experience of counsellor; number of sessions attended, gap between sessions, number of missed sessions, presenting problem, number of times taken to supervision, etc. There are many interesting hypotheses that can be tested against this data set, without collecting any new information.

Given the difficulties associated with collecting good-quality new data, it is worth giving consideration to using documentary sources where these are available. The classic introduction to documentary research remains Allport (1942). A more recent account of this method of data collection can be found in Macdonald and Tipton (1993).

Personal experience

Personal, subjective accounts of the meaning of experience or phenomena can also be used as research data. Again, this is not a technique that has been widely employed, because it conflicts with the requirements of the objective 'scientific' approach which is so highly valued by the academy. On the other hand, one of the most influential studies in the mental health field has been the research carried out by Rosenhan (1973) and his colleagues, in which, basically, they got themselves admitted to mental hospitals and then wrote about their experiences. Another example of the use of self-report can be found in the collection of essays edited by Feltham (1998), in which a number of experienced therapists write about what their work has taught them about the human condition. The *Changes* journal is another good source of first-person reflexive studies. There are perhaps two dangers inherent in using personal experience. The first danger is that it is in fact enormously difficult to gain enough critical distance from personal experience to get to the point of being able to write sensibly about it. Sometimes, the attempt to write about personal experience for a professional or academic audience can be painful, paralysing and self-destructive. There are some experiences that are better conveyed through novels, poems and paintings. The second problem with using personal experience as data is that the 'research' can degenerate into authority-saturated pronouncements from experts on high. Despite these difficulties, there is certainly great scope for the creative use of personal experience methods in practitioner research in counselling.

Conclusions: data collection in the context of counselling practice

The central message of this chapter is that there are many different ways to collect interesting and useful data. It can be valuable to employ more than one method of data collection in a study. Combining methods makes it possible to 'triangulate' across data sources, and to some extent to overcome the limitations of any one specific method. Although questionnaires and interviews are practicable and flexible methods, it is important to keep in mind that there are many different ways of interviewing and of using questionnaires. There are also many methods that are perhaps less widely used in counselling research, but which have a lot to offer.

There are many issues to consider when choosing a method of data collection in the context of a counselling research study. One of the key issues, and one which is generally given little attention in research methods textbooks, concerns the degree to which participation in the research can enhance the therapy. For example, asking a person to fill in a long questionnaire before a counselling session may annoy them, distract them or confuse them. On the other hand, filling in a brief and highly relevant questionnaire can help the person to sharpen the issues that he or she wishes to explore that day with their counsellor. Similarly, a research interview carried out six months after the end of counselling can be a superb means of enabling the person to reflect on their experience of therapy and to extract more meaning from it. Yet it is easy to see that a poorly conducted follow-up interview could open up unresolved issues and block further personal development. I believe that, whatever method is used to collect new data, it is very important to give the informant/respondent an opportunity to comment on their experience of giving that data. We need to know more about how research either facilitates or impedes different aspects of counselling practice. My sense is that most of the time collecting data has a positive effect on the counselling process, but that the occasions where it interferes with the process are hugely important even if they occur much less often.

7

Analysing and Presenting Quantitative Data

One of the key moments in any research study is the time when the data has been collected, and is ready to be analysed. Perhaps more than any other stage of the research process, data analysis requires the application of specific skills. The data analysis element of research is the aspect of inquiry that is perhaps furthest from counselling practice. Interviewing, administering assessment questionnaires and report writing are competencies that should have been developed in counsellor training. Using a statistics package or coding interview transcripts, by contrast, are not competencies that would be part of the everyday repertoire of most counselling practitioners.

The aim of this chapter is to offer an outline of the kinds of skills that are needed in analysing quantitative data. It is important to emphasise that the best way of acquiring these skills is to learn directly from other people, rather than relying solely on books. Many universities offer short courses on statistical techniques. Alternatively, a colleague or research supervisor may represent a source of guidance. It is very difficult to learn about data analysis in the abstract. 'Hands-on' experience is vital, either through working with someone else on the analysis of their data, or by trying out different ways of analysing one's own data.

When reading this chapter, it is also worth bearing in mind that the possibilities for analysing data are always constrained by the preceding stages in a study. For example, if the wrong questions have been asked in a questionnaire, no amount of statistical analysis will retrieve the situation. If questionnaire items have employed a simple yes/no response format, rather than a five-point Likert scale, then the type of statistical analysis that can be carried out is very limited. The point here is that the design and planning of a study should involve looking ahead to the analysis stage and being clear about how the data will be analysed. This is a difficult task for beginning researchers who may not have carried out a research study previously.

Analysing quantitative data

Quantitative data is information about some aspect of human experience, or some personal attribute, that has been transformed into numbers. Always, when quantitative methods are being used, it is essential to remember that what is being measured can also be described in words. For instance, we can say that one person is 'tall' and another is 'short' and therefore that one of them is 'taller' than the other. Quantitative methods allow these kinds of statement to be made with greater precision. We can then say that the first person is 6 feet 4 inches in height and the second person is 5 feet 4 inches in height and that the difference between them is 12 inches. The application of quantitative methods in research has a number of advantages:

1   Statements can be made over which there is a large degree of inter-subjective agreement. We may dispute just what counts as 'tall' (does 5 feet 9 inches count as 'tall'?), but we can all agree on what we mean by a foot or an inch. Quantification therefore introduces objectivity and reliability into research.

2   Quantification makes it easier to make aggregate statements that sum up the characteristics of large numbers of people. Say, for example, a researcher wished to explore the relationship between the therapeutic alliance and outcome in counselling. He or she might interview a large number of clients and collect lots of verbal descriptions of their experience of being in a relationship with their counsellor. Analysing and making sense of this would be interesting but highly time-consuming. It is much easier to administer the Working Alliance Inventory, which measures the important dimensions of the therapeutic relationship.

3 Quantitative methods make it easier to carry out comparisons between different groups of people. Staying with the example of therapeutic alliance research introduced above, it might become clear that there were some clients who had benefited a great deal from counselling, and others who had not. However, it would be difficult to tease out any contrasting experiences of the therapeutic relationship between the members of these two groups using open-ended qualitative interviews. This is because the people being interviewed would most likely all be using the same words to describe their experience ('trust', 'liking', 'warmth', 'bond') and so the researcher would need to be sensitive to perhaps very subtle nuances of difference in the way each of them talked. A researcher using quantitative methods, on the other hand, could use a standardised outcome measure to identify those clients who were 'good outcome' and 'poor outcome' cases, and then compare the Working Alliance scores of the two groups. This method would quickly detect whether there was a reliable difference between the two groups.

4 Transforming experience into numbers opens up many ways of looking for patterns in that experience. For instance, it could be helpful to look at whether male or female clients had better relationships with their counsellors, or whether the strength of the relationship was associated with the total number of sessions used, or the number of appointments missed. Statistical techniques make it easy to check whether such patterns exist in a quantitative data set.

5 Quantification allows researchers to estimate the confidence with which they can claim that their results are reliable or representative. A researcher using the Working Alliance Inventory, for example, can look at the 'norms' or average scores of clients in other studies, and will then be in a position to tell whether his or her particular sample is unusually high or low in terms of relationship factors. If a researcher finds that there is a difference in scores between good or poor outcome groups, there are statistical techniques that will show whether this difference is reliable (i.e. would be likely to occur again) or is due to chance.

There are therefore a number of good reasons for using quantitative methods in counselling research. For many counselling

---

Box 7.1

Steps in quantitative analysis of data

Collect quantitative data (e.g. scores on questionnaire scales)
Enter data into a spreadsheet or matrix, usually in a computer statistics
  package
Decide on which statistical operations are appropriate in testing
  particular hypotheses
Apply statistical tests
Interpret the results of statistical tests
Display and report data

---

practitioners, quantitative research appears to destroy all that is meaningful in therapeutic work, and to generate research findings that are impossible to translate into practice. They would see quantitative research as denying the ambiguity, richness and complexity of human experience, losing the individual in a welter of group averages, and contributing to a distanced, abstracted form of knowing that can never contribute to real understanding. It is essential to be aware of the strengths and weaknesses of quantitative methods. There are some things it does well and others that it does badly.

The series of sub-tasks involved in analysing quantitative data are set out in Box 7.1. Decisions need to be made at each of these stages. The initial data collection procedure, usually in the form of questionnaire, rating scale or coding manual, must be designed in such a way as to produce numbers that are appropriate for the kinds of statistical analysis that are intended. For example, as mentioned earlier, using questionnaire items with simple dichotomous yes/no responses restricts the type of analysis that can be carried out. In most circumstances a five-point or seven-point scale opens up more possibilities for subsequent analysis. Using a 'not applicable' response category can also lead to difficulties in quantitative analysis, because the person is being offered two quite different types of answer to a question. They can indicate that, for instance, they agreed with a statement to a greater or lesser extent. Alternatively, they can indicate that the question is not meaningful to them. This kind of question inevitably ends up dividing research subjects into two sub-groups. Another consideration is whether it is envisaged that it would be useful in a final report to be able to estimate whether a certain proportion of people definitely did or did not agree with a statement or report a particular problem. If a five- or seven-point scale is used, it can become impossible to make such statements with confidence, because subjects are given the option of using the mid-point on the scale (3 or 5) to indicate an ambivalent response. It may be more appropriate to use a four-point or six-point scale which forces a choice one way or the other. These are just some of the ways in which questionnaire design is (or should be) determined by the way that the data will eventually be analysed.

Once the data is collected, it is usually helpful to enter it into a data matrix for ease of analysis. A matrix can be created on paper or on a computer spreadsheet, and comprises a display of rows and columns in which the variable being measured (e.g. age, gender, number of counselling sessions, anxiety score, working alliance score, etc.) are arrayed in the first row along the top and the case numbers are listed in the first column on the left. The data for each person or 'case' can therefore be read by looking along the row that begins with their case number. The range of scores for each variable can be examined by looking down the column which is headed with that variable name. Each cell or box in the matrix can only include one number. While you are free to write text in these cells or boxes (and most computer packages will allow this), this qualitative data clearly cannot be 'added up' or analysed numerically. If you have collected only a limited amount of data (less than 30 variables) on a relatively small number of people (again, less than 30), *and* only plan to carry out a descriptive analysis (see below), then it is easiest to create the data matrix on a large piece of paper (or several sheets of paper taped together). For larger data matrices, or when inferential analysis (see below) is to be carried out, it is better to use a statistics package on a personal computer. Many PCs come supplied with spreadsheets that will handle simple statistical operations. Anything more ambitious will need a purpose-designed software package such as the *Statistical Package for the Social Sciences* (SPSS) or *Minitabs* (see Appendix). SPSS and Minitabs are widely used, and user-friendly books on how to apply them are available. The expense of buying a statistics package may be a factor for some practitioner-researchers. All colleges and universities make these packages available on open-access PCs and may be willing to allow community members to use them. Alternatively, most medium to large organisations will possess, somewhere, a PC loaded with such a package (and may even employ someone who knows how to use it).

Once the data is in a matrix, there are basically two different kinds of statistical operations that can be carried out – *descriptive* and *inferential*. Descriptive statistics aim to provide a summary of the main characteristics of the scores that have been collected. Examples of descriptive statistics are the *mean* (the average score of all subjects on one variable), the *median* (the score which represents the mid-point of the sample, with 50 per cent scoring higher and 50 per cent lower) and the *standard deviation (sd)* (an estimate of how spread-out the scores are; a low *sd* indicates that scores are clustered tightly around the mean, whereas a high *sd* indicates that scores are distributed across the whole range).

Inferential statistics, by contrast, are used to answer questions or to test hypotheses. For example, a research hypothesis may be that women clients report better therapeutic alliance scores than do male clients. It is fairly easy to work out the mean therapeutic alliance scores of the male and female clients respectively. What is harder is to know whether the difference between their mean scores reveals a real difference, or merely reflects random or chance differences in the particular groups of men and women that have been included in the study. After all, another sample of women clients would yield a slightly different mean score. What inferential statistics make possible, in this kind of situation, is to estimate the degree of confidence with which a result can be regarded as due to chance. All inferential statistics, one way or another, function to calculate the probability with which a particular pattern of scores might be obtained by chance. If the statistical calculation shows that it is relatively unlikely that the result would be found by chance, then we can accept that what we have found is (in some sense) a 'true' difference.

The way in which a statistical programme reports on the likelihood of a pattern of results being due to chance is through a *probability* figure. Statisticians have decided on a convention in which an absolute certainty that something will happen (e.g. the sun rising tomorrow) is reported as a probability of 1, whereas an absolute impossibility (e.g. Elvis Presley being discovered alive) is reported as a probability of 0. An event that is very unlikely is indicated by a number close to zero and an event that is highly likely is indicated by a number close to 1. For example, when tossing a coin the chance of getting a head or a tail is even, so the probability of either is 0.5 (it will happen 5 times in 10). The chances of Scotland winning the World Cup are, alas, remote, and so this event may be said to have a probability of 0.01 (one chance in 100).

In research on counselling and psychotherapy it is generally accepted that if a pattern of results is shown to be likely to occur by chance more than 1 time in 20 (a probability of 0.05) then it cannot be taken to be a 'true' result. When reading research reports and articles, you will find that the terminology generally used is $p < .05$. This means that the probability of the result being due to chance is *less than* 1 in 20 (.05) and that therefore on balance we can assume that the result is due to a real difference between the groups rather than attributable to chance factors. (In some studies probabilities of .01 – one in 100 – are used, which are more rigorous still.) The p value is known as the *significance level*, and results that meet the $p < .05$ criterion are regarded as *statistically significant*.

Statistical tests have been designed to assess the significance of differences found when data is analysed in a variety of ways. For example, it is possible to compare the mean scores of one group of people with those of another. The statistical test used here is the *t-test* or *analysis of variance* (ANOVA). On other occasions it may be more relevant to look at whether high scores on one variable are associated with high scores on another variable. The test used for this purpose is the *correlation* coefficient. There are many statistical tests available, depending on the analysis that is required to answer the specific research question. Any statistics textbook will provide clear guidelines on the circumstances under which particular tests can and cannot be applied.

This section has not attempted to supply a comprehensive introduction to quantitative methods, but instead to offer a framework within which practitioners can make sense of what statistics can and cannot do, and how they operate. Anyone intending to use statistics in a counselling research study is advised to attend a training course. There are many excellent textbooks available, some of which are listed below.

The key to using quantitative methods in practitioner research is to accept that they represent a way of knowing that is at odds with much of what happens in counselling practice. Quantification requires reducing the complex reality of the person to a set of variables. Getting something out of the data requires formulating precise hypotheses with which to interrogate these variables.

Further reading

Bausell, R.B. (1986) *A Practical Guide to Conducting Empirical Research*. New York: Harper and Row.

Bryman, A. and Cramer, D. (1990) *Quantitative Data Analysis for Social Scientists*. London: Routledge.

Cozby, P.C. (1985) *Methods in Behavioral Research* (3rd edn). Palo Alto, CA: Mayfield.

Howell, D.C. (1987) *Statistical Methods for Psychology* (2nd edn). Boston: Duxbury.

Knapp, T.R. (1996) *Learning Statistics through Playing Cards*. Thousand Oaks, CA: Sage.

Lewis-Beck, M.S. (1993) *Basic Statistics*. Thousand Oaks, CA: Sage.

Pilcher, D.M. (1990) *Data Analysis for the Helping Professions: A Practical Guide*. London: Sage.

Wright, D.B. (1996) *Understanding Statistics: An Introduction for the Social Sciences*. London: Sage.

8

Doing Qualitative Research

Qualitative research can be considered as 'a process of systematic inquiry into the meanings which people employ to make sense of and guide their actions'. The key idea here is that of uncovering, articulating, elucidating or illuminating *meaning*. The focus on meaning denotes a fundamental difference between qualitative and quantitative research that reaches beyond the fact that the latter is mainly concerned with the analysis of numbers and the former with the analysis of words and text. Ultimately, in attempting to measure or 'scale' human behaviour and attributes, the quantitative researcher needs to conceive of people, and life, as comprising of a set of interacting *variables*. The knowledge technology represented by quantitative research is designed to ascertain the degree of association, or the cause and effect linkage, between one variable and another. By contrast, a qualitative researcher views people as active, purposeful agents, engaged in co-constructing a world of meaning. There is a basic contrast here in the image or concept of the person being employed by researchers from these two traditions. It is ultimately a philosophical difference. These are two alternative ways of understanding the world.

There are a number of important implications that arise from the distinctive philosophical position within which qualitative research is rooted. These are:

1 At school, college or during their professional education (e.g. in any of the health professions) many people have acquired

a notion of 'science' and 'knowledge' as being objective, precise, detached, involving numbers and experiments and so on. To do good qualitative research it is necessary to unlearn these assumptions, in order to be able to learn anew how to make sense in a different way. The core skills of qualitative research include not only technical knowledge and procedures (some of which are described later in this chapter), but also an understanding of philosophical concepts around social constructionism, phenomenology and hermeneutics.

2   For other people, whose schooling or professional education may have been in the arts and humanities, the notion of working with meaning may represent familiar territory. For these people, one of the challenges involved in becoming a qualitative researcher is to realise that, unlike inquiry and scholarship in fields such as history and literary criticism, making sense of meaning within the domain of counselling and psychotherapy research has an added dimension. The goal of counselling research is to produce *practical* knowledge. There is therefore more of an emphasis on validity, credibility and method in qualitative counselling research than there is in scholarship in the humanities.

3   There has been a tendency for supporters of the qualitative and quantitative world-views to see themselves as being in competition: 'We are right and you are wrong.' For counselling researchers this tension can be encountered in the medical world, where some doctors can see no merit whatsoever in qualitative research, and regard randomised controlled trials as the only method of achieving valid knowledge. In the world of classical psychoanalysis, by contrast, many analysts would view any attempt to measure the phenomena of the analytic hour as completely ridiculous. Given that in most situations the quantitative/experimental scientific tradition is institutionally dominant, this conflict can make life difficult for qualitative researchers, and can lead to time being wasted in defending methods rather than in getting on with useful research.

4   Problems can arise in attempting to carry out research which mixes qualitative and quantitative methods. My own personal position is that qualitative and quantitative methodologies both represent useful ways of knowing, and that an adequate understanding of counselling requires using both (in fact, involves using anything that comes to hand). Nevertheless, it

is important to recognise that each approach is built around its own 'logic of justification' or set of rules and procedures, and that something that makes sense within one approach may look odd and misguided within another. A simple example relates to the issue sample size, the number of participants or 'subjects' to be included in a study. Within quantitative research there are clear guidelines for how to achieve a representative sample which is large enough to enable sufficiently powerful statistical analyses to be carried out. On the whole, these guidelines tend to suggest that bigger samples are better. Within qualitative research, there are many instances where bigger samples are disastrous, because the researcher becomes swamped with data and is then unable to carry out an analysis that has sufficient sensitivity and depth. Anyone seeking to combine qualitative and quantitative methods in a single study is well advised to think and plan carefully (see Brannen, 1992 or McLeod, 1994b, for further discussion of this issue).

People doing a piece of qualitative research for the first time typically seek out an introductory practical text such as Marshall and Rossman (1995) or Strauss and Corbin (1990). These are excellent books, but they concentrate mainly on the practicalities of qualitative research, on 'how to do it'. There is a time for practical detail, but my advice would be to begin the process of preparing to carry out a qualitative study by spending some time reading about the historical and philosophical background to this kind of work, and also reading some actual qualitative research studies. The original core philosophical texts are, I find, pretty hard going and take a long time to read (even longer to understand). Ultimately, your philosophy of qualitative research reading journey may take in seminal texts such as Rorty (1980), Gadamer (1975) and Gergen (1994). But it is much better to start with something that offers a general over-view of the philosophical terrain, such as Denzin and Lincoln (1994a) or the essays in Hammersley (1993). There are many good examples of qualitative research in counselling and psychotherapy that have been published in recent years. A list of qualitative research 'thrillers' is given in Box 8.1. As you read some of these books and papers, it may be helpful to reflect on the following questions:

Box 8.1

Good examples of qualitative research in counselling

Angus, L.E. and Rennie, D.L. (1988) 'Therapist participation in metaphor generation: collaborative and noncollaborative styles', *Psychotherapy*, 25: 552–60.

Bachelor, A. (1988) 'How clients perceive therapist empathy: a content analysis of "received" empathy', *Psychotherapy*, 25: 227–40.

Cummings, A. et al. (1994) 'Templates of client change in short-term counseling', *Journal of Counseling Psychology*, 41 (4): 464–72.

Davis, K. (1986) 'The process of problem (re)formulation in psychotherapy', *Sociology of Illness and Health*, 8: 44–74.

Elliott, R. and Shapiro, D.A. (1992) 'Client and therapist as analysts of significant events', in S.G. Toukmanian and D.L. Rennie (eds), *Psychotherapy Process Research: Paradigmatic and Narrative Approaches*. London: Sage.

Ellis, C., Kiesinger, C.E. and Tillmann-Healy, L.M. (1997) 'Interactive interviewing: talking about emotional experience', in R. Hertz (ed.), *Reflexivity and Voice*. Thousand Oaks, CA: Sage.

Gubrium, J.F. (1992) *Out of Control: Family Therapy and Domestic Disorder*. Newbury Park, CA: Sage.

Hill, C.E., Nutt-Williams, E., Heaton, K.J, Thompson, B.J. and Rhodes, R.H. (1996) 'Therapist retrospective recall of impasses in long-term psychotherapy: a qualitative analysis', *Journal of Counseling Psychology*, 43: 207–17.

Howe, D. (1989) *The Consumer's View of Family Therapy*. Aldershot: Gower.

McKenna, P.A. and Todd, D.M. (1997) 'Longitudinal utilization of mental health services: a time-line method, nine retrospective accounts, and a preliminary conceptualization', *Psychotherapy Research*, 7: 383–96.

Rennie, D.L. (1994a) 'Clients' deference in psychotherapy', *Journal of Counseling Psychology*, 41: 427–37.

- What do I like and appreciate about this study? Is there anything that annoys and frustrates me?
- How does the author persuade me that what he or she is writing is true?
- What might this study offer my practice as a counsellor?
- What can I take from this book or paper that I would wish to use in my own research? How could I improve on what the author of this book/paper has done?

Reading qualitative papers from the outset can provide a useful sense of what to be aiming for. One of the characteristics of qualitative research is that it generates vast amounts of material (interview transcripts, notes, memos). In the end all this material must be condensed down into the results section or chapter of a dissertation (perhaps 10,000 words) or of a paper (perhaps

1,000–2,000 words). It is very helpful to have some idea of how to pull off the condensing trick. But more than that, it is essential to gain a feel for the *spirit* of qualitative research, and to make up one's own mind about what constitutes good work in this area.

Another useful source of insight and guidance when setting out on qualitative inquiry is to read about the experiences of other researchers. The actual process of doing qualitative research is beset with anxiety, ambiguity and uncertainty. It is easy to get downhearted and to start to believe in one's unique incompetence. It is reassuring to learn that other people have visited this place and have survived. Interesting personal accounts of the experience of doing qualitative research in counselling or counselling-related fields can be found in Etherington (1996), Grafanaki (1996), Kiesinger (1998) and Rennie (1996).

The diversity of qualitative research

The use of qualitative methods draws upon a number of research traditions or genres, each of which has made a distinctive contribution to the development of this approach to what might be known as *human science* (Rennie, 1994d): hermeneutics, phenomenology, ethnography, feminist research, grounded theory analysis, co-operative inquiry, discourse analysis, narrative research, conversational analysis. The various traditions that constitute the field of qualitative research are represented in the authoritative *Handbook of Qualitative Research*, edited by Norman Denzin and Yvonna Lincoln (1994b). Current debates and developments in qualitative research can be found in the journals *Qualitative Inquiry* and *Qualitative Health Research*, and in the ever-expanding Sage qualitative methods book list.

The existence of diversity within the qualitative research domain can be scary for new researchers, since it immediately introduces a requirement to choose between approaches that may only be dimly understood at that point. Many novice qualitative researchers find that the best strategy for coping with the confusing richness of methodological options is to opt for one of the *generic* approaches offered in books such as Mason (1996) or Marshall and Rossman (1995). Another perfectly sensible strategy that many people follow is to decide to use a *grounded theory* approach (Strauss and Corbin, 1990). Grounded theory is undoubtedly the current 'market leader' in qualitative research. It is well understood and there is a wide literature on applications of grounded theory to different research topics.

However, it seems to me that the diversity of qualitative research genres is not merely a matter of confusion or of competitiveness between different research groups, but is an inescapable feature of this way of knowing. Quantitative research practice espouses a 'positivist' or 'realist' view that there is a single, knowable objective world out there, and it is the job of the scientist to arrive as closely as possible at the one true set of laws which explain the workings of that world. Qualitative research, by contrast, adopts a *social constructionist* perspective (Gergen, 1985, 1994) which takes the position that the reality of everyday life is co-constructed through the cultural and historical activities of people. There are therefore multiple realities, reflecting the interests and worlds of different cultural groups. Moreover, it is important for the researcher to locate himself or herself within their own cultural tradition. The basic tool of qualitative research is the researcher. Individual researchers and research teams are therefore engaged in a process of *constructing* knowledges. To arrive at a single unitary knowledge or at a unitary method of creating knowledge is not only impossible from a social constructionist standpoint but is also undesirable. A unified 'God's eye' view of things is totalitarian, and can only serve the interests of the dominant power elite in a society. One of the primary aims of social constructionist qualitative research is to keep the human conversation open, to keep pointing out that there is no *one* truth.

But enough of the ideological ranting. The point here is that multiple genres are intrinsic to the qualitative package. Denzin and Lincoln (1994a) urge qualitative researchers to celebrate diversity and to regard themselves as 'bricoleurs', assembling whatever concepts and techniques are necessary to advance their particular research project. Returning to some of the themes introduced in Chapter 1, I would argue that the image of the practitioner-researcher as bricoleur is consistent with the requirement that good practitioner research involves *ownership* of what is found, that the researcher is willing to engage with the challenge of examining his or her own participation in the research process. One of the gifts that we bring to research is our understanding of what it means to know. I believe that there is much to be learned from approaching qualitative research with the attitude that what is at stake is not just learning more about counselling process and outcome (important though these issues are), but includes learning about how I learn. Some of the issues here are:

- To what extent am I willing to trust my own interpretation of an interview transcript? How important is it to know that other readers agree with my interpretation?
- Do I believe what someone (e.g. a research informant) tells me? Is this person deceiving him/herself? Could he or she be driven by unconscious forces outside of their awareness? Can I know their truth better than they do? What kind of a relationship needs to be established before I can say that I know this other person's 'truth'?
- Who or what is my research *for*? What is my responsibility toward the people I interview for research purposes? What right do they have to comment on or even to veto what I have written?

These are just some of the questions that arise in making choices between different qualitative genres. Clearly, these are issues that also have a great deal of relevance for us as counselling practitioners.

Gathering qualitative data

There is a wide range of methods that have been employed in gathering data in qualitative inquiry into counselling and psycho-therapy. These are discussed in McLeod (1994b, ch. 6). The technique which has been used most often is the semi-structured interview, where the researcher invites an informant to talk freely in response to a series of general questions. Open-ended ques-tionnaires can also serve a similar function, but without the expense of arranging face-to-face meetings. The aim of all quali-tative data collection techniques is to generate a qualitative *text* which will form the basis for analysis and interpretation. The problem of how best to begin to analyse and make sense of qualitative research texts, which can quite easily comprise hundreds of pages of transcripts or notes, is addressed in the following section. Before moving there, however, it is important to reflect on the significance of collecting qualitative data, from a practitioner perspective.

In my experience many counsellors doing qualitative research studies both enjoy and are frustrated by the act of carrying out research interviews. I think they enjoy this activity because they are good at it, or good at parts of it. Listening to people, helping them to express themselves, is what counsellors are trained to do. What is frustrating is keeping the balance between a research interview and a counselling session. Sometimes, counselling researchers are so wary of moving into therapeutic or emotional material that their research interviews end up being curiously flat and detached. At other times, the researcher may follow the informant so deeply into personal stuff that the research goals of the interview are not met. I believe that it is rare that a counsellor-researcher would leave a research participant, at the end of an interview, in an exposed or vulnerable state. Counsellors are aware of the dangers of this, and know what to do about it. (My sense is that non-counsellor qualitative researchers frequently do leave informants in a harrowed state.)

In principle, counsellors possess the interpersonal skills and awareness to collect really good qualitative data. The problem is to work out how to align these skills and awareness with the research task. Here are some suggestions:

- Begin a research study by interviewing one or two informants whom you know to be tame, friendly, co-operative and robust. These people will often be friends or contacts of friends. Tape-record the interview. Transcribe it. Look closely at the *process* of the interview, and review it with your supervisor or colleagues. Where did you try to go too deep? Where could you have gone deeper?

- Make sure that you allocate plenty of time for interviews. Explain the structure and aims of the interview right at the start (it can be helpful to send the questions to the informant two or three days in advance of the interview). If possible, make an agreement where you can contact the informant more than once, for example by asking if they will comment on the transcript or your analysis, or would be willing to discuss any follow-up questions that might occur to you once you have listened to the tape.

■ Develop a collaborative relationship with the informant. He or she is the expert; you are there to learn. Be willing to share your own ideas and assumptions.

■ Do everything possible to avoid a dual relationship with the informant. One's own clients may be willing to be interviewed, but who are they speaking to – a researcher or their therapist?

■ Allow the informant maximum control. Informed consent should be a *process*, where the person consents to being interviewed, consents to you keeping the tape of the interview and can then withdraw their consent at any point thereafter (i.e. can claim back the tape and withdraw from the study). The informant should be given your name, address and telephone number and those of your research supervisor.

■ The final question in the interview should be an invitation to comment on the experience of being interviewed. Does the person feel that he or she has been able to speak openly? Has he or she learned anything new about herself or himself in the course of the interview? What recommendations would they make for improving the interview procedure for future participants in the study?

Applying these guidelines can help to create a situation in which a counsellor-researcher can feel able to apply with appropriate sensitivity his or her therapeutic skills. The informant or participant, too, may find that these 'rules' signal an invitation to take part in a serious and far-reaching conversation, but not in therapy. Many of the issues around collecting qualitative data through interviews are discussed very fully in the book by Kvale (1996). Here, Kvale argues that one of the hallmarks of a good qualitative interview lies in the extent to which the *informant* learns or gains from the experience. A qualitative research interview is not a situation where a person is passively reporting facts or opinions, but is better seen as an 'encounter' where the person is actively engaged in exploring the meaning of events or experiences that have been significant for them.

Finally, before beginning to carry out interviews it is perhaps worth considering the type of 'text' that you aim to produce. In recent years, there has been a growing realisation in the social sciences that in everyday life people make sense of and communicate their experience through telling stories. It is therefore, essential in research to allow informants to tell their stories, and indeed to encourage them to tell stories. Although there is a long history of using narrative accounts for research purposes, including for instance the 'critical incident' technique (Flanagan, 1954), there has been a strong tendency for interviewers to switch off once the informant gets into narrative mode, and to try to guide them back to the 'point' (Mishler, 1986). The difference between narrative and non-narrative approaches to qualitative interviewing can be highlighted by considering alternative questions that can be asked. For example, in a study of the client's experience of counselling, a participant could be asked the question 'How did counselling help you?' The person might then respond that counselling helped her to 'be more self-confident', 'make decisions about my career direction' and 'understand the effect of my childhood on the way I am now'. This is useful information, but it is fairly abstract and generalised. On the other hand, if the investigator were to ask the participant to describe 'two or three significant events in counselling that were particularly helpful for you', the informant may then tell a story of a problem which she took to counselling, how she and the counsellor worked together on the problem, and how this had an impact on her life. This narrative could be summed up as, or given the title of, 'making decisions about my career direction', but in conveying this experience in a narrative form the person is able to say so much more. The story, as a form of communication, conveys information about setting, relationships, values, intentionality, feeling, and moral evaluation. The notion of the story as a uniquely powerful carrier of personal information is explored more fully in McLeod (1997, ch. 2). Returning to the first version of the research question ('How did counselling help you?'), even this kind of question can elicit stories if the interviewer is patient enough to allow the informant to give his or her response through storytelling.

Of course, in a research interview it is always reassuring to get at least some straightforward and readily analysable answers ('counselling helped me to be more self-confident'). But narrative accounts provide the basis for the complex and contextualised understandings which are at the heart of good qualitative research. In reading books and papers which report on qualitative studies, especially those which do not explicitly espouse a narrative perspective, it is instructive to be on the alert for the number of times researchers build their analysis around stories told by informants, and use these stories as the focal points of their writing. Further discussion of the issues involved in adopting a narrative approach to qualitative research interviewing can be found in Mishler (1986) and Riessman (1993).

Lofland and Lofland (1984) and Kvale (1996) are recommended guides to good interviewing practice. It is important to keep in mind that interviews are not the only way of collecting qualitative research material. Other approaches are reviewed in McLeod (1994b).

Analysing qualitative data

The actual process of collecting research data is often the most enjoyable part of a qualitative study. Collecting data involves meeting people and listening to them talk about things that are important to them. Making sense of this material is usually much more challenging. The basic tasks are those of developing an understanding and then conveying that understanding in writing. In counselling, the process of understanding one client's world or reality proceeds step by step, session by session. In qualitative research there are multiple realities provided by different informants, each in the form of one-off blocks of interview. In counselling the counsellors' understanding of the client is usually given back fairly tentatively, piece by piece. In research, the investigator needs to create a much more definite and unambiguous statement of understanding.

The challenge of analysing qualitative data can be appreciated better by reflecting in practical terms on what needs to be done. A researcher may carry out 60-minute interviews with eight people. Each of these interviews will take at least five hours to transcribe (40 hours). Whatever method is used to analyse this material, each transcript will need to be read carefully and notes made – at least another eight hours of work, at the minimum. The researcher then needs to find a way of drawing together the different themes or meaning categories discovered in this data, which will now comprise a thick volume of transcripts, notes and memos. This takes an unpredictable amount of time. Then, finally, all of this needs to be condensed down to a 'results' section or chapter of between 1,000 (a short paper in a medical journal) and 10,000 words (chapter of a Doctoral dissertation).

Over and above the various analytic tasks outlined above, the researcher may wish to involve other people. Research informants may be supplied with transcripts or sections of analysis and asked to comment on accuracy and/or interpretive sensitivity. Colleagues, supervisor or members of a collaborative research group (see Chapter 11) may carry out parallel analyses of the material. All this adds to the complexity of the analytic work.

The different qualitative research approaches or genres each suggest different ways of coping with the problem of analysis. Phenomenological analysis, grounded theory, narrative analysis, co-operative inquiry and the other qualitative research genres are basically constructed around different ways of finding meaning in qualitative data. Although each of these approaches provides its own set of analytic guidelines, I would suggest that one way or another all of them are structured around the following stages:

1 Immersion in the material, for example through personally transcribing tapes and making notes, or reading transcripts over and over again. At this stage the aim is to get a sense of the meaning of the text as a whole.
2 Identifying elements of meaning. This can involve categorising or coding the meaning of segments of the text, highlighting key sections of narrative, or locating significant and meaningful conversational sequences. At this stage, the aim is to look for detail, focus on the meaning of fragments of the text. One of the important skills is to continue to be open to new meanings, to read and categorise the meaning of a section of text and then to ask oneself 'what *else* could it mean?'
3 Moving back and forward between the parts and the whole to the point where general themes or categories become apparent. This stage includes checking the validity of these general themes within the data, through asking questions such as 'do they occur in all cases?' and 'are there counterinstances?'
4 Constructing a written representation of the understandings that have been developed in earlier stages.

Anyone attempting to do this is advised *not* to rely on this highly schematic account of qualitative analysis, but to study carefully some of the practical manuals of qualitative inquiry such as

Strauss and Corbin (1990) on grounded theory, Colaizzi (1978) on phenomenological research, and Heron (1996) on co-operative inquiry. In addition to these manuals, the book by Miles and Huberman (1994) gives a wealth of hints on how to handle qualitative data.

There are three issues which, I believe, weave through any discussions of qualitative analysis and which need to be considered by anyone doing qualitative research for the first time. These are: the use of memos, technology and interpretive intent. These issues are discussed next.

The use of memos

Although the concept of the research 'memo' appeared to arise originally within the grounded theory approach (Glaser and Strauss, 1967; Strauss and Corbin, 1990), it is nevertheless applicable to any type of qualitative research. One of the characteristics of good qualitative research is the capacity to give very close attention to the meaning of short segments of texts, sometimes even individual words or short phrases. It is this close attention to detailed, multifaceted meaning that enables qualitative research to go beyond journalistic description. Common to all qualitative approaches is the idea that, in carrying out this close analysis of fragments of meaning, it is necessary to 'bracket off' any wider speculation of where each fragment might fit into the bigger picture. As Strauss, Glaser and Corbin would say, the priority is to stay 'grounded', to keep any interpretation very clearly linked to the actual data. This practice can lead beginning qualitative researchers to believe that all that is involved in analysis is coding or categorising little units of meaning, and that the final interpretive framework just appears through an accumulation of these codes. I believe that this is a big mistake. I would argue that the qualititative researcher finds meaning wherever it becomes available, and that the meaning of what informants say may 'strike' the researcher at any point: while planning the project, during the interview, on the bus home after the interview, in the middle of the night, while transcribing tapes, while discussing the material with a supervisor or colleague, while reading a book. The experience of qualitative research is that of many moments of illumination and insight. It is essential to capture these moments, and keeping a personal research journal, or writing analytic *memos* to oneself, is the way to begin to piece together a basis for understanding the topic being studied. In the Stage 3 described earlier (moving back and forward between the parts and the whole to the point where general themes or categories become apparent) the aim is to generate both a micro-analysis of the text (line-by-line coding) *and* a macro-analysis (what is written in the memo book or file). It is from the interplay between the detail of the former and the imaginative scope of the latter that something new can be created.

Technology

There is always in qualitative analysis a problem in keeping track of information: transcripts, memos, notes. Whatever qualitative approach is used, information needs to be taken from one place (e.g. lines 202 to 224 of Interview 1) and put somewhere else (Example 6 of Category 3). At the same time, it must be possible to track back from the new bit of information (e.g. within the Category 3 file) to see where it came from. All this can become messy and fiddly, and lead to enormous frustration. One of the solutions to this problem that has become available in recent years has been the use of software packages that can be used on personal computers. The longest established packages, such as Ethnograph, NU-DIST and ATLAS provide structures for assisting in the storage and coding of written text. The newer packages, such as Code-a-Text, can also work with written text but additionally have the facility to operate on audio or video tapes that are copied on to a computer file. A supplier of these packages is listed in the Appendix. It is important to be aware that some people find these packages invaluable, and others do not. There are two main drawbacks associated with qualitative software packages. The first is that it can take a long time to master them. This is fine if a researcher has sufficient time, or is engaged in a long-term project where there will be a time saving in the end. It can lead to frustration if the researcher is constrained by a tight schedule. The second difficulty for some people is that putting the material on computer limits the scope for *visual* exploration, for example by tagging codes on big charts on the wall, annotating notes with different coloured highlighter pens, or spreading index cards over the kitchen table to see which codes/ cards seem to have similar meanings and cluster together. Although anything on a computer can be printed off, using a software package creates an expectation that the analytic work will be done on the screen. This does not suit everyone. Another issue to bear in mind is that some qualitative researchers find that their familiar word-processing packages, such as Word or Word-perfect, allow them to do much of what they could achieve with a specialist package, but without the costs of buying the package or getting trained. There is not definitive advice that can be given about the use of qualitative software. It is a matter of developing one's own style as a researcher. It is also a matter of who one works with – it is much easier to learn about a package from a colleague who can already use it, rather than working through the manual. It is maybe also a matter of age. Researchers who have grown up with PCs may just not see any of this as problematic.

Interpretive intent

The final issue to be considered by anyone embarking on a piece of qualitative counselling research is that of *interpretive intent* – how far to go in analysing the material. Wolcott (1994) has introduced a useful distinction between three goals of qualitative research: description, analysis and interpretation. A researcher seeking to *describe* an area of human experience seeks to do the best possible job in documenting how a person or group of people act or perceive in relation to a topic. Much of the time, we fail to grasp the fullness of a phenomenon, we jump to conclusions. A comprehensive description which lays out all the different aspects of the phenomenon can therefore make a significant contribution to understanding. Research carried out in the phenomenological tradition takes as its aim the careful description of human experience, for instance through studies of the experience of learning, of being anxious, of being criminally victimised (see Valle and Halling, 1989, for further examples). Useful though description may be in illuminating experience, some researchers wish to take another step in working with qualitative material, in attempting to *analyse* patterns or themes within the data. Grounded theory studies tend to focus on analysis, by using a framework of main categories and a core category to provide a sense of how the phenomenon is struc-tured. In carrying out this kind of analysis, the goal is to derive a model, but one which is 'grounded' inductively in description. Analysis, in itself, does not look beyond the data set to build conceptual bridges between a current study and other studies or theoretical perspectives. For Wolcott (1994), a third step in which some qualitative researchers engage is that of building that bridge, and developing an *interpretive* understanding of the data which introduces ideas from elsewhere, usually from social science theory. Hermeneutic research is an example of a qualitative tradition that emphasises interpretation. The point that Wolcott is making is that none of these three activities – description, analysis, interpretation – can claim to be 'better' than the others. Each has its own valuable part to play in qualitative inquiry. Wolcott shows that all different combinations of the three can be effective. For anyone beginning qualitative research, it may be useful to give some thought to the particular mix of description, analysis and interpretation that would be most effective in fulfilling the aims of the research. Another consideration lies with the amount of time available to carry out the research. In my view, good description comes first. Credible analysis and interpretation rely on convincing and authentic descriptive detail. On the other hand, arriving at a satisfactory interpretation of qualitative data can take a long time. It is as though the material needs to filter through to some unconscious level before its deeper meaning can be appreciated. If time is limited in a study, it may be more realistic to go for description, or description and analysis, rather than trying to arrive at an interpretive breakthrough.

Quality control in qualitative research

What makes for a good qualitative study? Traditional quantitatively oriented concepts of reliability and validity (see Chapter 6) are not readily applicable to qualitative research. The distinctive philosophical stance of qualitative research, discussed earlier in this chapter, means that it is necessary to think about the question of what constitutes good practice in qualitative research. Qualitative research appears pitiful when judged in terms of criteria of objective measurement, sample size, experimental control and the other hallmarks of good quantitative research. It is important for the self-belief of qualitative researchers, and for their ability to defend their work against criticism, that the grounds for assessing the value of qualitative research are made as explicit as possible.

In this section I do not intend to go into very much detail. Stiles (1993) has written an excellent paper on issues of validity in qualitative research, which should be mandatory reading for anyone embarking on this kind of work. Although in McLeod (1994b) I offer a summary of the main points of the Stiles (1993) paper, it is well worth reading the original. Here, I would like to do no more than suggest three themes which inform all discussions about the adequacy of qualitative investigations:

Good qualitative research is personal

The person, the researcher, is the instrument of qualitative research. Knowledge is produced through a person or persons attempting to make sense and find meaning. The quality of the person's immersion in the research task, and the nature of the pre-understandings which they bring to that task, are therefore crucial.

Good qualitative research is dialogical

Knowledge is not a detached objective mirror of nature. Knowledge is co-constructed, is created between people. The kind of relationship that exists between 'co-researchers' is therefore a key factor in assessing a qualitative study. Another aspect here is the extent to which different voices and perspectives are incorporated into a research report. Are informants/participants asked to comment on 'findings', or are they silenced?

Good qualitative research enhances understanding

The experience of understanding involves a sense of being closer to a phenomenon, of being able to 'grasp' its meaning, of being able to 'see', becoming able to view in perspective, to engage empathically in the experience of the Other. These are subjective categories, but nevertheless vitally important. The goal of qualitative research is to make an impact in this sphere. In the end, only the reader can say whether he or she understands something better after reading your paper on it. In achieving this criterion, there is an elusive interplay between reiterating the familiar (good description) and offering a new image or metaphor that allows the familiar to be viewed in a new light.

Behind these unique criteria for qualitative research, there are of course also many values that this approach shares with positivist quantitative research. There is a basic sense of work that is *well done* that arises when reading a study which offers careful analysis and conceptualisation, a comprehensive critique of previous knowledge, and a clear account of research procedures.

Writing qualitative research

There are big differences between quantitative and qualitative research at the beginning and then again at the end of a study. At the beginning of a study it is necessary to think about the research in a different light. At the end of a study it is necessary to give a different kind of attention to the job of writing it up. There exist tried and trusted formats for reporting on quantitative, experimental or survey research. These formats leave little or no scope for creative writing or literary skill. By contrast, qualitative research makes major demands on the writing skills of the researcher. It can be helpful to write all the way through a project. If there are words 'in the bank', in the form of memos, sections of a research journal and draft papers, then the final writing task becomes more a matter of editing than the awful prospect of sitting in front of a word-processor and inserting an empty disk. It can also be helpful to realise that, in qualitative research, writing is part of analysis and interpretation. It is all very well to work out a structure of codes or categories by arranging index cards or NUD-IST files, but if the structure cannot be written it needs further revision. The act of writing introduces the demand that the understanding of the material that you have developed should now be told as a coherent story. A good story has a clear plot-line. If in writing a qualitative report you find that you have 'lost the plot' then you need to track back until you find it again. This is not really a matter of not being able to write, but a question of *what* is being written. The whole question of how to cope with the problem of writing up a qualitative study is discussed very well in a short book by Wolcott (1990), and also by Golden-Locke and Biddle (1997).

In recent years, there has been an influential movement within the social sciences to try out alternative ways of writing social research. A useful paper which sums up some of the key factors behind this movement is Gergen (1997). What has happened is that social researchers have realised that conventional forms of 'scientific' writing left no place either for their personal voices, or for the voices of participants. Typically, scientific writing presents what has been called a 'God's eye' view, or a 'view from nowhere'. Researchers have therefore started to experiment with autobiographical and 'multi-voiced' texts. So far, this has not caught on in counselling and psychotherapy research circles, but in many ways it is possibly even more appropriate in counselling research than in other areas of qualitative inquiry. Sources of further information on this new writing are Ellis and Bochner (1996), Hertz (1997) and Richardson (1991, 1992, 1994).

Conclusion: getting started in qualitative research

Qualitative research is felt by many counsellors to represent a form of inquiry that complements practice. In this chapter, some suggestions have been offered to anyone beginning qualitative research in counselling:

■ keep a research diary;
■ read about the philosophy of qualitative research and the experiences of qualitative researchers, and get hold of some inspirational examples of qualitative inquiry in action.

This advice needs to be placed alongside the ideas about getting started, finding a question and reading the literature, outlined in earlier chapters. While it is always important to do the best research that one can, it is also necessary to be realistic about what can be achieved in a first study. All good research is cyclical, with one cycle of inquiry generating understandings and new questions that are tested out in the next cycle. Another issue concerns the context within which the research is carried out. On the whole, this chapter has been written as though the research was being carried out on an individual basis. It is often much more enjoyable and valuable to work collaboratively with other people on qualitative projects. Some ideas about how to use practitioner inquiry groups are introduced in Chapter 11.

Further reading

In recent years, there has been an explosion of books and articles on qualitative research, many of them published in the Sage Methodology catalogue. Listed below is a set of key readings that will provide a comprehensive overview of the contribution of different qualitative approaches.

Denzin, N. and Lincoln, Y.S. (eds) (1994) *Handbook of Qualitative Research*. London: Sage. (An authoritative overview of the field, contains some reference to anything you might be interested in. Start with Lincoln and Denzin's historical account.)

Heron, J. (1996) *Co-operative Inquiry: Research into the Human Condition*. London: Sage. (Although the co-operative inquiry/human inquiry approach has been mainly associated with the work of Peter Reason, Heron's book provides the best practical introduction to this method.)

Hertz, R. (ed.) (1997) *Reflexivity and Voice*. Thousand Oaks, CA: Sage. (An introduction to some of the newer styles of qualitative research, which experiment with different forms of writing and alternative types of researcher–informant relationships.)

Lofland, J. and Lofland, L. (1984) *Analyzing Social Settings: A Guide to Qualitative Observation and Analysis* (2nd edn). Belmont, CA: Wadsworth. (An accepted classic. Written from a sociological point of view but captures better than any other book the spirit of qualitative inquiry.)

Marshall, C. and Rossman, G.B. (1995) *Designing Qualitative Research* (2nd edn). London: Sage. (Basic recommended introductory text.)

McLeod, J. (1996) 'Qualitative research methods in counselling psychology', in R. Woolfe and W. Dryden (eds), *Handbook of Counselling Psychology*. London: Sage. (A discussion of some of the ways in which qualitative approaches have been used in counselling research, structured around examination of a series of exemplar studies.)

Miles, M. and Huberman, A. (1994) *Qualitative Data Analysis: A Sourcebook of New Methods* (2nd edn). London: Sage. (Full of good ideas. Exhibits an eclectic approach to qualitative analysis.)

Moustakas, C. (1994) *Phenomenological Research Methods*. London: Sage. (An introduction to the use of phenomenological methods. Philosophically well-informed.)

Rennie, D.L., Phillips, J.R. and Quartaro, J.K. (1988) 'Grounded theory: a promising approach for conceptualization in psychology?', *Canadian Psychology*, 29: 139–50. (A very useful account of how grounded theory methods can be applied in psychotherapy research.)

Riessman, C.K. (1993) *Narrative Analysis*. London: Sage. (A short book which introduces the principles of using stories as the basic focus of qualitative analysis.)

Stiles, W.B. (1993) 'Quality control in qualitative research', *Clinical Psychology Review*, 13: 593–618. (An excellent review of the issues associated with the concept of validity in qualitative research.)

Strauss, A. and Corbin, J. (1990) *Basics of Qualitative Research: Grounded Theory Procedures and Techniques*. London: Sage. (Generally regarded as the best manual of how to do a grounded theory study.)

9

Evaluating Outcomes

One of the core questions that has motivated many hundreds of counselling researchers has been the issue of 'does it work?' The topic of *outcome* has been a major theme in the counselling and psychotherapy research literature. Some outcome studies have looked at the relative effectiveness of different types of therapy. For example, there have been many studies comparing the outcomes of psychodynamic and cognitive-behavioural approaches. Other outcome studies have been driven by external pressures around accountability. Increasingly, institutional purchasers of counselling services need to be convinced that what they are paying for is effective and good value for money. Yet other outcome studies have been inspired by a wish to improve services, for example by identifying those groups of clients who may or may not benefit from a particular approach, or by looking at the effects of different forms of service provision (e.g. time-limited counselling versus open-ended contracts).

On the whole, the majority of outcome studies that are to be found in the current published literature are *not* practitioner studies. Most of the published outcome research tends to consist of fairly large-scale studies that are externally controlled and inspired. Many outcome studies are initiated by academic researchers interested in contrasting different theoretical approaches, or by organisations and institutions (e.g. the NHS) interested in developing a rational (evidence-based) system for allocating health-care funding. It can be argued that this situation has led to at least three sets of negative consequences. First, the types of outcome studies that have been carried out generate a kind of over-abstract knowledge that can subsequently be quite hard to apply in practice. Second, externally controlled studies often employ quantitative methods that silence the voice of the counsellor (and often that of the client too). Given that counsellors represent an important source of information on what may have happened in any case, this is a significant loss. Third, large-scale outcome studies are expensive and complex, with the result that relatively few of them can be set up. The consequence here is that there are many forms of counselling, or client groups, for whom little or no outcome data exists.

There are several good reasons why practitioners should become more involved in outcome research. Practitioner outcome studies are more likely to produce results that can be applied in practice, that have some tangible payoff for clients. However, more than this, in many counselling settings counsellors receive very little in the way of reliable or 'objective' feedback regarding how helpful they have been to their clients. I believe that this can contribute to a certain degree of professional insecurity in counsellors and psychotherapists. It is relatively easy for members of other, less 'boundaried' professional groups (such as social work, medicine or teaching) to learn about the fate of former service users, or even to keep in touch with them. The strict confidentiality and voluntariness of the counsellor–client contract generally restrict the channels of post-counselling feedback for counselling practitioners, unless formal follow-up evaluation procedures are in place. There is a sense, then, that outcome data can play a valuable part in counsellor development and avoidance of burnout (how do I know that I am doing any good?).

What is essential in practitioner outcome research is to understand what is possible, and what are the key methodological issues. There is no point, as a practitioner, in attempting to carry out a multi-site controlled trial with large numbers of clients. At the same time, it is necessary to be aware that research audiences will need to be convinced that the results of an outcome study have not been biased by the practitioner's biases or fantasies. Who would believe an outcome study that reported a 100 per cent success rate on a counsellor's work with his or her own clients? Counsellors also have a primary responsibility to promote the well-being of the client. The method of collecting outcome data must be integrated into practice in a way that does not threaten the therapy itself.

The remainder of this chapter examines the issues and skills involved in designing and implementing practitioner outcome research. Different models of outcome research are introduced, followed by an exploration of some of the dilemmas faced by counsellors attempting this sort of work. In a book of this length, it is not possible to provide a comprehensive guide to how to carry out each of these different types of outcome study. Instead, in each case references are given that lead to the best sources of information for further study and implementation.

Client satisfaction studies

A client satisfaction study is a piece of research which evaluates the benefits of counselling by asking clients to complete a short, simple questionnaire once they have finished seeing their counsellor. Some of the issues involved in using this method have been discussed in Chapter 2. Basically, even though this method is both economical and necessary as a means of enabling clients to register their feelings about a service, it has some quite significant limitations. Those clients who complete satisfaction questionnaires tend to give uniformly positive ratings, which do not necessarily relate to the amount of actual benefit they have received. This makes it difficult, or impossible, to use satisfaction data to differentiate between sub-groups of clients who may be gaining more or less from counselling; the satisfaction questionnaire is a blunt instrument. There are no standard satisfaction scales that are particularly widely used. Most counsellors or agencies adapt existing scales to fit their own local requirements. Sources of further information about constructing satisfaction scales can be found in Box 9.1. The study by Sloboda et al. (1993) illustrates what can be done with satisfaction data. Although not in any sense a practitioner study, an influential paper by Seligman (1995) illustrates an interesting application of satisfaction research methods, in the form of a client survey carried out by a consumer organisation in the USA.

Randomised controlled trials

At the other extreme from client satisfaction studies, in terms of methodological rigour and scientific credibility, are what are

---

Box 9.1

Key sources of information on designing a client satisfaction questionnaire

Attkisson, C.C. and Greenfield, T.K. (1994) 'Client Satisfaction Questionnaire-8 and Service Satisfaction Scale-30', in M.E. Maruish (ed.), *The Use of Psychological Testing for Treatment Planning and Outcome Assessment*. Hillsdale, NJ: Lawrence Erlbaum.

Berger, M. (1983) 'Toward maximising the utility of consumer satisfaction as an outcome', in M.J. Lambert, E.R. Christensen and S.S. DeJulio (eds), *The Assessment of Psychotherapy Outcome*. New York: Wiley.

Lebow, J. (1982) 'Consumer satisfaction with mental health treatment', *Psychological Bulletin*, 91: 244–59.

Webb. Y. (1993) 'Consumer surveys: an overview', in R. Leiper and V. Field (eds), *Counting for Something in Mental Health Services: Effective User Feedback*. Aldershot: Avebury.

---

known as *randomised controlled trials* (RCTs) of therapy. A randomised trial involves first of all finding a pool of people who are all seeking help and who have a similar problem (e.g. as diagnosed through a psychiatric interview or through their scores on a questionnaire). These clients are then randomly assigned to different 'treatment conditions'. These conditions may comprise two or three different kinds of therapy, or a therapy compared with a control condition (e.g. remaining on a waiting list for six months) or a comparison with a placebo condition (e.g. being given regular meetings with a helper who does not use actual therapeutic skills or interventions). The client's level of anxiety, depression, phobia, or other problems, are assessed before therapy, at the end of therapy and then again at a follow-up period. RCTs are widely used in medicine, for example in trials of the effectiveness of new drug treatments. In drugs research (but not in counselling and psychotherapy research) it is possible to conduct 'double blind' studies in which neither doctor nor patient knows whether the drug being administered is active or is an inert placebo. In medicine, the randomised controlled trial is regarded as the 'gold standard' in terms of credible research evidence. In a well-conducted RCT, if truly random allocation of clients or patients to treatments is achieved, then any subsequent differences in outcome can *only* be attributed to the impact of the treatment, rather than to other factors. An RCT is therefore a highly logical and convincing method of evaluation.

In the world of counselling and psychotherapy, many hundreds of RCTs have been carried out over the years. Reviews of this literature can be found in Garfield and Bergin (1994) and Roth and Fonagy (1996). There are, however, some very serious problems associated with the application of this research genre within counselling and therapy. Some of the issues are:

- *true randomisation may be hard to achieve.* Clients may have preferences regarding the kind of therapy they would like to have. Most clients report a mixed set of problems, and would receive multiple diagnoses (if they were to be diagnosed), thus making it difficult to achieve the kind of clear-cut diagnostic samples that a good RCT requires.
- *inadequate sample sizes.* The statistical operations which are needed to decide whether an RCT has produced a clear result require reasonably large numbers (i.e. over 20) clients in each condition. In counselling and psychotherapy research, this can be expensive and impracticable.
- *distortion of usual therapeutic practice.* To produce the level of methodological control that is necessary in an RCT, counsellors are usually asked to practice according to a manual which specifies a standard mode of treatment that all practitioners in the study are expected to deliver (including number of sessions). Given that the majority of counsellors and psychotherapists describe themselves as eclectic or integrative in orientation, this requirement greatly limits the 'external validity' of such studies (i.e. the extent to which their results can be generalised to real-world practical settings).

The complexity of the RCT method means that it is only possible to implement this kind of study in a well-financed elite establishment. Most RCTs are associated with university medical schools or clinical psychology departments. There are great tranches of everyday counselling practice that have not and will not ever be included in an RCT, short of massive governmental investment in counselling research. It is important therefore for practitioner-researchers to be clear that an RCT is *not* the method of choice for them. It is also important for practitioner-researchers to be critically aware of the limitations and problems in the application of RCTs to the evaluation of counselling, so that they are in a position to counter the arguments of those who would seek to deny the relevance of the other types of evaluation research which counsellors can carry out. For example, the authoritative survey of RCT studies of psychotherapy commissioned by the Department of Health in England (Roth and Fonagy, 1996) is dismissive of the value of counselling in primary care, on the basis of a small number of questionable RCTs of counselling in this setting. I believe that the best response of counselling practitioners to this kind of argument is to make the strongest possible case that RCTs are neither the only nor the best way of discovering the value of employing counsellors as members of primary care teams. Indeed Roth and Fonagy (1996) themselves take the view that the results of randomised controlled trials need to be carefully 'translated' before they can be applied to actual practice.

Naturalistic outcome studies

Somewhere between the client satisfaction study and the full-blown RCT is what can be called a *naturalistic* outcome study. This kind of study is similar to a client satisfaction study in so far as it involves collecting data on every client who is seen in a clinic or counselling agency. It is similar to an RCT in that before and after measures of change are taken, rather than relying on a one-shot questionnaire completed only at the end of counselling. Naturalistic outcome studies are basically built around routine administration of questionnaires or other data collection methods by the staff of counselling agencies. While client satisfaction questionnaires can be completely anonymous (the client fills it in and either posts it back or places it in a box in the reception area), in an outcome study where repeated measures are employed it is necessary to use some kind of code number so that client questionnaires from different occasions can be matched up. It is also useful to keep a record within the agency of other data (e.g client age, gender, occupation, and area of residence, and perhaps also counsellor-supplied data on outcome, presenting problem and number of sessions) against which the client questionnaires can be compared. This is important because in a typical naturalistic outcome study only 50–60 per cent of clients will return questionnaires, and it is necessary to be able to estimate whether those who do complete questionnaires are representative of the group of clients as a whole. This kind of comparative data is less important in satisfaction studies, which can reach 80–90 per cent response rates, or in tightly controlled RCTs, where the presence of research assistants can ensure 100 per cent compliance rates.

In naturalistic outcome studies it can be helpful if some degree of separation can be established between the provision of counselling and the administration of questionnaires. For example, if it is the responsibility of the counsellor to give the client a questionnaire at an initial assessment session, there is the possibility that he or she may 'forget' to include difficult or highly distressed clients, thus skewing the results of the study. If clients either receive a questionnaire directly from their counsellors, or return it to them, the questionnaire can become a form of communication with the counsellor, one which will probably inhibit the passing on of bad news. It is generally more satisfactory for questionnaires to be distributed and collected either by agency reception staff or by external evaluators.

It is important to be clear that the amount of change or benefit to clients that will be demonstrated in a naturalistic outcome study is likely to be significantly lower than in an RCT, for the following reasons:

- In RCTs therapists trained in a specific approach work with clients around tightly defined problems. In naturalistic studies, counsellors are usually in a situation where they are called upon to adapt their approach to meet the needs of a wide variety of clients.
- In an RCT, a client is only included in the study if he or she has an initial score within a certain range (i.e. high enough problem score to allow some improvement, but not too high as to be intractable). In generic or naturalistic settings, there are some clients who appear to have zero or near-zero problem scores at the outset (probably because of some form of denial or lack of awareness) and others who record extremely high scores.
- RCTs are 'special' counselling situations where counsellors are given a great deal of supervision and support, have high expectations for success, and do their best work all the time because they know they are being closely monitored.

Sometimes, naturalistic outcome studies are carried out in situations where there is a known population of people from whom clients are drawn. For example, in a staff counselling unit in a Hospital Trust, all clients will be employees of the Trust. In a student counselling centre in a university, all clients will be students of the university. In these situations, it can be useful to collect data on the 'baseline' level of problems (anxiety, stress, depression, etc.) in that population. This data can be helpful in calculating what is called the *clinical significance* of the degree of change found in counselling clients (Jacobson et al., 1984; Jacobson and Revenstorf, 1988; Tingey et al., 1996). In most outcome studies of counselling, clients' problems and distress can be seen to improve to some extent. The question is whether this degree of change is just marginal (is merely 'statistically' significant) or whether it represents a real difference in terms of quality of life (clinical significance). It has become accepted that the latter can be calculated by estimating whether each client has shifted from having scores in the problem range to having scores that are within the 'normal' range. There are various formulae that can be used to work out whether this has occurred. However, on many scales of anxiety or stress, the normal score for a particular group of people can be quite different from that of the population of the country as a whole. For instance, nursing is a stressful occupation, and norms for stress, anxiety and depression in nurses in a Hospital Trust will usually be much higher than in the general population. In using a naturalistic outcome study to evaluate the effectiveness of employee counselling in a Hospital Trust, therefore, the collection of 'norms' from the Trust non-client workforce can help in the interpretation of results from actual clients. When this 'baseline' data is being collected (usually through questionnaires distributed to a random sample of around 10 per cent of the staff in the case of a workplace survey) it can be valuable to add in to the questionnaire a few items asking about the need for counselling, perceptions of the counselling unit, etc.

Naturalistic outcome studies represent a highly useful research strategy for counsellors. This kind of data can form the basis for monitoring and audit demanded by external funding bodies or for inclusion in annual reports to trustees, etc. However, if an agency or clinic routinely gathers outcome data, then over a period of time a number of practice-relevant questions can be addressed:

- trends in the data can be analysed (Has the new training course had an effect? Did the introduction of a pre-counselling leaflet have an impact on the rate of no-shows?);
- comparisons can be made between different sub-groups of clients (e.g. men versus women, different presenting problems, postcodes, age bands) to examine whether there are types of client who may need a new approach or who might be better referred to another agency;
- successful and non-successful cases can be selected and subjected to a more detailed case analysis.

The answers to these questions can be fed back into supervision, training and policy-making, and eventually contribute to the improvement of practice. In addition, the collection of routine outcome data can make it possible to build on more focused research studies to look more closely at particular issues of interest. For example, if the outcome data indicate that, say, men appear to benefit less from counselling, then some male former clients can be contacted and interviewed about their experience of the help they received, and what might be done to make it more useful for them.

One of the main challenges in naturalistic outcome research is to assemble a package of data collection methods that give sufficient coverage of the factors that are of interest to counsellors, counselling agency administrators and representatives of external funding bodies, but are not so lengthy, intimidating and unwieldy as to deter clients from responding or to make unreasonable demands on agency staff. Over the years, there has been much debate over the desirability of identifing a standard all-purpose battery of questionnaires that can be used in counselling and psychotherapy settings. The existence of agreed standardised procedures for evaluating counselling would have the advantage of making it much easier to compare the outcomes achieved by different agencies; 'benchmarking' would become possible. This debate continues. Nevertheless, it seems to me that a sensible outcome-monitoring package would include the following elements, which clients would be asked to complete before and at the end of counselling, and then at a three-month or six-month follow-up:

- Brief questions on the demographic characteristics (age, gender, occupation, etc.) of the client. This kind of information is relevant in most analyses or reports that would be compiled, but also makes it possible to assess the representativeness of the sample of people who participate in the evaluation, by comparing them to the total population of clients who use the agency.

- A questionnaire which assesses the general level of 'symptoms' or 'dysfunction' in the person's life. There are several questionnaires which do this kind of thing, for example the General Health Questionnaire (GHQ) and the Brief Symptom Index (BSI). However, the questionnaire of choice at present is probably the CORE scale, which has been recently developed at the Psychological Therapies Research Centre at the University of Leeds to provide an easy-to-use general purpose evaluation tool for counsellors and psychotherapists (see Chapter 6).

- Client rating of the severity of their actual problem. This enables the measurement of the specific issue around which the client has sought help. As a measure of change, this technique can be highly sensitive, and can pick up evidence of change that may be missed by other techniques. In a few cases the client may re-define the problem after a few sessions of counselling, with the result that their initial problem rating becomes irrelevant. In practice, however, this does not appear to occur often enough to invalidate the problem rating method.

- Opportunities for clients to describe their experience in their own words. It is helpful to include a few open-ended questions, so that clients can report on aspects of their counselling that are important to them but are not covered in the more structured areas of the questionnaire.

- Some general satisfaction questions. In the questionnaire completed at the start of counselling, clients can be asked how easy it was to contact the service, their views on the waiting time, etc. At the end of counselling clients can be asked about their assessment of the counselling as a whole, the relationship with the counsellor, their satisfaction with the number of sessions, etc. These satisfaction questions can be drawn from the satisfaction scales described earlier in this chapter.

This combination of symptom change, problem change, satisfaction and an invitation to add anything else that they feel is relevant is viewed by most clients as a reasonable and credible way of gathering their opinions on their counselling. It represents a manageable package for agency staff to deal with and an invaluable resource for practitioner-researchers.

n = 1 'single case' studies

The single case outcome study is a variant of the naturalistic outcome study. This type of study is often described as 'n = 1', where 'n' is the number of 'subjects' in the study. Apart from the difference in number of cases, this type of research differs from other quantitative outcome research in that information on the client is collected not just at the beginning, at the end and at follow-up, but on a much more regular basis. In many n = 1 studies outcome data are collected at each session, or even every day or several times each day. At the heart of the n = 1 study is a graph which charts the change in key problem variables over at least three phases of the therapy: a baseline period before therapy has commenced, the period when therapy is being received, and the period following the end of therapy. The analysis of this data does not usually involve statistics, but relies on visual inspection of the graph. The classic n = 1 case graph will show a high level of problems at baseline, followed by a rapid reduction once treatment has started, remaining at or around the same low level over follow-up. In writing up a single case outcome study, the graph is used as a device to demonstrate to readers that change has occurred, with an accompanying narrative based on case notes or counsellor observations used to explain what happened during the case. There are several alternative ways of structuring single case studies, and useful sources of further information on this method can be found in Box 9.2.

The strength of this method lies in its unique capacity to generate systematic research evidence on new or unusual forms of counselling. For example, a counsellor using time-limited counselling in a primary care setting may believe that guided imagery exercises may be helpful for some clients who are depressed. It would be unethical to begin to use imagery with all depressed clients, until the process was understood better. There may not be enough depressed clients in this counsellor's caseload to make the collection of data over several cases a feasible proposition. The n = 1 method allows data to be collected on

---

Box 9.2

How to carry out an 'n = 1' outcome study

The single case study that includes repeated measures of some aspect of problem behaviour (preferably before, during and following counselling) is a research tool that is flexible, practicable and has the potential to enhance work with clients. There are a number of useful sources of further information about how to use this technique:

Barlow, D.H. and Hersen, M. (1986) *Single Case Experimental Designs: Strategies for Studying Behavior Change* (2nd edn). New York: Pergamon.

Barlow, D.H., Hayes, S.C. and Nelson, R.O. (1984) *The Scientist Practitioner: Research and Accountability in Clinical and Educational Settings*. New York: Pergamon.

Galassi, J.P. and Gersh, T.L. (1991) 'Single-case research in counseling', in C.E. Watkins, jr, and L.J. Schneider (eds), *Research in Counseling*. Hillsdale, NJ: Lawrence Erlbaum.

Kratochwill, T., Mott, S. and Dodson, C. (1984) 'Case study and single-case research in clinical and applied psychology', in A. Bellack and M. Hersen (eds), *Research Methods in Clinical Psychology*. New York: Pergamon.

Morley, S. (1996) 'Single case research', in G. Parry and F.N. Watts (eds), *Behavioural and Mental Health Research: A Handbook of Skills and Methods* (2nd edn). London: Lawrence Erlbaum.

---

perhaps two or three cases where the use of imagery seemed appropriate to the counsellor and her supervisor, and the client was keen on this approach. Using the n = 1 format, the success of imagery would be revealed by clients' depression ratings being stable (and high) in the sessions before imagery, and falling in the weeks following the imagery intervention. By applying a single case method, the counsellor is able to explore in some detail what has happened in these cases, and is able to communicate her findings in a way that is more convincing than a simple descriptive case study that relies on the counsellor's case notes. The single case or n = 1 method is a good way of establishing what is *possible*.

In principle, the n = 1 approach is very practitioner-friendly, and indeed was first developed in the USA in the 1950s as a means of enabling practitioners to carry out research as part of their everyday work. However, the idea of collecting regular information on such things as ratings of target problems may not sit easily with some counsellors. A behaviourally oriented counsellor can perhaps see many advantages in a socially anxious client keeping a diary of how often they spoke to people each day. A counsellor aiming to work with this client around the unconscious meaning of his relationships might well regard such a diary as counter-productive. Nevertheless, much current practice in counselling is built around short-term or time-limited contracts. There is strong evidence that, even when using relationship-oriented or insight-oriented approaches, the success of brief counselling depends on finding a *focus* for the work. In the end, the n = 1 method only requires that this focus be scaled in some manner that is meaningful for the client. It is my belief that the n = 1 method has a lot to offer counselling practitioners interested in documenting innovatory or 'newsworthy' practice. Although it is a method that originated in behavioural psychology, it is flexible enough to be applied in many other counselling settings.

Cost-benefit studies

It is necessary for practitioners to be aware of the increasing use of *economic* measures in studies of the outcome of counselling and psychotherapy. Health care providers, insurance companies and other agencies who pay for counselling are concerned whether counselling produces equivalent benefit for each pound or dollar spent as other interventions, such as medication. This is the issue of 'cost-effectiveness'. They are also interested in the 'cost-benefit' analysis of counselling, where the economic savings that result from counselling are calculated. For example, employing a counsellor for car factory workers may reduce the number of days off sick of shift workers, which will save the company money. The economic analysis of therapy is a relatively recent development, and methods are still being devised to capture the complex and often subtle economic factors associated with this area. All of the economic studies of therapy that I have seen have relied on the participation of health economists. It seems to be unlikely that, at this point in time, a lone practitioner could carry out a meaningful or credible cost-effectiveness study without significant interdisciplinary collaboration. On the other hand, practitioners may become involved in economic research through the agencies or clinics which employ them, and so it is important to know about this form of inquiry. The most useful sources for further reading are listed in Box 9.3. Obviously, in the

---

Box 9.3

Sources of information on evaluating the cost-effectiveness of counselling

Mallett, P. (1991) 'Cost-benefit analyses of psychotherapeutic treatments', *Psychiatric Bulletin*, 15: 575–6.

Mangen, S. (1988) 'Assessing cost-effectiveness', in F.N. Watts (ed.), *New Developments in Clinical Psychology*, vol. II. Chichester: Wiley.

McGrath, G. and Lowson, K. (1986) 'Assessing the benefits of psychotherapy: the economic approach', *British Journal of Psychiatry*, 150: 65–71.

Tolley, K. and Rowland, N. (1995) *Evaluating the Cost-Effectiveness of Counselling in Health Care*. London: Routledge.

---

end economic research has profound implications for the employment of counsellors, and the availability of counselling for different groups of people. It is therefore necessary for counsellors to be aware of this kind of research and to be willing to be involved. The economic equation around counselling is complex, and there is a danger that research teams that do not take adequate account of the perspectives of counselling practitioners may end up using over-simplistic models.

Qualitative outcome studies

Another way of evaluating outcome is to carry out qualitative, open-ended interviews with clients. Perhaps surprisingly, this approach has not been used to any great extent in counselling research, probably because of the domination of quantitative, statistical methods in the outcomes literature. There is further discussion of this method in Chapter 2, and Greene (1998) provides an interesting discussion of some of the ways in which qualitative evaluation has been employed in educational research. Leiper and Field (1993) is a good source of ideas about how qualitative methods have been applied with a participative, user-oriented focus in mental health outcome evaluation research.

Issues in evaluating outcomes

It is my view that much of the current research on outcome is directed more towards establishing the legitimacy of therapy than towards actually finding out more about the different kinds of benefits that people get (or don't get) from seeing a counsellor or psychotherapist. The drive has been to show that it 'works', in order to promote counselling and make sure that funds are invested in counselling services. This has led to research in which virtually the sole aim is to show that there are changes in questionnaire scores before and after counselling. Partly this concentration on brute outcomes reflects the difficulty of doing outcome research, of setting up a situation in which data can be collected from the same people on two or more occasions. But there are also some very difficult issues associated with the *concept* of change in counselling (not just with the problem of measuring it reliably). These underlying dilemmas are discussed in the following sections.

Attrition from the study
In randomised controlled trials, research assistants are typically employed to be on hand to ensure that clients and therapists complete questionnaires. By contrast, in practitioner outcome research, the researcher is usually relying on other people such as receptionists and colleagues, to collect data. These people have other jobs to do, and may 'forget' to follow the research protocol. Clients may forget to complete questionnaires, or may fill them in and forget to send them back to the office. A fair number of clients leave therapy without any advance warning. All of these factors can result in missing data, and the ensuing problem of how to interpret the data that is there. The key question is whether data and cases are missing on a random basis, or whether there are any identifiable causal factors responsible for the pattern of attrition. In one study in which I was involved (Sloboda et al., 1993) we found that, by looking at counsellor ratings of outcome, it was possible to see that clients who did not return end-of-counselling questionnaires were those who appeared (in the view of the counsellors) to have been helped less by the counselling. We could then interpret the very positive client satisfaction ratings more appropriately. In real-life situations where only 40–60 per cent of clients complete questionnaires, it is essential to be able to say something about those 50 per cent or so who disappeared from the study. Unexplained attrition undermines the credibility of outcome research. It is important to do everything possible (encouragingly worded covering letters, well designed questionnaires which are not too long,

reminders, posters on waiting room walls, motivating agency colleagues, etc.) to ensure the highest return rate. It is also important to
collect alternative sources of information (demographic data from
index cards or case files, case notes, reception interview notes,
waiting times, numbers of sessions attended, counsellor ratings)
that can be used as a basis for comparing those who did participate
in the study with those who did not.

Stakeholder perspectives

In the early years of therapy outcome research, every effort was
made to collect information from different sources, such as the
client, the therapist, significant others, objective clinical judges
who interviewed the client, employers and ward staff (see
Auerbach, 1983; Davidson and Davidson, 1983). More recently,
outcome research has narrowed down the search to include only
the self-report of the client. To some extent this shift has
occurred for reasons of cost and practicality (it is much cheaper
just to ask clients to answer questionnaires). But I would argue
that another crucial factor has been that different 'stakeholders'
tend to have quite different views of whether a person has been
helped by therapy. Including multiple stakeholders gives a truer
picture of the benefits of therapy, but also a picture that is so
complex that it is virtually impossible to interpret. In addition,
different stakeholders are interested in different things. For
example, in an evaluation of the effectiveness of workplace
counselling, the counsellors might want to know whether there
were types of clients who needed more or fewer sessions. The
counsellors might also believe that, for them, qualitative case
descriptions were more useful than statistical displays. The
management of the counselling agency might want to know
whether there were any individual counsellors who were less
effective than others. They would also like to see nice graphs that
would be persuasive to those who were purchasing the service.
Finally, the purchasers, who might be personnel managers in a
large company, might well want to know about 'stress hot-spots'
in the company, and would be very pleased to see a reduction in
rates of sickness absence. For any practitioner carrying out an
outcome study, it is therefore essential to be clear from the start
about who or what the study is *for*, who the stakeholders are.
Almost always, clients represent an invisible stakeholder group.
Outcome data is seldom made available to clients, or collected

with their interests in mind. There are some projects which have attempted to build a consumer perspective into counselling outcome research (e.g. Seligman, 1995; Lieper and Field, 1993) and this is an area of work which, it is hoped, will continue to develop.

Theoretical perspectives

Over the last 20 years, there has been a tendency for counselling and psychotherapy research and practice to become less theoretical and more 'integrative' or 'generic' (McLeod, 1994b, 1998). For example, the research carried out by Carl Rogers and his colleagues in the 1950s into the effectiveness of client-centred counselling used a specially devised Q-sort measure of self-acceptance, reflecting the theoretical underpinnings of that approach. Now, outcome researchers are much more likely to use measures of generic factors such as 'depression, 'stress' and 'anxiety'. There is a gain here, in that results can be more readily compared across studies, but there is also a loss. What has been lost, to a great extent, is the capacity for outcome data to feed back into the theory and thereby help practitioners to get better at what they are doing. It is useful to consider the example of the development of *process experiential therapy* (Greenberg, Rice and Elliott, 1993). This is a form of humanistic therapy that draws on both person-centred and Gestalt methods. In a series of studies, the founders of this approach have used outcome data on how this therapy works (and does not work) with different groups of clients. From their theoretical model, they predict which outcomes (defined in terms of client ratings of what was helpful or not helpful) they would expect. If the predicted outcomes are not observed, then the model can be adjusted and tried out again with more clients. In this way a series of outcome studies can be used to improve practice. The link between the outcome data and the practice is the theoretical model. When designing an outcome study, therefore, it is useful to begin by drawing up a model of the counselling that you use, or that is used in your agency or clinic. Once you have mapped out this model (which can be an interesting and informative exercise in itself), the next step is to think about the kinds of evidence that you might collect to test different aspects of the model or to expand your understanding of pieces of the process. Examples of approaches to counselling which have developed out of several cycles of research inquiry can be found in Rennie (1998) and Barkham et al. (1996).

Applying the results of outcome studies

On the whole, the outcome research which finds its way into the published literature is carried out by people with academic, policy or theory concerns, rather than from a practitioner stand-point. This research belongs in a useful but nevertheless abstract realm of conferences and papers. For people who are primarily practitioners, the pressing need is to know what to do *now*, with *this* client. Where naturalistic outcome data is being collected within a counselling agency or clinic, it would seem important to find ways of using that information to be able to maximise the quality of the service to the clients who are currently in the building and filling in questionnaires, rather than just hoping that, some time in the future, the results of research will help to shape agency practice in a positive direction. But in fact very little is known, or has been done, around how to close the feedback loop and allow clients and counsellors to use research data in their work together. In some of the 'managed care' schemes in the USA, which offer time-limited therapy to those who take out private health insurance, there are systems through which client ratings are sent directly to supervisors, who can then use them to assist or monitor the work of counsellors. This may be helpful, but at the same time it is easy to see how it could turn into a form of workplace surveillance that could limit the professional autonomy of counsellors. There do exist collaborative ways that counsellors and clients can work together on the interpretation of the meaning of test data, but this approach has not been widely adopted. In my experience, researchers have little understanding of how to communicate research findings to counsellors, while the latter have little idea of how to make sense of the data they get. There is clearly much to be learned about strategies for the *direct* use of research information in practice.

The ethics of outcome research

In Chapter 1, and throughout this book, there has been an emphasis on the moral basis for counselling practice, and the requirement for the work of the counsellor to be in the service of the client and their community. Doing outcome research involves

Box 9.4

How can the findings of outcome research be used to improve practice?

A Special Issue of the *Journal of Counseling and Development* (vol. 74, July/ August 1996) was devoted to the relevance of research for counselling practice. Three papers in this symposium explored the implications of outcome research findings:

Lambert, M.J. and Cattani-Thompson, K. (1996) 'Current findings regarding the effectiveness of counseling: implications for practice', *Journal of Counseling and Development*, 74: 601–8.
Nelson, M.L. and Neufeldt, S.A. (1996) 'Building on an empirical foundation: strategies to enhance good practice', *Journal of Counseling and Development*, 74: 609–15.
Sexton, T.L. (1996) 'The relevance of counseling outcome research: current trends and practical implications', *Journal of Counseling and Development*, 74: 590–600.

addressing a number of ethical issues. These issues are probably more important for practitioner-researchers than they are for 'external' investigators. This is not to question the ethical standards or integrity of academic researchers. However, practitioners have to live with the consequences of their ethical decisions in a way that external researchers may not be called upon to do. The key ethical tasks are those of addressing issues of informed consent and confidentiality. It is essential to make sure that clients consent to taking part in a study, that they understand what they are consenting to, and that they do not imagine that counselling is contingent on completing questionnaires. Most counselling agencies have evolved reliable procedures for ensuring that client information remains confidential. The existence of research data makes confidentiality more complex, and introduces additional ways in which information may leak out. One of the basic safeguards is to use code numbers at all times to identify client data, with the key to the code (the list of actual names) being kept locked away. People participating in research not only have a right to confidentiality but have a right to know about the arrangements for confidentiality. The more that clients trust these arrangements, the more likely they are to answer research questions honestly and fully. It is also important to bear in mind the moral responsibility toward the counsellors taking part in an outcome study. Several studies

have shown that individual counsellors differ in their effectiveness. It is therefore probable that an outcome study carried out in
a clinic or agency will show that, over a period of time, some
counsellors have better success rates than others. This kind of
result needs to be handled very carefully. Even very skilled
counsellors can have cases that go badly wrong. A research
questionnaire can, occasionally, function as a channel for client
complaints about the inadequacies of their counsellors. The
questionnaire can also be used by some clients as a desperate cry
for help. Thought needs to be given about what to do in these
cases. Who opens the envelope and reads the questionnaire first?
What do they then do? If the questionnaire contains disturbing
information, whose responsibility is it to act, and how?

Conclusions

The question of outcome has been and probably always will
remain a major preoccupation of those who engage in research
into counselling and psychotherapy. I have tried to argue here that
it is important for practitioners to take a fresh look at what is
involved in evaluating outcomes. This is an area of research that
has been dominated for too long by medical model assumptions
and randomised controlled trials. It seems to me that it is necessary
to move beyond these somewhat narrow definitions of evaluation,
and to be willing to create approaches that more fully reflect the
world of counselling. We have to learn to live with randomised
trials and cost-effectiveness studies, because they will probably
continue to express some of the core values of modern bureau-
cratic forms of governance. But we can learn how to deconstruct
and critique these forms, and point out their limitations in relation
to our area of activity. And we can do more to create an alternative, practice-focused, perspective on evaluating the outcomes of
counselling.

Further reading

Two excellent chapters which look at outcome evaluation from a
counselling practitioner perspective are:

Barkham, M.J. and Barker, C. (1996) 'Evaluating counselling psychology
  practice', in R. Woolfe and W. Dryden (eds), *Handbook of Counselling
  Psychology*. London: Sage.

Mellor-Clark, J. and Barkham, M.J. (1997) 'Evaluating effectiveness: needs, problems and potential benefits', in I. Horton and V. Varma (eds), *The Needs of Counsellors and Psychotherapists*. London: Sage.

10

Studying the Therapeutic Process

Investigating the process of counselling or psychotherapy has always been a favourite topic for practitioner research. After all, the moment-by-moment process of counselling is what a practitioner *does*, and is therefore a persistent source of puzzlement, fascination and frustration. Although there are many ways of understanding the concept of 'process' (see McLeod, 1998, ch. 12), probably the best way of understanding this idea is to regard process as comprising the elements or ingredients of counselling, the parts which make up the whole. In a lot of research, the distinction is made between 'process' and 'outcome', with process being the skills or intervention strategies that contribute toward final outcome. Some of this research is described as 'process–outcome' research, and has the aim of identifying the contribution that different process elements may make to outcome. Other process research has restricted itself to describing and identifying processes, without making any claims about the extent to which these processes either do or do not lead to good outcomes. Clearly, descriptive research, which identifies or maps out different types of process, is a necessary precursor to research which evaluates the impact of process on outcome.

One of the great challenges of process research, and what makes this kind of research difficult, is the fact that the process of counselling is highly complex. For example, Elliott (1991) argues that there are different kinds of processes associated with different timescales:

- *micro-processes*, such as a speaking turn or a non-verbal gesture, may last from a few seconds to one or two minutes in length;
- a therapeutic episode or *event*, such as 'making sense of why I got so angry yesterday', may last for several minutes;
- a whole counselling *session* may represent an important process unit, for example the process of agreeing a contract in the first session;
- the process taking place over the entire *course of treatment* may be of interest, for example in terms of models of stages in treatment (beginning–middle–end).

In addition to these different time units, the counselling process at any moment can be explored in terms of either individual processes (what either the counsellor or client is thinking/feeling/doing) or in terms of dyadic or relational processes (how the client responded to the counsellor's statement; what the quality of the therapeutic alliance is between counsellor and client).

If process is being related to outcome, it is essential to keep in mind that outcome itself is not a monolithic entity but can, too, be broken down into different components. For example, one way of looking at outcome is to ask a client how helpful their counselling has been. These helpfulness ratings can be made in relation to the whole of their counselling, to their perception of the helpfulness of a single session, to the usefulness of a single event within a session, or to the usefulness of a specific intervention or counsellor statement. Just as there is a macro-process (the whole of the counselling treatment episode) and a micro-process (detailed analysis of one minute during a session), there are 'big outcomes' (how helpful counselling was as a whole) and 'little outcomes' (how helpful that last thing the counsellor said was).

To add to the complexity of process research, it is also necessary to think about the *source* of data. Is information about process to be collected from clients, counsellors, external observers, or from some combination of these sources? This is a tricky decision, because it is quite likely that observers from these different perspectives will report quite different perceptions of what happened during a session. It is as though client and counsellor each have their own 'reality' within a counselling session, with an external observer (for instance, someone watching a video of the session) being able to gain no more than a partial glimpse into these realities.

The intrusiveness of process research has also presented difficulties for some researchers. There can be concern that collecting process data may interfere with the actual therapy, and much of the time counsellors and psychotherapists are reluctant to give permission for process data to be collected because of this fear. In some studies, researchers have set up 'analogue' situations, such as one-off counselling sessions with volunteer clients, so that key processes can be studied in depth without any threat to the confidentiality or well-being of 'real' clients. Analogue studies can provide useful insights, but their generalisability to actual counselling is always uncertain until similar data can be collected from actual clients.

Finally, research on process is heavily influenced by the theoretical assumptions of the researcher. For example, a psychodynamic researcher will want to set up a process study in such a way that *unconscious* transference processes can be observed. The work of Luborsky et al. (1986) and Silberschatz et al. (1986, 1989) are good examples of how psychoanalytically informed researchers make sense of process. Alternatively, humanistic process researchers such as Elliott (1986) or Rennie (1990) design their studies in such a way as to do everything possible to explore the client's capacity for *conscious* reflexive awareness of his or her intentions or 'agency'.

The message here, therefore, is that the complexity of the literature on the process of counselling and psychotherapy mirrors the complexity of the process itself. Perhaps even more than in other areas of counselling research, it is advisable for beginning researchers to stick to one *genre* of process research and to accept its limitations. Specifically, it is useful to find an exemplar paper that illustrates an approach to understanding and researching process that strikes a chord, and to use that paper (or series of papers) as a template for one's own research. Better to walk than to fall over.

Collecting process data

The process that takes place during a counselling session is multi-dimensional and ephemeral, and therefore hard to pin down. For most practitioners, it is difficult to make detailed notes on the process of a particular counselling session, even if one sits down immediately after the session and tries to remember everything that has happened. One of the main problems in process research, therefore, is that of devising a way of getting access to the 'interior' of a counselling session, and then record-ing that information in a form that can be analysed. There have been six main approaches that have been used to collect process data:

- questionnaires completed after the counselling session;
- quantitative ratings of tapes (or transcripts of sessions);
- in-session recording (e.g. Barkham and Shapiro, 1986);
- qualitative analysis of tapes/transcripts of sessions;
- 'assisted recall' interviews following sessions using Inter-personal Process Recall (IPR);
- retrospective interviews or written accounts, for example in some of the recent work of Clara Hill and her colleagues.

These methods of data collection vary in terms of their close-ness to the actual therapy experience. Asking clients to press a hidden button every time they feel understood by their coun-sellor is *very* close to the experience (Barkham and Shapiro, 1986) but is not likely to be acceptable to many people. Asking a client or counsellor to complete a questionnaire immediately after a session, or to answer questions in response to hearing or watching a tape of the session (IPR) is still fairly close to the experience. Retrospective interviews or questionnaires, which invite counsellors or clients to recollect sessions that may have happened days or weeks previously, obviously run the risk that what is reported is a rationalised or generalised account that omits important experiential detail. A transcript or recording gets over the problem of time distance, by providing a direct record of what happened as it happened. However, listening to or watching a tape introduces a different kind of distancing, as does reading a transcript. The point here is that each mode of data collection can do no more than supply a version of the process.

There are many questionnaires that clients and/or counsellors can fill in at the end of sessions to indicate their experience of process factors. There are also several ratings scales which can be used to analyse video or audio recordings of sessions. Sources of information about these tools can be found in Box 10.1.

Box 10.1

Quantitative scales for measuring process factors

Barrett-Lennard, G.T. (1986) 'The Relationship Inventory now: issues and advances in theory, method and use', in L.S. Greenberg and W.M. Pinsof (eds), *The Psychotherapeutic Process: A Research Handbook*. New York: Guilford Press.

Gendlin, E.T. and Tomlinson, T.M. (1967) 'The process conception and its measurement', in C.R. Rogers, E.T. Gendlin, D.J. Kiesler and C.B. Truax (eds), *The Therapeutic Relationship and its Impact: A Study of Psychotherapy with Schizophrenics*. Madison: University of Wisconsin Press.

Hill, C.E. (1986) 'An overview of the Hill counselor and client verbal response modes category systems', in L.S. Greenberg and W.M. Pinsof (eds), *The Psychotherapeutic Process: A Research Handbook*. New York: Guilford Press.

Horvath, A.O. and Greenberg, L.S. (1986) 'Development of the Working Alliance Inventory', in L.S. Greenberg and W.M. Pinsof (eds), *The Psychotherapeutic Process: A Research Handbook*. New York: Guilford Press.

Horvath, A.O., Gaston, L. and Luborsky, L. (1993) 'The Therapeutic Alliance and its measures', in N.E. Miller, L. Luborsky, J.P. Barber and J.P. Docherty (eds), *Psychodynamic Treatment Research: A Handbook for Clinical Practice*. New York: Basic Books.

Klein, M.H., Mathieu-Coughlan, P. and Kiesler, D.J. (1986) 'The Experiencing Scales', in L.S. Greenberg and W.M. Pinsof (eds), *The Psychotherapeutic Process: A Research Handbook*. New York: Guilford Press.

Luborsky, L. and Crits-Christoph, P. (eds) (1990) *Understanding Transference: the CCRT Method*. New York: Basic Books.

Orlinsky, D.E. and Howard, K.I. (1986) 'The psychological interior of psycho-therapy: explorations with the Therapy Session reports', in L.S. Greenberg and W.M. Pinsof (eds), *The Psychotherapeutic Process: A Research Handbook*. New York: Guilford Press.

Rice, L.N. and Kerr, G.P. (1986) 'Measures of client and therapist voice quality', in L.S. Greenberg and W.M. Pinsof (eds), *The Psychotherapeutic Process: A Research Handbook*. New York: Guilford Press.

Stiles, W.B. (1986) 'Development of a taxonomy of verbal response modes', in L.S. Greenberg and W.M. Pinsof (eds), *The Psychotherapeutic Process: A Research Handbook*. New York: Guilford Press.

Tichenor, V. and Hill, C.E. (1989) 'A comparison of six measures of the working alliance', *Psychotherapy*, 26: 195–9.

A significant development in counselling process research over the last decade has been the growth in the number and variety of qualitative process studies that have been carried out. Many practitioner-oriented researchers would argue that, while remaining rigorous and systematic, qualitative methods make it possible to achieve a more sensitive insight into what is happening within a therapy session. The qualitative approaches listed in Box 10.2 are all highly appropriate means of carrying out practitioner research.

Box 10.2

Qualitative methods for researching therapeutic process

Barker, C. (1985) 'Interpersonal Process Recall in clinical training and research', in F.N. Watts (ed.), *New Developments in Clinical Psychology*. Chichester: Wiley/BPS.

Elliott, R. (1984) 'A discovery-oriented approach to significant change events in psychotherapy: Interpersonal Process Recall and Comprehensive Process Analysis', in L.N. Rice and L.S. Greenberg (eds), *Patterns of Change: Intensive Analysis of Psychotherapy Process*. New York: Guilford Press.

Elliott, R. (1986) 'Interpersonal Process Recall (IPR) as a psychotherapy process research method', in L.S. Greenberg and W.M. Pinsof (eds), *The Psychotherapeutic Process: A Research Handbook*. New York: Guilford Press.

Elliott, R. and Shapiro, D.A. (1988) 'Brief Structured Recall: a more efficient method for studying significant therapy events', *British Journal of Medical Psychology*, 61: 141–53.

Greenberg, L.S. (1984) 'Task analysis: the general approach', in L.N. Rice and L.S. Greenberg (eds), *Patterns of Change: Intensive Analysis of Psychotherapy Process*. New York: Guilford Press.

Mearns, D. and McLeod, J. (1984) 'A person-centred approach to research', in R. Levant and J. Shlien (eds), *Client-Centered Therapy and the Person-Centered Approach: New Directions in Theory, Research and Practice*. New York: Praeger.

Rennie, D.L. (1992) 'Qualitative analysis of the client's experience of psychotherapy: the unfolding of reflexivity', in S.G. Toukmanian and D.L. Rennie (eds), *Psychotherapy Process Research: Paradigmatic and Narrative Approaches*. London: Sage.

A practitioner perspective on process research

Process research provides many opportunities for counsellors interested in reflecting on their practice. Useful studies can be carried out on the basis of transcribed recording of single sessions, as in the work of Robert Elliott or in my own research on narrative process (McLeod and Balamoutsou, 1996). There are many brief questionnaires, such as the Working Alliance Inventory, or parts of the Barrett-Lennard Relationship Inventory or Therapy Session Report scales (see Chapter 6), which clients can be asked to complete immediately following sessions. There are also well-proven methods for collecting retrospective accounts of aspects of process (for example in the research by David Rennie or Clara Hill) through the use of interviews or written statements. There are methods which are well attuned to specific theoretical models, for example in the psychodynamic research by Luborsky and Silberschatz. Finally, there are styles of process research suited to lone researchers and to those who prefer to work as members of a team.

It is through process research that many of the most burning practitioner questions can be addressed: What difference does empathy make? Does providing a pre-counselling induction leaflet lead to more effective engagement in therapy? What are the characteristics of key moments of change? This chapter has done no more than touch on some of the different types of process research that have been carried out. Further discussion of this type of research can be found in McLeod (1994b) and in the list of recommended reading at the end of the chapter.

Finally, the moral and ethical issues associated with process research are significant. All of the ethical issues discussed in previous chapters apply, with the added complication that some forms of process research involve collecting actual in-session data through recording, or re-opening therapeutic issues in follow-up interviews. Because of these ethical issues, some counsellors can be wary about being involved in process research (Vachon et al., 1995).

Further reading

Greenberg, L.S. and Pinsof, W.M. (eds) (1986) *The Psychotherapeutic Process: A Research Handbook*. New York: Guilford Press. (A key text – contains information on most of the main approaches to studying process.)

Hill, C.E. (1989) *Therapist Techniques and Client Outcomes: Eight Cases of Brief Psychotherapy*. London: Sage. (Series of case studies that demonstrate the application of a range of process methods.)

Hill, C.E. (1991) 'Almost everything you ever wanted to know about how to do process research on counseling and psychotherapy but didn't know who to ask', in C.E. Watkins, jr, and L.J. Schneider (eds), *Research in Counseling*. Hillsdale, NJ: Lawrence Erlbaum. (Useful discussion of the practicalities of using quantitative methods in process research.)

Rice, L.N. and Greenberg, L.S. (eds) (1984) *Patterns of Change: Intensive Analysis of Psychotherapy Process*. New York: Guilford Press. (Examples of the application of both humanistic and psychodynamic process methods.)

Toukmanian, S.G. and Rennie, D.L. (eds) (1992) *Psychotherapy Process Research: Paradigmatic and Narrative Approaches*. London: Sage.

(Good examples of process research in action, and valuable concluding chapter which reviews important issues in process research methodology.)

11

Practitioner Inquiry Groups

For some counsellors, research can become an isolated and isolating experience. It may be that no immediate colleagues share your interest in a particular topic, or it may be that they are interested but have neither the time nor commitment to participate fully in looking at data or transcripts. Some colleagues may feel threatened by research, or regard it as irrelevant to their clinical concerns. As mentioned in Chapter 1, there has been a tendency for research support to be based in academic rather than clinical settings, with the result that the meaning of research can become divorced from practice. In the end, academic research produces words – books, articles, reports – whereas counselling practice produces action. The 'knowing that' of research can sometimes be difficult to integrate with the 'knowing how' of actual counselling practice. In an attempt to address these issues, there have been various attempts to develop *collective* approaches to research. The assumption is that if a number of people work together on a research study, they should be able to provide mutual support and synergy, and generate findings that are both more reliable and more creative than could be achieved by an individual working alone. In addition, when the members of the group are practitioners, the process of discussing research-based insights in the group should provide a better basis for applying research findings to practice.

The aim of this chapter is to give an outline of some of the different ways in which groups of practitioner-researchers have worked together in counselling and allied fields. The three most influential traditions in collective research have been the *human inquiry* model developed by Peter Reason, Judy Marshall and their colleagues at the University of Bath, the *consensual qualitative research* approach pioneered by Clara Hill at the University of Maryland, and finally the *comprehensive process analysis* method created by Robert Elliott at the University of Toledo in Ohio. These three approaches can be considered as versions of a more general research strategy built around the use of *practitioner inquiry groups*. The chapter will conclude with a look at some of the wider issues raised by this style of research.

Human inquiry groups

The multiple influences that have contributed to the human inquiry method can be found in the book *Human Inquiry: A Sourcebook of New Paradigm Research*, published in 1981 and edited by Peter Reason, an organisational theorist with an interest in co-counselling, and John Rowan, a psychotherapist with a background in market research. *Human Inquiry* included chapters on the sociology and philosophy of science, psycho-analytic, existential and personal construct and feminist perspectives, heuristic, endogenous and action research, and the importance of researcher reflexivity. The message was that there existed an emerging new way of doing social and psychological research which would be subjective yet also systematic, and would cut through the objectivist dogma of mainstream quantitative positivist methodology. During the 1980s and 1990s one strand of this 'new paradigm' methodology crystallised into an approach that is variously known as 'human inquiry', 'collabora-tive inquiry', 'co-operative inquiry' or 'participatory research'. The key texts describing this approach are Reason (1988a, 1994a) and Heron (1996). The latter book is in effect a manual of how to do human inquiry research. Reason and Heron (1986) and Reason (1994b) offer useful brief summaries of the principles of this method. In addition, the Centre for the Study of Organisational Change and Development at the University of Bath publishes an international newsletter, *Collaborative Inquiry*, which provides a means of contact and networking for those using this approach.

The main features of the human inquiry method are that it is: group-based, involving active participation and self-reflection from all members of the group, proceeds through a series of stages, and generates knowledge that is (primarily) practical rather than cognitive/intellectual.

A human inquiry project begins when a group of co-researchers meet to inquire into some aspect of their life and work. Reason (1988b) describes the ensuing cycle of inquiry in these terms:

- negotiation and agreement over what is to be researched, and how the research is to be carried out;
- active immersion in relevant aspects of life and work, accompanied by sensitive collection of authentic experiential data, for example self-observation, observations of each other, doing interviews, keeping a diary, making tapes of counselling or supervision sessions, etc.;
- reflection on experience. In this phase, co-researchers attempt to make sense of experiential data, and to use it to challenge and extend the concepts, models and pre-understandings which were identified at the outset of the inquiry process;
- further cycles of inquiry, in which new understandings lead to the collection of further experiential material, which is in turn the source of reflection and analysis.

Reason (1988b: 6) proposes that 'the essence of co-operative experiential inquiry is an aware and self-critical movement between experience and reflection which goes through several cycles as ideas, practice, and experience are systematically honed and refined'.

The process of carrying out a human inquiry study successfully involves overcoming a number of challenges. There can be practical difficulties in collecting together a group of people who are motivated to act as co-researchers and understand what this role involves. Usually, people expect to be 'subjects' of a sovereign researcher, and it can be hard for the person who initially sets up the group to avoid the role of leader, facilitator or 'expert', or being seen as the real 'owner' of the project. While it is inevitable that individual members of a human inquiry group will each have their own level of interest in and commitment to the project, for the inquiry process to flow it is necessary that a sufficiently collaborative, co-operative or egalitarian group culture is created from the outset. It is also necessary to build in procedures (e.g. regular review sessions) to ensure that the process of the group does not get stuck or diverted into group dynamics issues such as interpersonal conflict and scapegoating, lack of trust and safety, shared fantasies and collusion, or task avoidance. At least some of the members of the group probably need to have prior experience or training in principles of effective group or team working. The group also needs to develop a framework for coping with distress, since the process may involve the challenging of strongly held personal beliefs and values. If all of these 'group maintenance' factors are in place to a sufficient degree, then an inquiry culture is created in which authentic collaboration is possible (Heron, 1996).

Examples of the products of human inquiry research can be found in Reason (1988a). Perhaps the most widely known and celebrated published study carried out using this method is the project facilitated by Heron and Reason (Reason 1988c; Reason et al., 1992), based in Marylebone Health Centre in London, into the development of 'whole person' practice in GP clinics within the British National Health Service. This study involved 16 medical practitioners interested in holistic medicine, who met on seven occasions over a period of several months. Something of the intensity of this experience is conveyed by Reason:

> we met regularly for encounter sessions during the whole inquiry, dealing with issues such as uneven contribution levels, the domination of the group by particular vocal men, personal attractions and antipathies, and so on. Similarly we took time in pairs and small groups to explore the personal distress that was restimulated by the inquiry process. Group members discovered, for example, that they hated both doctors and doctoring; that they had been grievously hurt and their aspirations to do good work crushed by their experience of medical school; that they had lost their way both professionally and personally. The changes in practice brought about through membership of the project stimulated some violent disagreements with both professional and personal partners. And group members found the challenge of new ways of practice deeply disturbing. For some group members the significance of the learning which emerged from these personal confrontations was far more important than the formal research findings. . . . (1988c: 107)

This final point, concerning the way that personal learning took on more significance than did the final written report, represents a crucial issue in human inquiry work. For Reason and his colleagues, knowledge is fundamentally bound up with *action* rather than with the creation of text. It can therefore be difficult to find ways of representing what has been learned from a human inquiry that will enable those who were not members of the group (the wider research audience) to learn from the experience of those who were the actual participants. As far as I am aware, the findings of the Marylebone project were never written up in detail for any of the widely read establishment medical journals. The paper by Reason et al. (1992) in the *Journal of the Royal Society of Medicine* provides a highly abstracted version of what went on. This dilemma is part of a broader 'crisis of representation' within qualitative research, discussed by several of the contributors to Denzin and Lincoln (1994b). To do justice to the depth of learning that may take place in a human inquiry group calls for the construction of truly 'multi-voiced' text.

It has taken some time for human inquiry methods to be applied to research in counselling and psychotherapy. This is perhaps surprising, since the experiential and constructivist emphases of the method are consistent with the values and world-view of many counsellors. On the other hand, counselling research, until recently, has been very much dominated by the methods of quantitative psychology. Also, it is probably the case that there are special difficulties involved in using inquiry groups with people who currently define themselves as belonging in a help-seeking 'client' or 'patient' role. Such people may seek to pull an inquiry group in the direction of therapy, and be unwilling to see themselves as 'co-researchers'. However, it may well be that these difficulties can be overcome, and that the human inquiry can be employed in research into clients' experiences of counselling.

The work of William West (1996, 1997) comprises the clearest currently published example of a human inquiry study of a counselling/psychotherapy topic. West was interested in the experiences of therapists who also regarded themselves as spiritual healers. His aim was to explore the ways in which practitioners integrated these two approaches in their day-to-day work. In this study, West (1997) collected data using a combination of individual interviews and a human inquiry group. Having gathered this material, he carried out a form of grounded theory analysis to identify core categories and themes. The results of the study therefore predominantly convey West's way of making sense of the phenomena, rather than being collectively written by the inquiry group members themselves. However, as someone who was involved with this study (as academic supervisor) I can add my own observation that the inquiry group sessions generated material that would not have come up in interviews; there was a clear 'added value' in the use of the group. Also, as West (1997) notes, the group was so meaningful for participants that they continued to meet even after the end of the research. This study therefore exemplifies both the potential of the human inquiry method and also some of its challenges.

At the present time, there are a number of human inquiry studies of counselling and psychotherapy in the process of being carried out. As the findings of these studies enter the public domain, the influence of this approach within counselling is likely to increase.

Consensual qualitative methods

In Chapter 8, a number of different approaches to qualitative research were introduced. It is clear that there exist contrasting inquiry traditions and methods of data collection and analysis within the qualitative research arena. One of the issues which is debated less often, but is nevertheless an important question for many therapy practitioners embarking on qualitative research, arises from the decision of whether to carry out a study as a lone researcher, or to seek to work as part of a team. There are powerful arguments in support of the lone researcher approach, arising from the fact that the kind of total immersion within the data, and intimate familiarity with all the details of the study, that is necessary for sensitive and original qualitative analysis, is more likely to be achieved by a single person working alone; it is difficult or impossible to assemble a team who all share the same level of commitment to the research task. On the other hand, many qualitative researchers enjoy their research more if they work in a team. Collaboration between a set of people analysing the same qualitative texts can both help in the generation of new ideas, arising from creative interaction between members. Working together can also contribute to a sense that what is being written is in some sense 'true' because it is supported by the shared judgements of a group of people, rather than being based only on the views of one investigator. One of the major challenges of team-based qualitative research, however, is that of deciding how to structure the efforts of different members of the group. Analysing qualitative data is a complex enough business in single-researcher projects. When a team of people is involved, avoidance of chaos depends on everyone knowing how, when and why they will work together. There have been two principal methods of team-based qualitative research developed in recent years, the *consensual qualitative research* model of Hill, Nutt-Williams and Thompson (1997), and the *comprehensive process analysis* procedure created by Elliott (1986).

Consensual qualitative research

The *consensual* approach associated with the research group led by Clara Hill at the University of Maryland consists of a set of guidelines for collecting and analysing qualitative data on (usually) counselling and psychotherapy process issues. The method has been influenced by grounded theory (see Chapter 8) and to some extent represents an attempt to reconcile the more fluid and intuitive methods of traditional qualitative research with the demand for rigour and objectivity characteristic of mainstream psychology. Critics of the consensual approach have drawn attention to some of the costs incurred at arriving at such a compromise (Hoshmand, 1997; Stiles, 1997). However, for the present purpose the main aim is to explore the ways in which Hill and her colleagues work as a research group.

Consensual qualitative research (CQR) is structured around four main research tasks (Hill et al., 1997: 522–3):

1 Qualitative data is collected using open-ended questions from questionnaires or interviews in order not to constrain the responses of participants.
2 These responses are divided into general domains or topic areas, usually decided in advance by the research team.
3 Core ideas (abstracts or brief summaries) are constructed for all the material within each domain for each individual case.
4 A cross-analysis is conducted through which categories are generated to capture consistencies in the core ideas across domains.

These procedures are carried out by a primary team of three to five researchers, along with one or two auditors. The role of the auditors is to check the work of the primary team at every stage, but to be independent enough to avoid becoming enmeshed in the dynamics of the group. It is important to attend to the maintenance of an appropriate balance of safety and challenge within the primary team, for example by giving enough time for group meetings, dealing with process issues whenever they arise, and rotating who talks first.

Participation in the research team involves sharing initial expectations and biases about the research topic, reflecting on clients' or therapists' experiences captured in open-ended questionnaires or interviews, making sense of these accounts, listening to colleagues' analyses of interviews, challenging colleagues and being challenged, placing what has been learned into a narrative form that will communicate effectively to other people, and working out how what has been discovered meshes with other research evidence. In all this, there are many opportunities for practitioners to develop self-awareness, learn about collaboration, extend their capacity for useful conceptualisation, and be part of a supportive network. Hill et al. observe that

> the steps of the process mimic much of what often occurs in supervision or case consultation, in that the team members make sense of the data and then compare their understanding of the data with the other team members, talking through differences in perceptions to arrive at a 'good enough' truth. (1997: 563–4)

There are many examples of studies that have employed the CQR approach, for example investigations of therapeutic impasses (Hill et al., 1996), helpfulness of therapist self-disclosure (Knox et al., 1997) and sexual attraction toward clients (Ladany et al., 1997).

Comprehensive process analysis

The comprehensive process analysis (CPA) approach was devised by Robert Elliott as a means of intensive exploration of the meaning of significant events in therapy sessions. Some time following a counselling session, the client is asked to identify the most significant helpful or hindering event in that session. The session is also recorded on audio or video tape. Usually, the Helpful Aspects of Therapy (HAT) questionnaire (Llewelyn et al., 1988) is employed for this purpose. Then, within 48 hours, both client and counsellor are interviewed about their experience of this event. The interview is based on the client or counsellor listening (or viewing) the tape, and then pausing to report on what they had been thinking or feeling at that moment in the session. It is intended, or hoped, this technique of 'stimulated recall' will generate something close to a record of the actual experience of the event, rather than a constructed or rationalised post-hoc version of what happened.

This set of procedures therefore produces a research text which comprises a transcript of the relevant part of the counselling session, a brief description of the helpful event written by the client immediately after the session, and transcripts of 'structured recall' interviews with the client and the counsellor. There may also be quantitative ratings made by the client and/or counsellor on the helpfulness of the event and the counselling session as a whole, or other relevant variables. This material is then analysed by the members of a research team, starting with the actual words and statements uttered during the event, then moving out into the minute before and after the event, the session context and then finally the context of the therapy as a whole.

The outcome of a comprehensive process analysis investigation is a case study of the therapeutic process which contributed to the creation of a single significant moment in a therapy session. CPA research reports are normally given titles that reflect the key statement in the therapy session that captured, for the client, the 'essence' of the event. The title of a CPA paper therefore represents the *client's* title for the event, indicating the roots of CPA in a humanistic tradition which places emphasis on the client's experience. There is also clearly an acknowledgement here of the requirement that good qualitative research should pay heed to the 'poetics' of human experience. Examples of titles of CPA papers are: 'That in your hands . . .' (Elliott, 1983a) and 'Whingeing versus working' (Hardy et al., 1998).

Further information on how to carry out a CPA study can be found in Elliott (1984). It is planned that a detailed manual of the CPA method will be published in book form within the next two years.

Other examples of group-based practitioner research

Although the examples described so far in this chapter comprise methods of group-based practitioner inquiry that have been supported by a clear methodological rationale, there are several other studies that have also used a practitioner inquiry group approach. An important line of research in counselling and psychotherapy which has made use of a research team has been the programme of work carried out by Al Mahrer and his colleagues at the University of Ottawa into the nature of 'good moments' in therapy (Mahrer and Nadler, 1986; Mahrer et al., 1987). Mahrer's method is to use a large number of 'clinically sophisticated judges' to analyse the process occurring in moments of change during therapy sessions (Mahrer et al., 1986). The use of a collaborative research team can also be found in the study of therapist values carried out by Walsh, Perrucci and Severns (1999) and in the research on 'therapist difficulties' by Davis et al. (1987). A very interesting team-based approach to evaluation is described by Jones (1993), comprising the analysis of client evaluation sheets by a large group (16-20 members) of the management of a mental health unit.

Developing the practitioner inquiry group approach

The examples of team-based research described in this chapter certainly do not exhaust the possibilities of this approach. There are other ways in which research teams can be organised and deployed, and other types of research question for which they can be used. The methods devised by Reason, Hill, Elliott, Mahrer and their colleagues need to be seen as possible ways of carrying out group inquiry, not as fixed and rigid methodologies which must be replicated. Other groups of practitioners, with different priorities and local circumstances, will inevitably discover their own preferred styles of carrying out research through group collaboration. The increasing availability and flexibility of telephone and video conferencing and internet discussion groups open up new possibilities.

The further development of practitioner inquiry groups in counselling and psychotherapy research could be facilitated by a greater willingness to look at how researchers in other fields have applied this type of approach in their work. One of the themes in the writings of therapy researchers such as Hill, Mahrer and Elliott is that the value of a group approach lies in its capacity to demonstrate that a consensus interpretation has been reached. The inquiry group can therefore be seen as the qualitative equivalent of inter-rater reliability coefficients in quantitative research. The tendency has therefore been for all members of an inquiry group to carry out the same tasks (with the exception, in CQR, of external auditors who check the analyses carried out by members of the team). In some team-based research, however, there has been a deliberate strategy of using different members of the inquiry group to produce diverse and contrasting interpretations. In the health-care research of Olesen et al. (1994), for example, a research team consisting of nurses and sociologists was assembled, so that contrasting understandings of health behaviour could be integrated into a more holistic analysis. Much earlier, the pioneering studies of Henry Murray and his colleagues into personality (Murray, 1938) employed a research team drawn from different disciplines (psychology, sociology, anthropology, the arts) in order to maximise interpretive richness. In Murray's studies, members of the research group also collected information using different methods (interviews, observation, questionnaires, situational tests). Rather than all team members working on the same data set, members analysed their own data and then met as a group to look at the extent of agreement or disagreement between them (McLeod, 1992).

The point here is that it can be useful in a practitioner inquiry group not only to arrive at consensus, but to generate alternative perspectives that open up new interpretive possibilities. Individual members of the group can pursue their own interests, their own 'line' through the data, as long as there exists a robust enough group forum for joining these lines together. The inclusion in practitioner inquiry groups of critics or 'devil's advocates' is also worth consideration. In the Hill et al. (1997) consensual qualitative research studies, the external auditor was generally someone from the same professional community, who was sympathetic to the ideas and values held by the members of the research team. It is easy to imagine situations in counselling research where the credibility of a study (as well as the quality of the research analysis) could be enhanced by using auditors who were sceptical or hostile. For example, some GPs are far from convinced of the value of counselling in primary care. A practitioner inquiry group studying the effectiveness of counselling in primary care might well invite such a person to audit their analyses. In attempting to respond to the views of such a critic, the group would be forced to reflect deeply on the adequacy of its research. Perhaps a genuine dialogue might even be initiated. Levine (1974) has argued that researchers should seek out 'adversaries'. Bromley (1986) has suggested that it is useful for researchers to adopt a 'quasi-judicial' approach, in which they create a situation in which they have to defend their interpretations of their data in the face of strongly argued alternative interpretations (the prosecution).

Inquiry groups represent a form of research that is highly suitable for practitioners. Such groups create possibilities for open and non-hierarchical peer discussion between counsellors with different levels of experience, colleagues within a single agency or counselling setting, or colleagues from several agencies or counselling settings. Whatever group format or task is selected, the experience of participating in a practitioner inquiry group involves counsellors in sustained and challenging reflection on the concepts and assumptions that inform their practice. This should have the effect of contributing to professional development (Skovholt and Ronnestad, 1992) and counteracting many of the factors that lead to burnout, such as professional isolation, loss of meaning in the work, and emotional exhaustion. Inquiry groups can therefore be seen as playing a part in creating better counsellors and better counselling.

Finally, it is important to take into account the type of knowledge that is brought into being by research activities such as inquiry groups. The people who take part in inquiry groups are not raters trained not to deviate from the procedures laid down in a research protocol, of the kind who have formed the workforce for many hundreds of psychological studies (see Hill, 1991). Nor are they operating as expert judges chosen to function as sources of received clinical wisdom, as in the psychoanalytic research carried out by Luborsky or Silbershatz. Members of inquiry groups are in a situation where the quality of the research depends on their capacity to challenge their own understandings and extend their horizons. The knowledge generated by inquiry groups is the product of dialogue within the group, which is then disseminated beyond the group as a way of continuing and deepening the conversation around important issues within counselling. It is therefore not knowledge that comprises bundles of static 'fact modules', but knowledge that represents an active, applied understanding that is contextualised, personally owned and involving.

In further developing the practitioner inquiry group approach, counselling researchers need to take account of the experience of using research teams in other disciplines. The short book by Erickson and Stull (1998), for example, describes some of the issues that can arise when anthropologists engage in joint fieldwork.

12

Getting into Print . . . and Other Ways of Getting the Message Across

One of the fundamental differences between formal research and the kind of informal personal reflection on practice that is part of supervision and training is that the products of research are disseminated and become part of a general stock of knowledge and understanding. Usually, the findings of research are disseminated in written form. Although some researchers are beginning to experiment with other media such as video and live performance, or are publishing their work on the Internet, the main way of passing on research is through written articles, chapters, reports and books. The aim of this chapter is to offer some guidelines for getting into print. Many counsellors who do research do so in the context of studying for a degree, and initially write up their results in a Masters or Doctoral dissertation. Other counsellors carry out research as part of the audit and evaluation function of their agency or clinic, and their work remains hidden within internal memos and reports. I believe that it is important for counsellors who wish to continue their professional development to the stage of making an impact on their peers, of claiming their own authority and professional voice, to go beyond this and publish in the public realm. Here is how to do it.

There are four main types of publication outlet: journals, conference proceedings, books and monographs. These are discussed in turn.

Publishing in journals

There is a huge international journals industry which is largely invisible to those outside the academic world. Advances in desktop publishing and printing have made it much cheaper to produce journals. Whereas commercial magazines need to pay authors for every word that they publish, the contributors to professional and academic journals do not usually get paid, and in many journals the editor will receive an honorarium rather than a salary. Moreover, many journals enjoy fixed subscriptions tied in to the membership of professional bodies. For example, all 12,000 members of the British Association for Counselling receive the journal *Counselling*, which is paid for out of their membership dues. Professional and academic journals can survive with quite limited subscription bases (around 500 would appear to be sufficient for a viable journal). Publishing companies therefore like publishing journals, which provide steady income, low outgoings and a vehicle for promoting their book sales. The economics of the journals publishing industry has a number of implications for anyone wishing to get into print:

- There are *lots* of journals. If you cannot get your article accepted by a mainstream journal there will be some other niche journal, somewhere, that will in all likelihood be glad to have it. An (incomplete) list of journals that publish research or research-oriented articles in counselling and psychotherapy can be found in Chapter 4.
- Most journals are run on a shoestring. People who review articles for journals are not paid. There is no one paid to have the time to polish up your grammar, spelling and use of references or to give you general advice. You have to meet their deadlines (e.g. for proof reading) and follow their instructions.
- You must only submit your article to one journal at a time. If everyone were to submit their stuff to three or four journals simultaneously, the editing and reviewing system would collapse under the strain.

■ *You* will not be paid. Normally, if you have an article accepted in a journal you will get a free copy of the journal (the one with your paper in it) and a batch of free offprints.

A broad distincton can be made between *professional* and *research/academic* journals, although there are also some journals which straddle this divide. Professional journals are mainly concerned with publishing articles about professional issues. In the counselling and psychotherapy world such journals include *Counselling*, the *Journal of Counseling and Development*, *The Counseling Psychologist*, *American Psychologist* and the *Psychologist*. These journals are the official organs of professional associations. Although they may include excellent learned articles on theory and practice, they are unlikely to carry original research, and they tend to include fairly lengthy sections on announcements, meetings of professional committees, and general professional business. They also carry a lot of advertising for courses and conferences. By contrast, academic journals such as the *British Journal of Guidance and Counselling*, *Counselling Psychology Quarterly*, and the *Journal of Counseling Psychology* carry mainly research reports, reviews of the research literature and articles on theory and methodology. They do not cover professional business, and include only limited advertising. Some of the differences between the publication policies of these different types of journal are outlined in Box 12.1.

In deciding which journal to submit work to, it is essential to get hold of an actual copy of the journal. Look at the kind of articles that are published in the journal, and choose one which carries articles that are similar in style and content to the one that you intend to write. Inside the cover of every journal it is possible to find some sort of 'mission statement' describing the type of papers the journal would like to receive. Sometimes, this statement can be misleading, because editorial policies can outgrow the original journal remit, so it is always important to look at a few back issues to get a feel for the territory which the journal has carved out for itself. Inside the front or back cover of the journal there is usually other vital information, including:

■ minimum and maximum length of articles;
■ guidelines for preparing articles, for example referencing conventions, policy on sexist language, ethical waivers, and

Box 12.1

Publication policies of professional and academic journals

Professional journals	*Academic journals*
Publication criteria weighted toward topicality, interest value, readability	Publication criteria weighted toward research rigour
May commission articles	Publication almost wholly responsive to submissions sent in
Decision to publish often made by editor	Decision to publish always arrived at through peer review
Broad current readership	Limited circulation but more likely to be held in libraries as permanent record
More flexibility over writing	Strict writing style conventions and format
National readership	International readership

perhaps even rules on use of sub-headings, notes, tables, diagrams, photographs and figures. Here, journals may also ask that articles are submitted with the author's name and address on a separate page (to facilitate anonymous reviewing);
- who to send the articles to, how many copies (at least three, which are not returned) and how to print it (always double spaced on one side of the page);
- publication dates and deadlines, acceptance rates.

It is essential to follow these instructions as far as you can. A paper which at least *looks* as though it has been carefully prepared in accordance with the guidelines laid down by a journal will be viewed more favourably. One of hardest things (I find) is ensuring that references are laid out exactly according to the requirements of a particular journal. There are many different referencing formats in use, some of which differ only in the use of full stops. Bibliographic software packages such as *Papyrus* (see Appendix) can be invaluable in constructing reference lists.

There are other aspects of the 'house style' of a journal that tend not to be explained in their instructions for authors sections, and can only be discovered by looking at articles published in the journal itself. Most research journals expect articles to be structured around a series of sub-headed sections: Abstract; Introduction (including a brief literature review) leading into a statement of the research question(s) or hypothesis; Methods/ Procedures; Results; Discussion; References. However, specific journals may deviate from this structure slightly or may use different terminology. Qualitative studies are notoriously difficult to fit into this kind of linear format, and it is worth looking at how the particular journal handles qualitative material.

The normal procedure is to send in the required number of copies of the article with a short covering letter. Fairly soon there usually follows a brief acknowledgement of receipt of the article. Very occasionally editors may return an article at this point if it is clearly inappropriate for the journal, too long or otherwise unsuitable. However, most articles are sent off at this point for blind peer review. This means that anything that identifies the author(s) is deleted from the paper, which is reviewed by three experts nominated by the editor. Reviewers are customarily given three to four weeks to prepare their (anonymous) reports, although it is not uncommon for them to take longer. The standard practice is for reviewers to make ratings on the overall quality of the paper and its suitability for the journal. They also write a brief report on the paper, which may be quite brief (five or six lines) or more lengthy (two or three pages in some cases). The ratings may or may not be sent to the author, depending on journal policy, but the report will almost always be sent on, accompanied by a letter from the editor. This letter will either reject the paper, perhaps recommending other journals which might consider it, or will suggest alterations that need to be carried out. It is unusual for papers to be accepted for publication without any re-writing at all.

At this point many would-be authors become dispirited. Having opened their letter from the journal, they are faced with three critical and cryptic sets of anonymous comments, some of which may contradict each other. This experience can seem like an invitation to low self-esteem, frustrated rage and depression. Personally, I have often had to banish such reports to the outer reaches of my office for several days (or longer!) before being able to read them in a balanced and constructive fashion. It is helpful to remind oneself of what is happening in these circumstances. Reviewers are not being asked to be therapeutic or supportive, but to help the editor produce the best quality work for his or her journal. If an editor does not want to publish a paper at this stage, he or she will say so very clearly. Therefore, any invitation to re-submit the paper is an acknowledgement that it has the potential to make the grade.

Once the re-writing has been done (which may take months) it is usual to send in another three or four copies (the reviewers may well wish to see the paper again) along with a covering letter which explains briefly how the main points made by reviewers have been addressed. It may be necessary to explain why some of these points have *not* been addressed – reviewers can be wrong! Again there is a waiting period while the paper is being considered. Some journals may permit another round of revisions. Once the paper is accepted there is yet another delay while it takes its place in the queue of articles for publication. Some prestigious journals have publication delays of over 12 months.

It is clear that this whole process take time. It is common for at least 18 months to elapse between submitting an article to an academic journal, and seeing it in print. Some professional journals do not employ such elaborate review procedures, and can turn round articles more quickly. Less popular, or new journals may not receive many papers and may be in a position to put an article straight into the next edition.

Finally, it is sensible to be on the alert for upcoming special issues of journals. Editors or Editorial Boards of many journals like to reserve one or two editions each year for symposia or collections of articles on specific topics. Notification of these special issues is usually advertised in the journal about two years ahead, with a deadline for submission of articles around 12 months ahead of the eventual publication date. It can be easier to get an article accepted for a special edition (there is less competition) and once published it will receive more attention, since anyone interested in the topic will seek out the journal, even if they do not normally read it.

Conference proceedings

For many researchers, giving a paper at a conference represents a good way to get started in their writing career. The dates and venues of conferences are advertised about nine months in advance in relevant professional journals, or on the Internet, along with a call for papers. For most conferences, the act of submitting a paper merely involves writing an abstract (i.e. a 300-word summary). A few conferences demand to see the whole of the paper at the submission point, but this is rare. When the time for the conference comes round, a formal paper may or may not need to be written. Some people at conferences actually read out papers, but this form of presentation is almost always boring and static. Presentations where the speaker talks freely around overhead projector headings tend to be better received. At a conference, ordinary speakers will have 20–30 minutes for their talk (keynote or megastar speakers are allowed longer), which puts pressure on the presenter to express his or her ideas crisply and succinctly – a good discipline. Following the conference, the journal of the professional association responsible for the event will publish the title (and sometimes also the abstract) of each paper, along with the name and address of the presenter. It is quite common to receive several requests for copies of a conference paper. The people who want to read the paper are likely to be interested enough in it to give feedback if asked. Useful feedback can also be received during the conference itself, either through formal questions asked after the paper, or less formally in the bar or round the dinner table. If you have actually written a paper in advance of a conference, it is useful to take 10–20 copies to the event to distribute to people interested in your work. Another format that is increasingly employed at conferences is the *poster* presentation. Researchers display their work on a poster, and during a session of the conference stand beside it to answer questions. This can be a very rewarding way of meeting other people with similar research interests. It can also be less terrifying than standing up and delivering a paper. Contributing a paper or poster at a conference can be a useful way of achieving some degree of dissemination of research, and getting the material into the public domain. It is also an excellent way of rehearsing ideas that are later worked up into a published article.

Publishing a book

Most journal articles are between 3,000 and 6,000 words in length. A book can be anything between 60,000 and 100,000 words. There is therefore much more work entailed in writing a book, compared to writing a paper. Also, it is unusual, nowadays, to see book-length research reports in the field of counselling and psychotherapy. Nevertheless, there may be situations where the only way to do justice to a piece of research is to give it the space made possible by a book. Examples of widely read counselling and psychotherapy research books which have appeared in recent years are Hill (1989), Howe (1989) and Gubrium (1992).

Unlike a research paper, which is written and then sent off to a journal, no one in their right mind would ever write a research book and send it off cold to a publisher. The procedure is to submit a proposal to the publisher, which is then reviewed by two or three academic referees. Just as in deciding on which journal to approach with an article, it is important to investigate the previous work published by an imprint. A book proposal is more likely to be accepted if it fits in to the publisher's existing portfolio. A good proposal will include the following information:

- a title and general outline or aims;
- a synopsis of each chapter;
- information about the previous writing experience of the author(s). If the author(s) have limited experience, then a sample chapter should be included;
- the anticipated readership of the book;
- how the book compares with other texts in the same field;
- some indication of the timescale for finishing the manuscript.

As with journal article submissions, the process of getting a book proposal accepted may take some time and involve changes to the original conception. Once a publisher accepts a proposal, they will issue a contract and may pay a small advance on future royalties. It is perhaps important to stress here that earnings from academic or research books are meagre. The publisher will allocate an editor to the book, who can be treated as an ally. Book editors cajole and encourage their authors, and are willing to discuss the project quite openly. Editors also put a great deal of work into ensuring that the final copy of the book is as near perfect as it can be.

One of the crucial factors that needs to be understood in relation to book publishing is that publishers are partly interested in the quality of a book but are much more interested in whether it will *sell*. As explained earlier, the economics of journal publishing are fairly stable. Books, on the other hand are more hit or miss. It is not unusual for academic or research-focused books to struggle to break even. Publishers continually seek to be reassured that there is a market for a proposed book. The idea that the book will be bought by large numbers of students on courses in different colleges and universities (preferably all around the globe) is the kind of thing that publishers like to hear.

It is worth noting that publishers are traditionally cautious about edited collections, conference proceedings or unreconstituted Doctoral dissertations. The latter are often far too dry and technical to work in book form, and multi-author edited books can be fragmented and inconsistent. Obviously, many edited books are published every year in the counselling and psychotherapy domain, but many of them are put together by highly experienced academic editors. For example, in Britain, Professor Windy Dryden has edited many counselling books. Close examination of these books will reveal the extent to which he has provided a clear structure and aims for the authors he has included.

Being invited to contribute to an edited book is a good way of getting published for the first time. One of the ways of being asked to write a book chapter is to become known, for example by giving talks and conference papers.

Publishing a monograph

A monograph can be defined as an academic text that is shorter than a book (around 30,000 words), and is not usually published by a commercial company. Many university departments support their own monograph series, as do some voluntary and public sector agencies. Indeed, with the ready availability of desktop publishing and printing, any individual or group can produce their own monograph-length reports. There are many research projects which produce substantial reports, for example an end-of-project report to a funding body, which do not translate easily into journal articles. If such monographs are advertised in the appropriate professional journals, they can easily generate sales that are sufficient to cover costs. It is not difficult to get an ISBN number which will ensure that the monograph eventually finds its way into bibliographic listings. The people who are interested enough in a subject to seek out a monograph tend not to be particularly concerned about how 'glossy' the product is, as long as it is accurate and well edited. To some extent, a degree of unglossiness can help to give a monograph an aura of authenticity. A good example of a locally published monograph series has been the *Dulwich Centre* series, which has presented much of the work of narrative therapists Michael White and David Epston and their colleagues. This set of writings has been enormously influential, without any involvement or support from international publishing houses.

Writing practitioner research

A central theme of this book has been the distinctiveness of practitioner research in counselling. To do justice to the principles of practitioner research, for example a commitment to critical reflexivity and to the goal of producing knowledge in context, it is necessary to write more creatively and personally than is usually the case in the psychological and social scientific literature. Some of the ways in which practitioner writing may differ from conventional research writing are:

- A greater willingness to write in the first person where appropriate. It can be very hard for people who have been trained to be detached, scientific 'observers' to use the word 'I' in work that is to be publicly disseminated. The use of first-person writing is essential if the study is to be 'owned' and grounded in a context. At the same time, over-use of the first person can be a distraction. Beginning every sentence with 'I believe. . .' in the end diminishes the impact of the use of a personal voice;
- Including the voices of other people. As counsellors, we do not regard our clients as 'subjects' (or objects). Why, then, in research, are participants or informants written about as if they were passive 'response-machines' or specimens? Any attempt to engage in dialogical, collaborative research will mean that other people have the right to see their own words in the final articles or report;
- More space given to ethical and moral considerations. In mainstream research it is generally assumed that ethical issues

have been dealt with as part of the general methodological competence of the researcher, and as a result do not require detailed discussion. In practitioner research the closeness of the research to practice, and the over-riding priority given to positive empowerment and enhancing the well-being of participants, will often mean that ethical and moral issues are more complex and less resolved, and will therefore call for discussion in more depth;

■ Using different forms of writing to represent experience. Conventional social scientific writing adopts a highly detached and distanced perspective on experience, and does not allow the reader to 'dwell in' (Mair, 1989) the world of those being written about. In recent years, some social scientists have started to experiment with different approaches to writing, drawing on drama, fiction and poetry. Gergen (1997) provides a very useful discussion of the implications of different forms of writing;

■ Writing about implications for practice. If you carry out a piece of practitioner research and write it up, then what readers will want to know is what impact the research made on your practice. In practitioner research papers it is important to give examples of implications for practice, or to devote a section of the paper to this theme.

As a result of these considerations, practitioner research articles are likely to look somewhat different from the kinds of research articles that can be found in the current literature. There are likely to be additional sections giving reflexive and contextual information. There will be a section explicitly examining implications for practice. There may be more space given to ethical issues and the whole thing may be structured and written from a more dialogical standpoint.

Doing the writing

It is all very well to outline the various kinds of publication outlet that are available, and how they operate. For some people reading this, the main hurdle comes long before even starting to think about which journal to approach with a paper. The hurdle is writing. It is possible to be a gifted researcher and yet experience writing as an activity that is utterly painful and frustrating.

There is no easy way round this. It may be helpful, however, to consider three propositions:

1   Writing is a skill. Everyone who writes can write better. There are ways of learning how to write more effectively.
2   Everyone can write when they are sufficiently in tune with what they are writing, when they have found their own 'voice' or 'author-ity'. If you are stuck with your writing, approach the problem as a counsellor. What do you *really* want to say?
3   The kind of writing that tends to be expected in research publications is linear, abstract, middle-class, Western white male kind of stuff. There are other ways, better ways, of communicating.

If you find writing difficult, my suggestion is that you study writing. Dig out the work of writers in your field whom you admire. How do *they* do it, how do they structure sentences, paragraphs, chapters and even whole books? There are also several books which give good advice on how to write and how to create the conditions for writing. Among these are Becker (1986), Bell (1993), Golden-Locke and Biddle (1997), MacMillan and Clark (1998) and Wolcott (1990).

When looking at published work from a perspective of wondering 'how was this written?', it is useful to develop a sensitivity to the way that articles are structured. One of the most terrifying experiences is to sit down with a blank sheet of paper or empty word-processor file in the hope of being able to grind out an article or chapter. It is much better to already have a structure or template around which one's words and ideas can be woven. Box 12.2 provides some hints for constructing writing templates. These are not hard and fast rules. Many excellent social science writers have developed alternative ways of structuring their written output. To some extent the structure may be dictated by the requirements of a journal or book editor. But the point is that, virtually always, good writing involves having a clear structure which allows the reader to follow the thread(s) of the argument through from beginning to end. Poor writing occurs when this does not happen, when the author has 'lost the plot'.

Box 12.2

Some basic rules for structuring a paper, article or chapter

Anchor the beginning and the end. There should normally be some kind of introduction, which tells the reader why this is an important topic, outlines the aims of the paper, and may also briefly describe how the article is structured (i.e. what follows). There should also normally be a conclusion, which summarises the main argument and draws out implications for the future (e.g. implications for practice, for further research, for theory-building, etc.). Omitting a conventional introduction or conclusion can have great dramatic effect and impact, but also runs the danger of making your piece incomprehensible.

Use sub-headings and sections. It is difficult to write good stuff that flows on and on without any breaks. These breaks can be indicated by subheadings, section numbering or even by lines or asterisks in the middle of the page. Each section should be brought to a close with a brief summary or conclusion, and then there should be a brief statement at the beginning of the next section introducing the new theme or sub-topic. Look at published books and articles. There are many different levels of sub-heading that can be used. For instance, in this book there are major sub-headings (in bold) and minor sub-headings (in italics). In a few places there are also subsidiary divisions marked by the first word or phrase of a section being italicised. It is seldom effective to go beyond two or three levels of sub-heading, except in very technical writing.

Use quotations for special effect, not to carry the main argument. As a rock fan, I tend to think about a piece of writing as similar to recording a track on a record. First, the basic track is laid down quite simply, often with just voice and guitar or piano. Later, added musical layers are dubbed on, backing vocals, such as a full rhythm section, solos, etc. Applying this metaphor to writing, it can be seen that a quote is an embellishment, like a guitar or saxophone solo. If you write a piece that comprises a series of quotes (whether from published authors or from your research informants) it will be very difficult for a reader to follow the direction of the argument. You need to learn to rely first and foremost on your own 'voice' and bring in other voices to give emphasis or contrast.

Don't use the good stuff too early. In any paper or chapter there are perhaps two or three really good ideas and a lot of padding. If this is the case, then it is not sensible to include these glittering moments *before* the more mundane material. It is better to work up to the more interesting ideas, and to use them to critique and illuminate the background material.

Other ways of getting the message across

Because of the domination of research by academics, it is natural to assume that research outputs must always take the form of written texts. We live in a literate professional culture, in which authority is associated with written authorship. From a counselling perspective, however, it is clear that experiential learning is, most of the time, a more powerful medium for communication and learning than reading and writing could ever be. There are many ways of using research findings. Even at academic conferences, it is not unusual for research papers to be presented as pieces of 'performance art'. In other settings, research can be translated into workshops or video documentaries. In the context of the day-to-day work of counselling agencies, the results of research can be incorporated into protocols and training manuals. The impact of practitioner research will depend, in the long run, not only on the adoption of a diversity of methodologies, but also on the exploration of a multiplicity of channels of communication and learning.

13

Critical Reflexivity and the Reconstruction of Counselling

The aim of this final chapter is briefly to draw together some of the main themes of the book, and to suggest the idea of *critical reflexivity* as a means of conveying what is distinctive about practitioner research in counselling. In earlier chapters, issues associated with the process of beginning research for the first time were reviewed. Among the skills examined were those of formulating a research question, locating that question within the previous research literature, and planning a research project. An outline was also given of the different approaches or research genres that exist within counselling and psychotherapy research: quantitative, qualitative, outcome, process. Running through all this were some key assumptions about what it means to do practitioner research in counselling. These assumptions can be summed up under three main themes: the nature of practical knowledge in counselling; the role of the practitioner-researcher; the purpose of practitioner research. These are explored in turn.

The nature of practical knowledge in counselling

It seems to me that what counts as practical knowledge depends a great deal on the area of practice, on the type of practical work that is being carried out. The way that knowledge is structured in a profession like medicine, for example, is quite different from the way that it is structured in counselling. In medicine, a doctor collects information in order to arrive at a diagnosis, which in turn leads to treatment. The knowledge of the doctor can be viewed as a highly complex, but nevertheless fairly explicit, set of if–then causal links. If various diagnostic signs are present, then the most probable diagnosis is K, and the treatment of choice is drug X. If drug X is administered then symptoms A, B and C should begin to reduce within three days. If these symptoms do not reduce then a physician will consider the likelihood of diagnosis L and do tests P and Q to check its probability. . . . To describe medical knowledge in this fashion is of course an over-simplification which ignores important factors such as the relationship between doctor and patient. There is no way that the role of doctor can ever be wholly reduced to a set of if–then causal links. The point is merely that a significant part of the knowledge domain of the doctor can be seen to be structured in this way. The existence of this form of knowledge structure is what makes medical research so effective. The vast and complex interlocking field of medical knowledge can be broken down into its component if–then links, which can then be researched in isolation. New knowledge about one of the if–then links can result in it being replaced without any threat to the edifice as a whole. So, a doctor may read in a medical journal that drug Y has been shown to be more effective than drug X in cases where K has been diagnosed. That doctor can quite happily go into his or her surgery the next day and begin to prescribe the new drug and perhaps even never use the old drug again.

Research and knowledge in counselling and psychotherapy is not like this at all. Although many therapy theorists and researchers have attempted to develop knowledge structures of the kind used in medicine, their efforts have had no more than a marginal impact on therapy practice. For example, there have been many attempts to examine the links between psychiatric diagnoses and the effectiveness of specific therapeutic interventions. If a client is diagnosed as depressed, what is the treatment of choice? Is it interpersonal psychotherapy, anti-depressant drugs, long-term psychoanalysis, cognitive therapy. . .? The very existence of so many alternative interventions gives the answer. The differences in rates of effectiveness between these interventions is so marginal that there is little basis for selecting one over the others. Other research in counselling has attempted to establish if–then links not between diagnosis and treatment but between client behaviours and specific counsellor responses. This is generally known as process research. For example, under what circumstances is it best for a counsellor to use interpretation, empathy, vivid metaphoric language, self-disclosure, homework assignments. . .? While research on these process variables has certainly demonstrated the value of such therapist responses in general terms, it has not been precise enough to identify the kind of specific if–then links seen in medicine. I seriously doubt whether any counsellor or psychotherapist has *ever* read an article in a research journal that has resulted in him or her going in to work the next day having decided to replace one intervention with another whenever a client shows signs of a particular problem or symptom.

Why is the structure of knowledge in counselling so different from that in medicine (and other applied sciences)? The answer is that these are very different kinds of work. The fact that so many of the pioneers of therapy (Freud, Jung, Berne, Beck) were originally trained in medicine resulted in a large-scale importation into therapy of many medical assumptions (including its name – psychotherapy). But in a medical consultation a doctor remains in control, collects information, makes decisions and directs the treatment. It can be shown that, most of the time, the success of the treatment is attributable to the quality of the decision-making of the doctor (i.e. making the right diagnosis and choice of drug or operative procedure). In counselling, by contrast, the counsellor and client are engaged in a process of working together to develop an understanding. Research has shown that the effectiveness of counselling and psychotherapy is mainly related to three factors:

- the characteristics of the client (e.g. their readiness to change);
- the counsellor as a person (several studies have shown marked differences in effectiveness between individual therapists);
- the quality of the client–therapist relationship.

It is these *personal* factors, rather than specific techniques or if–then procedures, that have been shown over and over again in research to be associated with good outcomes. This suggests that the knowledge actually used by counsellors and psychotherapists to achieve good results is not of a detached, objective, if–then variety, but instead comprises knowledge that is both *personal* (concerning how I as a counsellor operate in this situation, and how the other person – the client – might be thinking and feeling) and *relational* (how client and counsellor work jointly together).

The word that is normally used to describe knowledge of personal and relational issues is *understanding*. The structure of knowledge used by counsellors, the knowledge that seems to make a difference to outcomes, does not comprise a network of if–then linkages but comprises a way of understanding.

In everyday life, when we talk about understanding oneself or understanding another person or a relationship, it seems to me that we assume a number of things. We mean that we understand a particular person or relationship, rather than persons or relationships in general. In other words, this is a situated or contextualised knowledge. We mean that we have drawn upon our feelings or emotional reactions to the person or relationship, and that there is a *felt* quality to the understanding itself. We mean that we have arrived at the understanding in a fairly intuitive manner, drawing upon multiple strands of knowing: awareness, imagery, memory, theories, stories.

If the knowledge that counsellors use can be viewed as a type of personal understanding, then practitioner research needs to be designed and written in a way that promotes understanding. Basically, practitioner-researchers must be willing to tell the story of what they have observed and experienced, and to produce 'accounts about particular clients, therapists and encounters, produced with a sincere intent to convey something that you could have witnessed if you had been in the right place at the right time' (Stiles, 1995: 125).

The role of the practitioner-researcher: finding the right posture

This book is written around an assumption that most people who would wish to use it would have completed a basic training in counselling or psychotherapy (or perhaps in an allied profession such as social work or psychiatric nursing) and would be at a stage of seeking to engage in research either as part of a postgraduate course or as part of their on-going professional development.

Anyone in this position will have established a fairly secure sense of their professional or occupational role. They would have arrived at a definition and set of expectations about their work that they and their colleagues could understand and accept. Moving from this kind of settled work role to something new and different can be hard. One of the most difficult tasks in doing research in counselling can be that of creating a viable identity or role for oneself. The role of counsellor is known and understood. The role of researcher can be alien and threatening. The role of practitioner-researcher is mysterious, unknown, vague.

I suspect that there are many counsellors who enjoy doing research and get a lot out of it, for example when they are doing a research project during a Masters degree, but who do not maintain this interest later in their career because they just cannot find a way of fitting it in. There are few role models of practitioner-researchers. Practitioners do not get paid for doing research. Sometimes even the mention of research findings during a super-vision session or training workshop will elicit attributions of elitism or over-intellectualisation.

So, one of the challenges of beginning counselling research is that of starting to develop ways of integrating research into a work role and occupational identity. The well-known qualitative education researcher, Harry Wolcott (1992), uses the notion of 'posturing' to describe this process. This is an odd idea, but also useful. There are two meanings of 'posturing'. In a negative sense it refers to the adoption of an affected or artificial stance. In a positive sense it means the act of taking a strategic position, making a policy statement. In proposing that the latter definition refers to something that is useful for new researchers to do, Wolcott is aware of the irony associated with the former meaning of the word. Wolcott argues that there are many alternative research approaches and genres currently around, and also many different theoretical models. There is a 'marketplace of ideas'. It is only when would-be researchers have assembled their own combinations of ideas and methods, made their policy state-ments, that they can really get on with the work.

There are several different ways in which practitioner-researchers in counselling can develop a posture which maintains a sustainable link between research and practice. One posture is to adopt the role of student. Registering for a Masters degree can legitimate research activity for maybe two years. Going on to take a Doctorate, particularly when studying part-time, can extend the shelf-life of this posture to around five or six years. The advantage of being a student is that this role can bestow the most amazing permission to do almost anything. The disadvantages are that it is necessarily a temporary role, and the price of the permissiveness is that the person being indulged is never taken completely seriously.

Another posture which can support both practice and research is to work within an organisation which takes research seriously. For instance, one voluntary agency offering bereavement counselling has for some years supported an on-going programme of research which is co-ordinated by a committee which is part of the management structure of the organisation. An acceptance of the value of research permeates the agency, with studies being carried out both by staff registered for degrees and by others who just see it as part of their job. Further information on the role of research in this particular organisation can be found in Machin and Pierce (1996). Even if a counselling or psychotherapy clinic or agency has not integrated research into its organisational ethos to this extent, most agencies will have links to external, national counselling networks. In any field of counselling (student, workplace, trauma, health) there can usually be found at least one national or international research forum or working group. Offering to be the liaison person between an agency and such an external group can be a good way of creating a work role that will enable research and practice to be combined.

Beyond being a student or finding a research niche within your organisation, the other way of being a practitioner-researcher is to develop your own voice. There are many conferences and journals that exist to promote the dissemination of knowledge about counselling. Anyone can submit a paper to a conference or journal. Taking part in such activities leads to meeting other people with similar interests. All this contributes to the development of an identity as a practitioner-researcher.

Practitioner research and the reconstruction of counselling

It is perhaps worth reflecting on the purpose of research in counselling and psychotherapy. In this book the idea that counsellors and psychotherapists should take more responsibility for the knowledge base of their profession has been emphasised. But what does this mean? Why do we do research? What is research *for*?

The immediate response to these questions is to answer that research is carried out to answer practical questions, to develop new understanding, to articulate theory. But why do we need to answer practical questions, develop new understandings, or expand our theoretical horizons? Returning to the comparison made earlier in this chapter between counsellors and doctors, if we were physicians we could argue with some justification that research leads to scientific progress which results in better forms of treatment. As counsellors we cannot make this kind of claim, or so it seems to me. Counselling and psychotherapy research does not add to an ever-accumulating stock of coherent scientific knowledge of therapy which feeds into new treatments. The research that we do has quite a different purpose. Counselling and psychotherapy are activities that are inevitably engaged in a process of continual reconstruction. Because of economic, political and technological change, the society that we live in is itself changing more rapidly than any other society in history (as far as we know). Counselling can be seen as a cultural practice which helps individual citizens to adapt to these changes, to re-adjust or re-author their life stories in the light of what is going on around them. Ever since its emergence at the back end of the nineteenth century, psychotherapy has periodically re-created itself in the face of cultural change (Cushman, 1995). The 'invention' of the humanistic therapies in the 1950s, cognitive therapies in the 1960s, feminist therapy and also multicultural approaches in the 1980s, narrative therapy in the 1990s . . . all these developments can be understood as the response of the therapy profession to changing cultural forces.

Some of the major research challenges in recent years can be recognised as arising from the need to find ways of accommodating counselling to new situations and issues:

- How best can counsellors work alongside other health professionals in primary care teams?
- What kind of psychological therapy can help people to cope with the moral, philosophical and personal demands of the new infertility treatments?

- How can counselling be meaningfully carried out between persons from very different cultural backgrounds?
- How do we find space in therapy for spiritual experience?
- What are the processes, outcomes and professional issues associated with counselling on the Internet?
- How can counsellor training best deal with the postmodern proliferation of theoretical perspectives?

These are just some of the contemporary research questions that were not being asked 20 or 30 years ago, because they did not need to be asked. Many other such questions could be added to this list.

The conclusion that I draw from these reflections is that, ultimately, the purpose of counselling research is the *reconstruction of therapeutic practice*. The general contours of what comprises a helpful therapeutic relationship are widely accepted as consisting of the kinds of principles articulated by writers such as Carl Rogers and Jerome Frank. However, these principles need to be constantly stretched or modified, for two reasons. First, once a set of therapeutic ideas and methods has been around for long enough it becomes assimilated into mainstream culture and gradually becomes less potent as a means of opening up new ways of being for clients. The therapies become part of everyday reality rather than a vantage point from which everyday reality can be seen afresh. Second, as has already been mentioned, the pace of social change means that counsellors and their clients are continually being faced by issues and possibilities that would be unrecognisable to their predecessors. Making sense of these issues and possibilities requires a capacity to reflect on self-in-role that is not only personal, but also critically informed by an appreciation of social and cultural meanings.

Conclusions: practitioner research in counselling

The purpose of this book has been to begin to sketch an outline of a what a practice-centred approach to research in counselling might look like. There is much to be done in this arena. Although most counselling research is, and has been, carried out by people who are also practitioners, the prevailing scientific and academicist ethos demands that they/we deny and conceal our real motives, practical experience and passionate interest when we do research. To reiterate, this book has defined practitioner research as grounded in:

- a concern to generate knowledge-in-context, rather than seeking to establish generalised, 'universal' truths;
- a commitment to critical reflexivity, encompassing elucidation of not only the personal but also the social, cultural, political and moral pre-understandings that inform our research;
- a willingness to deploy in research the basic tools of counselling practice: an acceptance of feeling and emotion, the disciplined use of self-in-relation, and the capacity to engage in a dialogical process with others;
- the intention to disseminate the results of research in ways that genuinely inform practice and empower users.

These are lofty goals, but why shouldn't they be? In Britain, at any rate, people do not become counsellors because it is a highly paid and respected profession that offers job security. Christopher (1996) reminds us of the 'moral vision' that underpins good practice in counselling. Surely counselling researchers should not be afraid to embrace a moral vision. It is right that research effort should be directed toward reassuring service managers that they are getting good value for money. But it is also right that practitioner-researchers should innovate and should question the basis of their practice.

Steiner Kvale (1996) has argued that the most successful body of research in the history of psychology has been the psychoanalytic case study. He points out that psychology textbooks would be almost empty if ideas derived from psychoanalysis were to be deleted. Yet why have psychoanalytic ideas been so influential? The methodological inadequacies of the psychoanalytic case study are extensive: failure to provide data that can be verified by others, failure to consider alternative interpretations, selective choice of case material to confirm hypotheses, an organisational structure that punishes dissent. But despite these very real inadequacies, psychoanalytic ideas and methods have survived innumerable attempts to declare them dead and buried.

Psychoanalytic case studies represent a tradition of *practitioner* research that has been in existence for almost 100 years. Personally, I do not believe that the strength of the psychoanalytic approach lies in the validity of psychoanalytic ideas and therapy.

It seems to me that its strength lies instead in the fact that it has constituted a form of inquiry that is based in practice and that has made use of a set of theoretical constructs. The utilisation of a shared theoretical language has not only facilitated communication between practitioners, but has required that practitioner-researchers move beyond describing phenomena and attempt to make sense of these phenomena.

But now there are research strategies and techniques that make it possible for practitioner-researchers to do more than interpret their process notes. Methods such as practitioner inquiry groups, IPR, analysis of transcripts, and different approaches to the evaluation of outcomes, open up new ways of understanding counselling.

Failure to develop a distinctive practitioner research base may have important consequences. Academic and managerial voices are given a great deal of authority in modern society, and there is a danger that if knowledge of counselling – the published literature – is dominated by academic and policy-oriented research and writing, the unique understandings that practitioners possess will not be taken seriously in debates over new services or funding. The silencing of practitioners goes hand in hand with the devaluing of practice. In allied professions such as nursing, teaching or social work, it is difficult to keep good practitioners in jobs that allow them to see clients, because to achieve professional respect and a decent salary they need to move into management. These professions have, not very successfully, been forced to develop incentives for keeping experienced workers in front-line practice roles. This has not happened in counselling yet, but it is not difficult to imagine that it might occur in the future. Practitioner research is one means of valuing practice.

It is perhaps necessary to state that practitioner research is just one among a range of forms of research that need to co-exist. It is inevitable that government departments will want to commission 'big' research that addresses 'big' policy decisions. It is inevitable that people in universities will develop programmes of theoretically driven research. These things will happen anyway. But practitioner research in counselling has not developed far enough to take its full place alongside these other forms of research. And the other type of research that is sadly lacking is consumer research. Most of the time, users of counselling services can only make their views heard through questionnaires devised and collated by practitioners or administrators. I am sure that users have a lot more to say than has ever emerged through the kinds of 'client experience' research that has been carried out until now.

Finally, an acknowledgement of the political dimension of practitioner research. In the past, counsellors and psychotherapists who have wanted to do research have been assimilated into a framework for inquiry that has been dominated by the methods and assumptions of behavioural psychologists and medical researchers. The passionate need-to-know of counsellors has been transformed into a series of (usually trivial) questions that were amenable to investigation by quantitative, disembodied, impersonal methodologies. Practitioner research is clearly in opposition to these dominant ways of knowing, whose proponents will undoubtedly deride it as irrelevant, invalid and unscientific. But here, it is important to ask: *in whose interest* is any piece of research? Whose interests are served by randomised controlled trials and whose interests are served by qualitative, reflexive practitioner research?

Appendix

Annotated List of Key Resources for Counselling Researchers

1 Books on counselling research
2 General research methods texts
3 Statistics packages
4 Qualitative analysis packages
5 Test publishers
6 Professional societies
7 Referencing/bibliography software

1 Books on counselling research

1.1 There are several textbooks that provide an overview of the issues and methods of counselling research. These texts represent the 'next step' beyond this book.

Barker, C., Pistrang, N. and Elliott, R. (1994) *Research Methods in Clinical and Counselling Psychology*. Chichester: Wiley. (Highly recommended. A comprehensive account of all facets of counselling research.)

Heppner, P.P., Kivlighan, jr., D.M. and Wampold, B.E. (1992) *Research Design in Counseling*. Pacific Grove, CA: Brooks/Cole. (Excellent, detailed coverage of all aspects of research. Written for a North American readership, so tends to assume a basic familiarity with psychological methods and statistics.)

McLeod, J. (1994) *Doing Counselling Research*. London: Sage. (Particularly recommended for readers who do not have a psychology background. Good on qualitative approaches.)

Parry, G. and Watts, F.N. (eds) (1996) *Behavioural and Mental Health Research* (2nd edn). London: Erlbaum. (A widely used introductory text that is not counselling-specific but has been written to reflect the interests of a range of different groups of mental health professionals.)

Watkins, jr., C.E. and Schneider, L.J. (eds) (1991) *Research in Counseling*. Hillsdale, NJ: Lawrence Erlbaum. (Has the advantage that every chapter is written by an acknowledged expert in the field. Written for a North American readership, so tends to assume a basic familiarity with psychological methods and statistics.)

1.2 Books which explore more advanced issues in counselling and psychotherapy research.

Aveline, M. and Shapiro, D. (eds) (1995) *Research Foundations for Psychotherapy Practice*. Chichester: Wiley. (A series of chapters on the challenges involved in carrying out research in different therapy settings.)

Bergin, A.E. and Garfield, S.L. (eds) (1994) *Handbook of Psychotherapy and Behavior Change* (4th edn). Chichester: Wiley. (This *Handbook* is published every eight years, and includes authoritative reviews of current knowledge written by the leading figures in the field. The first three chapters examine some of the main methodological issues in this area of research.)

Miller, N.E., Luborsky, L., Barber, J.P. and Docherty, J.P. (eds) (1993) *Psychodynamic Treatment Research: A Handbook for Clinical Practice*. New York: Basic Books. (Examines the issues in doing both process and outcome research that is consistent with the assumptions of psychodynamic theory.)

Russell, R.L. (ed.) (1994) *Reassessing Psychotherapy Research*. New York: Guilford Press. (A highly stimulating look at the current research scene. Particularly good chapters on the historical development of psychotherapy research and the issue of simplicity–complexity in process research.)

2   General research methods texts

There are many good research methods books written primarily for psychology, social science and health studies students, but which contain information that is useful for counsellor researchers. The short list below is not exhaustive, but is a selection of general texts that reflect a reflexive, practitioner-oriented perspective.

Bickman, L. and Rog, D.J. (eds) (1998) *Handbook of Applied Social Research Methods*. London: Sage.

Robson, C. (1993) *Real World Research: A Resource for Social Scientists and Practitioner-Researchers*. Oxford: Blackwell.

Sapsford, R. and Abbott, P. (1992) *Research Methods for Nurses and the Caring Professions*. Buckingham: Open University Press.

Shakespeare, P. et al. (eds) (1993) *Reflecting on Research Practice: Issues in Health and Social Welfare*. Buckingham: Open University Press.

Whitaker, D.S. and Archer, J.L. (1989) *Research by Social Workers: Capitalizing on Experience*. London: CCETSW.

3 Statistics packages

Statistical Package for the Social Sciences (SPSS)
SPSS
1st Floor
St Andrew's House
West Street
Woking
Surrey
GU21 1EB

MINITABS
Minitab Ltd
Brandon Court Unit EL
Progress Way
Coventry
CV3 2TE

4 Qualitative analysis packages

(NUD-IST, Code-a-Text, ATLAS-TI)
Sage Publications
6 Bonhill St
London
EC2A 4PU

5   Test publishers

(*MBTI*)
Oxford Psychologists Press
Lambourne House
311–321 Banbury Rd
Oxford
OX2 7JH

(*Beck Depression Inventory*)
The Psychological Corporation
Freepost
24–28 Oval Rd
London
NW1 7DX

(*STAI, GHQ, HADS*)
NFER/Nelson
Darville House
2 Oxford Rd East
Windsor
Berkshire
SL4 1DF

(*MMPI, SCL-90-R, BSI, PTSD Scale*)
NCS Assessments
c/o Afterhurst Ltd
27 Church Rd, Hove
E. Sussex
BN3 2FA

(*CORE*)
Psychological Therapies Research Centre
University of Leeds
17 Blenheim Terrace
LEEDS
LS2 9JT

6 Professional societies

Division of Counselling Psychology
British Psychological Society
St Andrews House
48 Princess Rd East
Leicester
LE1 7DR

Research Network Co-ordinator
British Association for Counselling
1 Regent Place
Rugby
Warwickshire
CV21 2PJ

7 Referencing/bibliography software

Papyrus
Research Software Design
2718 SW Kelly St
Suite 181
Portland
OR 97201
USA

References

Adler, P.A. and Adler, P. (1994) 'Observational techniques', in N.K. Denzin and Y.S. Lincoln (eds), *Handbook of Qualitative Research*. London: Sage.

Allport, G. (1942) *The Use of Personal Documents in Psychological Science*. New York: Social Science Research Council.

Angus, L.E. and Rennie, D.L. (1988) 'Therapist participation in metaphor generation: collaborative and noncollaborative styles', *Psychotherapy*, 25: 552–60.

Angus, L.E. and Rennie, D.L. (1989) 'Envisioning the representational world: the client's experience of metaphoric expressiveness in psychotherapy', *Psychotherapy*, 26: 373–9.

Atkinson, P. and Hammersley, M. (1994) 'Ethnography and participant observation', in N.K. Denzin and Y.S. Lincoln (eds), *Handbook of Qualitative Research*. London: Sage.

Attkisson, C.C. and Greenfield, T.K. (1994) 'Client Satisfaction Questionnaire-8 and Service Satisfaction Scale-30', in M.E. Maruish (ed.), *The Use of Psychological Testing for Treatment Planning and Outcome Assessment*. Hillsdale, NJ: Lawrence Erlbaum.

Attkisson, C.C. and Zwick, R. (1982) 'The client satisfaction questionnaire: psychometric properties and correlations with service utilization and psychotherapy outcome', *Evaluation and Program Planning*, 5: 233–7.

Aubrey, C., Bond, R. and Campbell, R. (1997) 'Clients' suitability for counselling: the perception of counsellors working in general practice', *Counselling Psychology Quarterly*, 10: 97–118.

Auerbach, A.H. (1983) 'Assessment of psychotherapy outcome from the viewpoint of the expert observer', in M.J. Lambert, E.R. Christensen and S.S. DeJulio (eds), *The Assessment of Psychotherapy Outcome*. New York: Wiley.

Aveline, M. and Shapiro, D.A. (eds) (1995) *Research Foundations for Psychotherapy Practice*. Chichester: Wiley.

Bachelor, A. (1988) 'How clients perceive therapist empathy: a content analysis of "received" empathy', *Psychotherapy*, 25: 227–40.

Baker, R., Allen, H., Gibson, S., Newth, J. and Baker, E. (1998)

'Evaluation of a primary care counselling service in Dorset', *British Journal of General Practice*, 48: 1049–53.

Banister, P. (1994) *Qualitative Methods in Psychology: A Research Guide.* Buckingham: Open University Press.

Barker, C. (1985) 'Interpersonal Process Recall in clinical training and research', in F.N. Watts (ed.), *New Developments in Clinical Psychology.* Chichester: Wiley/BPS.

Barker, C., Pistrang, N. and Elliott, R. (1994) *Research Methods in Clinical and Counselling Psychology.* Chichester: Wiley.

Barkham, M.J. and Barker, C. (1996) 'Evaluating counselling psychology practice', in R. Woolfe and W. Dryden (eds), *Handbook of Counselling Psychology.* London: Sage.

Barkham, M.J. and Shapiro, D.A. (1986) 'Counselor verbal response modes and experienced empathy', *Journal of Counseling Psychology*, 33 (1): 3–10.

Barkham, M.J., Stiles, W.B., Hardy, G.E. and Field, S.D. (1996) 'The Assimilation Model: Theory, Research and Practical Guidelines', in W. Dryden (ed.), *Research in Counselling and Psychotherapy: Practical Applications.* London: Sage.

Barkham, M.J., Shapiro, D.A. and Firth-Cozens, J. (1989) 'Personal questionnaire changes in prescriptive vs. exploratory psychotherapy', *British Journal of Clinical Psychology*, 28: 97–107.

Barlow, D.H. and Hersen, M. (1986) *Single Case Experimental Designs: Strategies for Studying Behavior Change* (2nd edn). New York: Pergamon.

Barlow, D.H., Hayes, S.C. and Nelson, R.O. (1984) *The Scientist Practitioner: Research and Accountability in Clinical and Educational Settings.* New York: Pergamon.

Barrett-Lennard, G.T. (1986) 'The Relationship Inventory now: issues and advances in theory, method and use', in L.S. Greenberg and W.M. Pinsof (eds), *The Psychotherapeutic Process: A Research Handbook.* New York: Guilford Press.

Battle, C.C., Imber, S.D., Hoehn-Saric, R., Stone, A.R., Nash, E.R. and Frank, J.D. (1966) 'Target complaints as criteria of improvement', *American Journal of Psychotherapy*, 20: 184–92.

Bausell, R.B. (1986) *A Practical Guide to Conducting Empirical Research.* New York: Harper and Row.

Becker, H.S. (1986) *Writing for Social Scientists: How to Start and Finish Your Thesis, Book or Article.* Chicago: University of Chicago Press.

Becker, C.S. (1992) *Living and Relating: An Introduction to Phenomenology.* London: Sage.

Beech, J.R. and Harding, L. (eds) (1990) *Testing People: A Practical Guide to Psychometrics.* Windsor: NFER-Nelson.

Bell, J. (1993) *Doing Your Research Project.* Buckingham: Open University Press.

Berger, M. (1983) 'Toward maximising the utility of consumer satisfaction as an outcome', in M.J. Lambert, E.R. Christensen and S.S. DeJulio (eds), *The Assessment of Psychotherapy Outcome.* New York: Wiley.

Bergin, A.E. and Garfield, S.L. (eds) (1994) *Handbook of Psychotherapy and Behavior Change* (4th edn). Chichester: Wiley.

Beutler, L.E. and Crago, M. (1983) 'Self-report measures of psychotherapy outcome', in M.J. Lambert, E.R. Christensen and S.S. DeJulio (eds), *The Assessment of Psychotherapy Outcome.* New York: Wiley.

Beutler, L.E. and Crago, M. (eds) (1991) *Psychotherapy Research: An International Review of Programmatic Studies.* Washington, DC: American Psychological Association.

Bickman, L. and Rog, D.J. (eds) (1998) *Handbook of Applied Social Research Methods.* London: Sage.

Bischoff, R.J., McKeel, A.J., Moon, S.M. and Sprenkle, D.H. (1996) 'Therapist-conducted consultation: using clients as consultants to their own therapy', *Journal of Marital and Family Therapy*, 22: 359–79.

Bond, T. (1993) *Standards and Ethics for Counselling in Action.* London: Sage.

Bowling, A. (1991) *Measuring Health: A Review of Quality of Life Scales.* Buckingham: Open University Press.

Bowling, A. (1995) *Measuring Disease: A Review of Disease-Specific Quality of Life Measurement Scales.* Buckingham: Open University Press.

Brannen, J. (ed.) (1992) *Mixing Methods: Qualitative and Quantitative Research.* Aldershot: Avebury.

Branthwaite, A. and Lunn, T. (1983) 'Projective techniques in social and market research', in R. Walker (ed.), *Applied Qualitative Research.* Aldershot: Gower.

Bridges, K. and Goldberg, D. (1989) 'Self-administered scales of neurotic symptoms', in C. Thompson (ed.), *The Instruments of Psychiatric Research.* Chichester: Wiley.

Bromley, D. (1986) *The Case-Study Method in Psychology and Related Disciplines.* Chichester: Wiley.

Bryman, A. (1984) 'The debate about quantitative and qualitative research: a question of method or epistemology?', *British Journal of Sociology*, 35 (1): 75–93.

Bryman, A. and Burgess, R.G. (eds) (1994) *Analyzing Qualitative Data.* London: Routledge.

Bryman, A. and Cramer, D. (1990) *Quantitative Data Analysis for Social Scientists.* London: Routledge.

Buckley, G. (1998) 'Partial truths – research papers in medical education', *Medical Education*, 32: 1–2.

Burton, M.V. and Topham, D. (1997) 'Early loss experiences in psychotherapists, Church of England clergy, patients assessed for psychotherapy, and scientists and engineers', *Psychotherapy Research*, 7: 275–300.

Christopher, J.C. (1996) 'Counseling's inescapable moral visions', *Journal of Counseling and Development*, 75: 17–25.

Clinton, J.J., McCormick, K. and Besteman, J. (1994) 'Enhancing clinical practice: the role of practice guidelines', *American Psychologist*, 49: 30–33.

Coffey, A. and Atkinson, P. (1996) *Making Sense of Qualitative Data.* London: Sage.

Cohen, L.H., Sargent, M.M. and Sechrest, L.B. (1986) 'Use of psychotherapy research by professional psychologists', *American Psychologist*, 41: 198–206.

Colaizzi, P.F. (1978) 'Psychological research as the phenomenologist views it', in R.S. Valle and M. King (eds), *Existential-Phenomenological Alternatives for Psychology.* New York: Oxford University Press.

Cornelius III, E.T. (1983) 'The use of projective techniques in personnel selection', in K. Rowland and G. Ferris (eds), *Research in Personnel and Human Resources Management*, vol. 1. London: JAI Press.

Cozby, P.C. (1985) *Methods in Behavioral Research* (3rd edn). Palo Alto, CA: Mayfield.

Crits-Christoph, P., Cooper, A. and Luborsky, L. (1988) 'The accuracy of therapists' interpretations and the outcome of dynamic psychotherapy', *Journal of Consulting and Clinical Psychology*, 56: 490–5.

Cronbach, L. (1970) *Essentials of Psychological Testing* (3rd edn). New York: Harper and Row.

Cummings, A.L., Hallberg, E.T. and Slemon, A.G. (1994) 'Templates of client change in short-term counseling', *Journal of Counseling Psychology*, 41 (4): 464–72.

Cushman, P. (1995) *Constructing the Self, Constructing America: A Cultural History of Psychotherapy.* New York: Addison-Wesley.

Csikzentmihalyi, M. and Rathunde, K. (1993) 'The measurement of flow in everyday life: toward a theory of emergent motivation', in J.E. Jacobs (ed.), *Nebraska Symposium on Motivation 1992. Developmental Perspectives on Motivation*. Lincoln, NB: University of Nebraska Press.

Cytrynbaum, S., Sinath, Y., Birdwell, J. and Brandt, L. (1979) 'Goal attainment scaling: a critical review', *Evaluation Quarterly*, 3 (1): 5–40.

Dale, P., Allen, J. and Measor, L. (1998) 'Counselling adults who were abused as children: clients' perceptions of efficacy, client–counsellor communication, and dissatisfaction', *British Journal of Guidance and Counselling*, 26: 141–58.

Davidson, C.V. and Davidson, R.H. (1983) 'The significant other as data source and data problem in psychotherapy outcome research', in M.J. Lambert, E.R. Christensen and S.S. DeJulio (eds), *The Assessment of Psychotherapy Outcome*. New York: Wiley.

Davis, K. (1986) 'The process of problem (re)formulation in psychotherapy', *Sociology of Illness and Health*, 8: 44–74.

Davis, J., Elliott, R., Davis, M., Binns, M., Francis, V., Kelman, J. and Schroder, T. (1987) 'Development of a taxonomy of therapist difficulties: initial report', *British Journal of Medical Psychology*, 60: 109–19.

de Vaus, D.A. (1990) *Surveys in Social Research* (3rd edn). London: Allen and Unwin.

Deane, F.P., Spicer, J. and Todd, D.M. (1997) 'Validity of a simplified target complaints measure', *Assessment*, 4: 119–30.

Delbecq, A.L., Van de Ven, A.H. and Gustafson, D.H. (1975) *Group Techniques for Program Planning: A Guide to Nominal Group and Delphi Techniques*. Glenview, IL: Scott, Foresman.

Denzin, N.K. and Lincoln, Y.S. (1994a) 'Introduction: entering the field of qualitative research', in N.K. Denzin and Y.S. Lincoln (eds), *Handbook of Qualitative Research*. London: Sage.

Denzin, N.K. and Lincoln, Y.S. (1994b) *Handbook of Qualitative Research*. London: Sage.

Derogatis, L.R. and Melisaratos, N. (1983) 'The Brief Symptom Inventory: an introductory report', *Psychological Medicine*, 13: 595–605.

deVries, M. (ed.) (1992) *The Experience of Psychopathology: Investigating Mental Disorders in their Natural Settings*. Cambridge: Cambridge University Press.

Dickens, P. (1994) *Quality and Excellence in Human Services*. Chichester: Wiley.

Douglass, B. and Moustakas, C. (1985) 'Heuristic inquiry; the internal search to know', *Journal of Humanistic Psychology*, 25: 39–55.

Dryden, W. (ed.) (1996) *Research in Counselling and Psychotherapy: Practical Applications*. London: Sage.

Duckworth, J.C. (1990) 'The Minnesota Multiphasic Personality Inventory', in C.E. Watkins, jr., and V.L. Campbell (eds), *Testing in Counseling Practice*. Hillsdale, NJ: Lawrence Erlbaum.

Elkin, I. (1994) 'The NIMH treatment of depression collaborative research program: where we began and where we are', in A.E. Bergin and S.L. Garfield (eds), *Handbook of Psychotherapy and Behavior Change* (4th edn). Chichester: Wiley.

Ellenberger, H.F. (1970) *The Discovery of the Unconscious: The History and Evolution of Dynamic Psychiatry*. London: Allen Lane.

Elliott, R. (1983a) '"That in your hands . . .": a comprehensive process analysis of a significant event in psychotherapy', *Psychiatry*, 46: 113–29.

Elliott, R. (1983b) 'Fitting process research to the practising psychotherapist', *Psychotherapy*, 20 (1): 47–55.

Elliott, R. (1984) 'A discovery-oriented approach to significant change events in psychotherapy: Interpersonal Process Recall and Comprehensive Process Analysis', in L.N. Rice and L.S. Greenberg (eds), *Patterns of Change: Intensive Analysis of Psychotherapy Process*. New York: Guilford Press.

Elliott, R. (1986) 'Interpersonal Process Recall (IPR) as a psychotherapy process research method', in L.S. Greenberg and W.M. Pinsof (eds), *The Psychotherapeutic Process: A Research Handbook*. New York: Guilford Press.

Elliott, R. (1991) 'Five dimensions of therapy process', *Psychotherapy Research*, 1: 92–103.

Elliott, R. and Shapiro, D.A. (1988) 'Brief Structured Recall: a more efficient method for studying significant therapy events', *British Journal of Medical Psychology*, 61: 141–53.

Elliott, R. and Shapiro, D.A. (1992) 'Client and therapist as analysts of significant events', in S.G. Toukmanian and D.L. Rennie (eds), *Psychotherapy Process Research: Paradigmatic and Narrative Approaches*. London: Sage.

Elliott, R., Barker, C.B., Caskey, N. and Pistrang, N. (1982) 'Differential helpfulness of counselor verbal response modes', *Journal of Counseling Psychology*, 29: 354–61.

Ellis, C. and Bochner, A. (eds) (1996) *Composing Ethnography: Alternative Forms of Qualitative Writing*. Thousand Oaks, CA: Sage.

Ellis, C. and Flaherty, M. (eds) (1992) *Investigating Subjectivity: Research on Lived Experience*. Thousand Oaks, CA: Sage.

Ellis, C., Kiesinger, C.E. and Tillmann-Healy, L.M. (1997) 'Interactive interviewing: talking about emotional experience', in R. Hertz (ed.), *Reflexivity and Voice*. Thousand Oaks, CA: Sage.

Ellis, R. (ed.) (1988) *Professional Competence and Quality Assurance in the Caring Professions.* London: Chapman and Hall.

Epston, D. and White, M. (1992) 'Consulting your consultants: the documentation of alternative knowledges', in D. Epston and M. White (eds), *Experience, Contradiction, Narrative and Imagination: Selected Papers.* Adelaide: Dulwich Centre Publications.

Erickson, K. and Stull, D. (1998) *Doing Team Ethnography: Warnings and Advice.* Thousand Oaks, CA: Sage.

Etherington, K. (1996) 'The counsellor as researcher: boundary issues and critical dilemmas', *British Journal of Guidance and Counselling,* 24 (3): 339–46.

Fairhurst, K. and Dowrick, C. (1996) 'Problems with recruitment in a randomized controlled trial of counselling in general practice: causes and implications', *Journal of Health Services Research and Policy,* 1: 77–80.

Feltham, C. (ed.) (1998) *Witness and Vision of the Therapists.* London: Sage.

Ferguson, B. and Tyrer, P. (1989) 'Rating instruments in psychiatric research', in C. Freeman and P. Tyrer (eds), *Research Methods in Psychiatry: A Beginner's Guide.* London: Gaskell.

Fielding, N.G. and Lee, R.M. (eds) (1991) *Using Computers in Qualitative Research.* London: Sage.

Finch, J. (1984) '"It's great to have someone to talk to": ethics and politics of interviewing women', in C. Bell and H. Roberts (eds), *Social Researching: Politics, Problems, Practice.* London: Routledge.

Firth, J., Shapiro, D.A. and Parry, G. (1986) 'The impact of research on the practice of psychotherapy', *British Journal of Psychotherapy,* 2 (3): 169–79.

Fish, L.S. and Busby, D.M. (1996) 'The Delphi method', in D.H. Sprenkle and S.M. Moon (eds), *Research Methods in Family Therapy.* New York: Guilford Press.

Flanagan, J.C. (1954) 'The critical incident technique', *Psychological Bulletin,* 51: 327–58.

Flick, U. (1998) *An Introduction to Qualitative Research.* London: Sage.

Freeman, C. and Tyrer, P. (eds) (1989) *Research Methods in Psychiatry: A Beginner's Guide.* London: Gaskell.

Friedli, K., King, M.B., Lloyd, M. and Horder, J. (1997) 'Randomised controlled assessment of non-directive psychotherapy versus routine general-practitioner care', *Lancet,* 350: 1662–5.

Froyd, J.E., Lambert, M.J. and Froyd, J.D. (1996) 'A review of practices of psychotherapy outcome measurement', *Journal of Mental Health,* 5: 11–15.

Gadamer, H. (1975) *Truth and Method*. New York: Continuum.

Galassi, J.P. and Gersh, T.L. (1991) 'Single-case research in counseling', in C.E. Watkins, jr., and L.J. Schneider (eds), *Research in Counseling*. Hillsdale, NJ: Lawrence Erlbaum.

Garfield, S.L. (1984) 'The evaluation of research: an editorial perspective', in A. Bellack and M. Hersen (eds), *Research Methods in Clinical Psychology*. New York: Pergamon.

Garfield, S.L. and Bergin, A.E. (1994) 'Introduction and historical overview', in A.E. Bergin and S.L. Garfield (eds), *Handbook of Psychotherapy and Behavior Change* (4th edn). Chichester: Wiley.

Gaston, L. and Gagnon, R. (1996) 'The role of process research in manual development', *Clinical Psychology: Science and Practice*, 3: 13–24.

Gendlin, E.T. (1986) 'What comes after traditional psychotherapy research?' *American Psychologist*, 41 (2): 131–6.

Gendlin, E.T. and Tomlinson, T.M. (1967) 'The process conception and its measurement', in C.R. Rogers, E.T. Gendlin, D.J. Kiesler and C.B. Truax (eds), *The Therapeutic Relationship and its Impact: A Study of Psychotherapy with Schizophrenics*. Madison: University of Wisconsin Press.

Gergen, K.J. (1985) 'The social constructionist movement in modern psychology', *American Psychologist*, 40: 266–75.

Gergen, K.J. (1994) *Toward Transformation in Social Knowledge* (2nd edn). London: Sage.

Gergen, K. (1997) 'Who speaks and who replies in human science scholarship?' *History of the Human Sciences*, 10 (3): 151–73.

Glaser, B. and Strauss, A. (1967) *The Discovery of Grounded Theory*. Chicago: Aldine.

Golden, C., Sawicki, R. and Franzen, M. (1984) 'Test construction', in A. Bellack and M. Hersen (eds), *Research Methods in Clinical Psychology*. New York: Pergamon.

Golden-Locke, K. and Biddle, K.D. (1997) *Composing Qualitative Research*. London: Sage.

Goss, S. and Mearns, D. (1997a) 'A call for a pluralistic epistemological understanding in the assessment and evaluation of counselling', *British Journal of Guidance and Counselling*, 25: 189–98.

Goss, S. and Mearns, D. (1997b) 'Applied pluralism in the evaluation of employee counselling', *British Journal of Guidance and Counselling*, 25: 327–44.

Grafanaki, S. (1996) 'How research can change the researcher: the need for sensitivity, flexibility and ethical boundaries in conducting qualitative research in counselling/psychotherapy', *British Journal of Guidance and Counselling*, 24 (3): 329–38.

Greenbaum, T.L. (1998) *The Handbook for Focus Group Research* (2nd edn). Thousand Oaks, CA: Sage.

Greenberg, L.S. (1984a) 'A task analysis of intrapersonal conflict resolution', in L.N. Rice and L.S. Greenberg (eds), *Patterns of Change: Intensive Analysis of Psychotherapy Process*. New York: Guilford Press.

Greenberg, L.S. (1984b) 'Task analysis: the general approach', in L.N. Rice and L.S. Greenberg (eds), *Patterns of Change: Intensive Analysis of Psychotherapy Process*. New York: Guilford Press.

Greenberg, L.S. (1992) 'Task analysis: identifying components of inter-personal conflict resolution', in S.G. Toukmanian and D.L. Rennie (eds), *Psychotherapy Process Research: Paradigmatic and Narrative Approaches*. London: Sage.

Greenberg, L.S. and Pinsof, W.M. (eds) (1986) *The Psychotherapeutic Process: A Research Handbook*. New York: Guilford Press.

Greenberg, L.S., Rice, L.N. and Elliott, R. (1993) *Facilitating Emotional Change: The Moment-by-Moment Process*. New York: Guilford Press.

Greene, J.C. (1994) 'Qualitative program evaluation: practice and promise', in N.K. Denzin and Y.S. Lincoln (eds), *Handbook of Qualitative Research*. London: Sage.

Greene, J.C. (1998) 'Qualitative, interpretative evaluation', in A.J. Reynolds and H.J. Walberg (eds), *Advances in Educational Productivity: Evaluation Research*. Greenwich, CN: JAI Press.

Guba, E. and Lincoln, Y.S. (1989) *Fourth Generation Evaluation*. London: Sage.

Gubrium, J.F. (1992) *Out of Control: Family Therapy and Domestic Disorder*. Newbury Park, CA: Sage.

Guy, J.D. (1987) *The Personal Life of the Psychotherapist*. New York: Wiley.

Hall, E., Hall, C., Biddulph, M., Duffy, T., Harris, B. and Hay, D. (1997) 'Group work in counsellor training: an evaluation', *Counselling Psychology Review*, 12: 179–86.

Hammersley, M. (ed.) (1993) *Social Research: Philosophy, Politics and Practice*. London: Sage.

Hardy, G. (1995) 'Organisational issues: making research happen', in M. Aveline and D.A. Shapiro (eds), *Research Foundations for Psychotherapy Practice*. Chichester: Wiley.

Hardy, G., Rees, A., Barkham, M., Field, S.D., Elliott, R. and Shapiro, D.A. (1998) 'Whingeing versus working: Comprehensive Process Analysis of a "vague awareness" event in psychodynamic-interpersonal therapy', *Psychotherapy Research*, 8: 334–53.

Heath, A.E., Neimeyer, G.J. and Pedersen, P.B. (1988) 'The future of cross-cultural counselling: a Delphi poll', *Journal of Counseling and Development*, 67: 27–30.

Hemmings, A. (1997) 'Counselling in primary care: a randomised controlled trial', *Patient Education and Counselling*, 32: 219–30.

Henry, W.P. (1998) 'Science, politics, and the politics of science: the use and misuse of empirically validated treatment research', *Psychotherapy Research*, 8: 126–40.

Heppner, P.P., Kivlighan, jr., D.M. and Wampold, B.E. (1992) *Research Design in Counseling*. Pacific Grove, CA: Brooks/Cole.

Herman, S.E., Marvenko, M.O. and Hazel, K.L. (1996) 'Parents' perspectives on quality in family support programs', *Journal of Mental Health Administration*, 23: 156–69.

Heron, J. (1996) *Co-operative Inquiry: Research into the Human Condition*. London: Sage.

Hertz, R. (ed.) (1997) *Reflexivity and Voice*. Thousand Oaks, CA: Sage.

Hill, C.E. (1986) 'An overview of the Hill counselor and client verbal response modes category systems', in L.S. Greenberg and W.M. Pinsof (eds), *The Psychotherapeutic Process: A Research Handbook*. New York: Guilford Press.

Hill, C.E. (1989) *Therapist Techniques and Client Outcomes: Eight Cases of Brief Psychotherapy*. London: Sage.

Hill, C.E. (1991) 'Almost everything you ever wanted to know about how to do process research on counseling and psychotherapy but didn't know who to ask', in C.E. Watkins and L.J. Schneider (eds), *Research in Counseling*. Hillsdale, NJ: Lawrence Erlbaum.

Hill, C.E. and O'Grady, K.E. (1985) 'List of therapist intentions illustrated by a case study and with therapists of varying theoretical orientations', *Journal of Counseling Psychology*, 32: 3–22.

Hill, C.E., Carter, J.A. and O'Farrell, M.K. (1983) 'A case study of the process and outcome of time-limited counseling', *Journal of Counseling Psychology*, 30 (1): 3–18.

Hill, C.E., Nutt-Williams, E. and Thompson, B.J. (1997) 'A rejoinder to Stiles's, Hoshmand's and Tinsley's comments about "A guide to conducting consensual qualitative research"', *Counseling Psychologist*, 25: 606–14.

Hill, C.E., Thompson, B.J., Nutt-Williams, E. (1997) 'A guide to conducting consensual qualitative research', *Counseling Psychologist*, 25: 517–72.

Hill, C.E., Nutt-Williams, E., Heaton, K.J, Thompson, B.J. and Rhodes,

R.H. (1996) 'Therapist retrospective recall of impasses in long-term psychotherapy: a qualitative analysis', *Journal of Counseling Psychology*, 43: 207–17.

Hilliard, R.B. (1993) 'Single-case methodology in psychotherapy process and outcome research', *Journal of Consulting and Clinical Psychology*, 61 (3): 373–80.

Hingley, S.M. (1995) 'Cognition, emotion and defence: processes and mechanisms of change in a brief psychotherapy for depression', *Clinical Psychology and Psychotherapy*, 2: 122–33.

Horvath, A.O. and Greenberg, L.S. (1986) 'Development of the Working Alliance Inventory', in L.S. Greenberg and W.M. Pinsof (eds), *The Psychotherapeutic Process: A Research Handbook*. New York: Guilford Press.

Horvath, A.O. and Greenberg, L.S. (1989) 'Development and validation of the Working Alliance Inventory', *Journal of Counseling Psychology*, 36: 223–33.

Horvath, A.O., Gaston, L. and Luborsky, L. (1993) 'The Therapeutic Alliance and its measures', in N.E. Miller, L. Luborsky, J.P. Barber and J.P. Docherty (eds), *Psychodynamic Treatment Research: A Handbook for Clinical Practice*. New York: Basic Books.

Hoshmand, L. (1997) 'The normative context of research practice', *Counseling Psychologist*, 25: 599–605.

Hoshmand, L. and Martin, J. (eds) (1994) *Method Choice and Inquiry Process: Lessons from Programmatic Research in Therapeutic Practice*. New York: Teachers' Press.

Howard, G.S. (1983) 'Toward methodological pluralism', *Journal of Counseling Psychology*, 30 (1): 19–21.

Howe, D. (1989) *The Consumer's View of Family Therapy*. Aldershot: Gower.

Howe, D. (1996) 'Client experiences of counselling and treatment interventions: a qualitative study of family views of family therapy', *British Journal of Guidance and Counselling*, 24 (3): 367–76.

Howell, D.C. (1987) *Statistical Methods for Psychology* (2nd edn). Boston: Duxbury.

Huberman, A.M. and Miles, M.B. (1994) 'Data management and analysis methods', in N.K. Denzin and Y.S. Lincoln (eds), *Handbook of Qualitative Research*. London: Sage.

Hunt, P. (1985) *Clients' Responses to Marriage Counselling*. Rugby: NMGC.

Hutchinson, S. and Wilson, H. (1994) 'Research and therapeutic interviews: a poststructuralist perspective', in J. Morse (ed.), *Critical Issues in Qualitative Research Methods*. London: Sage.

Jacobson, N.S. and Revenstorf, D. (1988) 'Statistics for assessing the clinical significance of psychotherapy techniques: issues, problems and new developments', *Behavioral Assessment*, 10: 133–45.

Jacobson, N.S., Follette, W.C. and Revenstorf, D. (1984) 'Psychotherapy outcome research: methods for reporting variability and evaluating clinical significance', *Behavior Therapy*, 15: 336–52.

Jeffery, G., Hache, G. and Lehr, R. (1995) 'A group-based Delphi application: defining rural counselling needs', *Measurement and Evaluation in Counseling and Development*, 28: 45–60.

Jenkins, D.A. and Smith, T.E. (1994) 'Applying Delphi methodology in family therapy research', *Contemporary Family Therapy*, 16: 411–30.

Jones, L. (1993) 'User input into Total Quality Management: the Critical Incident Technique', in R. Leiper and V. Field (eds), *Counting for Something in Mental Health Services: Effective User Feedback*. Aldershot: Avebury.

Josselson, R. (ed.) (1996) *Ethics and Process in the Narrative Study of Lives*. Thousand Oaks, CA: Sage.

Josselson, R. and Lieblich, A. (eds) (1993) *The Narrative Study of Lives*, vol. 1. London: Sage.

Josselson, R. and Lieblich, A. (eds) (1995) *Interpreting Experience: The Narrative Study of Lives*, vol. 3. London: Sage.

Josselson, R., Lieblich, A., Sharabany, R. and Wiseman, H. (1997) *Conversation as Method: Analyzing the Relational World of People who were Raised Communally*. Thousand Oaks, CA: Sage.

Kagan, N. (1980) 'Influencing human interaction: 18 years with IPR', in A.K. Hess (ed.), *Psychotherapy Supervision: Theory, Research and Practice*. Chichester: Wiley.

Kagan, N. (1984) 'Interpersonal Process Recall: basic methods and recent research', in D. Larsen (ed.), *Teaching Psychological Skills*. Monterey, CA: Brooks/Cole.

Katz, A.M. and Shotter, J. (1996) 'Hearing the patient's "voice": toward a social poetics in diagnostic interviews', *Social Science and Medicine*, 43 (6): 919–31.

Kazdin, A.E. (1994) 'Methodology, design and evaluation in psychotherapy research', in A.E. Bergin and S.L. Garfield (eds), *Handbook of Psychotherapy and Behavior Change* (4th edn). Chichester: Wiley.

Kiesinger, C.E. (1998) 'From interview to story: writing Abbie's life', *Qualitative Inquiry*, 4: 71–95.

Kitchener, K.S. (1984) 'Intuition, critical evaluation and ethical principles: the foundation for ethical decisions in counselling psychology', *Counseling Psychologist*, 12: 43–55.

Klein, M.H., Mathieu-Coughlan, P. and Kiesler, D.J. (1986) 'The

Experiencing Scales', in L.S. Greenberg and W.M. Pinsof (eds), *The Psychotherapeutic Process: A Research Handbook*. New York: Guilford Press.

Knapp, T.R. (1996) *Learning Statistics through Playing Cards*. Thousand Oaks, CA: Sage.

Knox, S., Hess, S.A., Petersen, D.A. and Hill, C.E. (1997) 'A qualitative analysis of client perceptions of the effects of helpful therapist self-disclosure in long-term therapy', *Journal of Counseling Psychology*, 44: 274–83.

Kolakowski, L. (1993) 'An overall view of positivism', in M. Hammersley (ed.), *Social Research: Philosophy, Politics and Practice*. London: Sage.

Kratochwill, T., Mott, S. and Dodson, C. (1984) 'Case study and single-case research in clinical and applied psychology', in A. Bellack and M. Hersen (eds), *Research Methods in Clinical Psychology*. New York: Pergamon.

Krueger, R. (1994) *Focus Groups: A Practical Guide for Applied Research*. London: Sage.

Kvale, S. (1996) *InterViews: An Introduction to Qualitative Research Interviewing*. London: Sage.

Ladany, N., O'Brien, K., Hill, C.E., Melincoff, D., Knox, S. and Petersen, D. (1997) 'Sexual attraction toward clients, use of supervision, and prior training: a qualitative study of psychotherapy predoctoral interns', *Journal of Counseling Psychology*, 44: 302–35.

Lambert, M.J. (1994) 'Use of psychological tests for outcome assessment', in M.E. Maruish (ed.), *The Use of Psychological Testing for Treatment Planning and Outcome Assessment*. Hillsdale, NJ: Lawrence Erlbaum.

Lambert, M.J. and Cattani-Thompson, K. (1996) 'Current findings regarding the effectiveness of counseling: implications for practice', *Journal of Counseling and Development*, 74: 601–8.

Lambert, M.J. and Ogles, B.M. (1988) 'Treatment manuals: problems and promise', *Journal of Integrative and Eclectic Psychotherapy*, 7 (2): 187–204.

Lambert, M.J., Christensen, E.R. and DeJulio, S.S. (eds) (1983) *The Assessment of Psychotherapy Outcome*. New York: Wiley.

Lambert, M.J., Masters, K.S. and Ogles, B.M. (1991) 'Outcome research in counseling', in C.E. Watkins and L.J. Schneider (eds), *Research in Counseling*. Hillsdale, NJ: Lawrence Erlbaum.

Lambert, M.J., Ogles, B.M. and Masters, K.S. (1992) 'Choosing outcome assessment devices: an organizational and conceptual scheme', *Journal of Counseling and Development*, 70: 527–32.

Larsen, D.L., Attkisson, C.C., Hargreaves, W.A. and Nguyen, T.D. (1979)

'Assessment of client/patient satisfaction: development of a general scale', *Evaluation and Program Planning*, 2: 197–207.

Lebow, J. (1982) 'Consumer satisfaction with mental health treatment', *Psychological Bulletin*, 91: 244–59.

Lee, R. (1993) *Doing Research on Sensitive Topics*. London: Sage.

Lewis, J., Clark, D. and Morgan, D. (1992) *Whom God Hath Joined Together: The Work of Marriage Guidance*. London: Routledge.

Lewis-Beck, M.S. (1993) *Basic Statistics*. Thousand Oaks, CA: Sage.

Levine, M. (1974) 'Scientific method and the adversary model', *American Psychologist*, 29: 661–77.

Liddle, B.J. (1997) 'Gay and lesbian clients' selection of therapists and utilization of therapy', *Psychotherapy*, 34: 11–18.

Lieberman, M., Yalom, I. and Miles, M. (1973) *Encounter Groups: First Facts*. New York: Basic Books.

Lieblich, A. and Josselson, R. (eds) (1994) *Exploring Identity and Gender: The Narrative Study of Lives*, vol. 2. London: Sage.

Lieper, R. (1993) 'User feedback and organisational change', in R. Leiper and V. Field (eds), *Counting for Something in Mental Health Services: Effective User Feedback*. Aldershot: Avebury.

Lieper, R. and Field, V. (eds) (1993) *Counting for Something in Mental Health Services: Effective User Feedback*. Aldershot: Avebury.

Lietaer, G. (1992) 'Helping and hindering processes in client-centered/experiential psychotherapy: a content analysis of client and therapist postsession perceptions', in S.G. Toukmanian and D.L. Rennie (eds), *Psychotherapy Process Research: Paradigmatic and Narrative Approaches*. London: Sage.

Linehan, M.M. (1997) 'Treatment development, evaluation, and dissemination: thoughts from the trenches', paper read at the Society for Psychotherapy Research (UK) Annual Conference, Ravenscar, 24 March 1997.

Llewelyn, S.P., Elliott, R., Shapiro, D.A., Hardy, G. and Firth-Cozens, J. (1988) 'Client perceptions of significant events in prescriptive and exploratory periods of individual therapy', *British Journal of Clinical Psychology*, 27: 105–14.

Lofland, J. and Lofland, L. (1984) *Analyzing Social Settings: A Guide to Qualitative Observation and Analysis* (2nd edn). Belmont, CA: Wadsworth.

Luborsky, L. (1993) 'Recommendations for training therapists based on manuals for psychotherapy research', *Psychotherapy*, 30 (4): 578–80.

Luborsky, L. and Crits-Christoph, P. (eds) (1990) *Understanding Transference: The CCRT Method*. New York: Basic Books.

Luborsky, L. and DeRubeis, R.J. (1984) 'The use of psychotherapy treatment manuals: a small revolution in psychotherapy research style', *Clinical Psychology Review*, 4: 5–14.

Luborsky, L., Crits-Christoph, P. and Mellon, J. (1986) 'Advent of objective measures of the transference concept', *Journal of Consulting and Clinical Psychology*, 54: 39–47.

Lukinsky, J. (1990) 'Reflective withdrawal through journal writing', in J. Mezirow (ed.), *Fostering Critical Reflection in Adulthood: A Guide to Transformative and Emancipatory Learning*. San Francisco: Jossey-Bass.

Macdonald, K. and Tipton, C. (1993) 'Using documents', in N. Gilbert (ed.), *Researching Social Life*. London: Sage.

Machin, L. and Pierce, G. (1996) *Research: A Route to Good Practice. A Case Study of the Role of Research in the Development of a Service to the Bereaved – Bereavement Care*. Keele, Staffs: Centre for Counselling Studies. (Available from Linda Machin, School of Social Relations, Keele University, Keele, Staffordshire, ST5 5BG.)

MacMillan, M. and Clark, D. (1998) *Learning and Writing in Counselling*. London: Sage.

Madill, A. and Barkham, M. (1997) 'Discourse analysis of a theme in one successful case of brief psychodynamic-interpersonal psychotherapy', *Journal of Counseling Psychology*, 44: 232–44.

Mahrer, A. and Nadler, W. (1986) 'Good moments in psychotherapy: a preliminary review, a list and some promising research avenues', *Journal of Consulting and Clinical Psychology*, 54 (1): 10–15.

Mahrer, A., Nadler, W., Gervaize, P. and Markow, R. (1986) 'Discovering how one therapist obtains some very good moments in psychotherapy', *Voices*, 22: 72–83.

Mahrer, A., Dessaulles, A., Nadler, W.P., Gervaize, P.A. and Sterner, I. (1987) 'Good and very good moments in psychotherapy: content, distribution and facilitation', *Psychotherapy*, 24: 7–14.

Mahrer, A., Paterson, W.E., Theriault, A.J., Roessler, C. and Quenneville, A. (1986) 'How and why to use a large number of clinically sophisticated judges in psychotherapy research', *Voices*, 22: 11–15.

Mair, M. (1989) *Between Psychology and Psychotherapy: A Poetics of Experience*. London: Routledge.

Mallett, P. (1991) 'Cost-benefit analyses of psychotherapeutic treatments', *Psychiatric Bulletin*, 15: 575–6.

Maluccio, A. (1979) *Learning from Clients: Interpersonal Helping as Viewed by Clients and Social Workers*. New York: Free Press.

Mangen, S. (1988) 'Assessing cost-effectiveness', in F.N. Watts (ed.), *New Developments in Clinical Psychology*, vol. II. Chichester: Wiley.

Marshall, C. and Rossman, G.B. (1995) *Designing Qualitative Research* (2nd edn). London: Sage.

Mason, J. (1996) *Qualitative Researching*. London: Sage.

Masson, J. (1988) *Against Therapy: Emotional Tyranny and the Myth of Psychological Healing*. Glasgow: Collins.

Masson, J. (1991) *Final Analysis: The Making and Unmaking of a Psychoanalyst*. London: HarperCollins.

Mayer, J. and Timms, N. (1970) *The Client Speaks: Working-Class Impressions of Casework*. London: Routledge and Kegan Paul.

McClelland, D.C. (1980) 'Motive dispositions: the merits of operant and respondent measures', in L. Wheeler (ed.), *Review of Personality and Social Psychology*. Beverley Hills, CA: Sage.

McGrath, G. and Lowson, K. (1986) 'Assessing the benefits of psychotherapy: the economic approach', *British Journal of Psychiatry*, 150: 65–71.

McKenna, P.A. and Todd, D.M. (1997) 'Longtitudinal utilization of mental health services: a time-line method, nine retrospective accounts, and a preliminary conceptualization', *Psychotherapy Research*, 7: 383–96.

McLennan, J. (1990) 'Clients' perceptions of counsellors: a brief measure for use in counselling research, evaluation and training', *Australian Psychologist*, 25: 133–46.

McLeod, J. (1990) 'The client's experience of counselling: a review of the research literature', in D. Mearns and W. Dryden (eds), *Experiences of Counselling in Action*. London: Sage.

McLeod, J. (1992) 'The story of Henry Murray's diagnostic council: case study in the demise of a scientific method', *Clinical Psychology Forum*, 44: 6–12.

McLeod, J. (1994a) 'The research agenda for counselling', *Counselling*, 5 (1): 41–3.

McLeod, J. (1994b) *Doing Counselling Research*. London: Sage.

McLeod, J. (1995) 'Evaluating the effectiveness of counselling: what we don't know', *Changes*, 13 (3): 192–200.

McLeod, J. (1996) 'Qualitative research methods in counselling psychology', in R. Woolfe and W. Dryden (eds), *Handbook of Counselling Psychology*. London: Sage.

McLeod, J. (1997) 'Reading, writing and research', in I. Horton and V. Varma (eds), *The Needs of Counsellors and Psychotherapists*. London: Sage.

McLeod, J. (1998) *An Introduction to Counselling* (2nd edn). Buckingham: Open University Press.

McLeod, J. and Balamoutsou, S. (1996) 'Representing narrative process in therapy: qualitative analysis of a single case', *Counselling Psychology Quarterly*, 9: 61–76.

Meara, N.M. and Schmidt, L.D. (1991) 'The ethics of researching the counseling/therapy process', in C.E. Watkins, jr., and L.J. Schneider (eds), *Research in Counseling*. Hillsdale, NJ: Lawrence Erlbaum.

Mearns, D. and McLeod, J. (1984) 'A person-centred approach to research', in R. Levant and J. Shlien (eds), *Client-Centered Therapy and the Person-Centered Approach: New Directions in Theory, Research and Practice*. New York: Praeger.

Mearns, D. and Thorne, B. (1988) *Person-centred Counselling in Action*. London: Sage.

Meier, S.T. (1994) *The Chronic Crisis in Psychological Measurement*. New York: Academic Press.

Meier, S.T. (1997) 'Nomothetic item selection rules for tests of psychological interventions', *Psychotherapy Research*, 7: 419–28.

Mellor-Clark, J. and Barkham, M. (1997) 'Evaluating effectiveness: needs, problems and potential benefits', in I. Horton and V. Varma (eds), *The Needs of Counsellors and Psychotherapists*. London: Sage.

Mellor-Clark, J. and Shapiro, D.A. (1995) 'It's not what you do . . . it's the way that you do it: the inception of an evaluative research culture in Relate Marriage Guidance', *Changes*, 13 (3): 201–7.

Mies, M. (1993) 'Towards a methodology for feminist research', in M. Hammersley (ed.), *Social Research: Philosophy, Politics and Practice*. London: Sage.

Miles, M. and Huberman, A. (1994) *Qualitative Data Analysis: A Sourcebook of New Methods* (2nd edn). London: Sage.

Miller, N.E., Luborsky, L., Barber, J.P. and Docherty, J.P. (eds) (1993) *Psychodynamic Treatment Research: A Handbook for Clinical Practice*. New York: Basic Books.

Mishler, E.G. (1986) *Research Interviewing: Context and Narrative*. Cambridge, MA: Harvard University Press.

Morgan, D.I. and Krueger, R.A. (1997) *Focus Group Kit*, vols 1–6. Thousand Oaks, CA: Sage.

Morley, S. (1996) 'Single case research', in G. Parry and F.N. Watts (eds), *Behavioural and Mental Health Research: A Handbook of Skills and Methods* (2nd edn). London: Lawrence Erlbaum.

Morley, S. and Snaith, P. (1989) 'Principles of psychological assessment', in C. Freeman and P. Tyrer (eds), *Research Methods in Psychiatry: A Beginner's Guide*. London: Gaskell.

Morrow-Bradley, C. and Elliott, R. (1986) 'Utilization of psychotherapy research by practicing psychotherapists', *American Psychologist*, 41 (2): 188–97.

Moustakas, C. (1967) 'Heuristic research', in J. Bugental (ed.), *Challenges of Humanistic Psychology*. New York: McGraw-Hill.

Moustakas, C. (1990a) *Heuristic Research: Design, Methodology and Applications*. Thousand Oaks, CA: Sage.

Moustakas, C. (1990b) 'Heuristic research, design and methodology', *Person-Centered Review*, 5: 170–90.

Moustakas, C. (1994) *Phenomenological Research Methods*. London: Sage.

Mulhall, D. (1976) 'Systematic self-assessment by PQRST', *Psychological Medicine*, 6: 591–7.

Munoz, R.F., Hollon, S.D., McGrath, E., Rehm, L.P. and VandenBos, G.R. (1994) 'On the AHCPR *Depression in Primary Care* guidelines', *American Psychologist*, 49: 42–61.

Murphy, S. and Tyrer, P. (1989) 'Rating scales for special purposes. I: Psychotherapy', in C. Freeman and P. Tyrer (eds), *Research Methods in Psychiatry: A Beginner's Guide*. London: Gaskell.

Murray, H.A. (1938) *Explorations in Personality*. New York: Oxford University Press.

Neimeyer, G.J. and Norcross, J.C. (1997) 'The future of psychotherapy and counseling psychology in the USA: Delphi data and beyond', in S. Palmer and V. Varma (eds), *The Future of Counselling and Psychotherapy*. London: Sage.

Nelson, M.L. and Neufeldt, S.A. (1996) 'Building on an empirical foundation: strategies to enhance good practice', *Journal of Counseling and Development*, 74: 609–15.

Oakley, A. (1981) 'Interviewing women: a contradiction in terms', in H. Roberts (ed.), *Doing Feminist Research*. London: Routledge and Kegan Paul.

Olesen, V. (1994) 'Feminisms and models of qualitative research', in N.K. Denzin and Y.S. Lincoln (eds), *Handbook of Qualitative Research*. London: Sage.

Olesen, V., Droes, N., Hatton, D., Chico, N. and Schatzman, L. (1994) 'Analyzing together: recollections of a team approach', in A. Bryman and R.G. Burgess (eds), *Analyzing Qualitative Data*. London: Routledge.

Orlinsky, D.E. and Howard, K.I. (1986) 'The psychological interior of psychotherapy: explorations with the Therapy Session reports', in L.S. Greenberg and W.M. Pinsof (eds), *The Psychotherapeutic Process: A Research Handbook*. New York: Guilford Press.

Orlinsky, D.E., Grawe, K. and Parks, B.K. (1994) 'Process and outcome in psychotherapy: noch einmal', in A.E. Bergin and S.L. Garfield (eds),

Handbook of Psychotherapy and Behavior Change (4th edn). Chichester: Wiley.

Osborne, J.W. (1990) 'Some basic existential-phenomenological research methodology for counsellors', *Canadian Journal of Counselling*, 24 (2): 79–91.

Parry, G. (1989) 'Writing a research report', in G. Parry and F.N. Watts (eds), *Behavioural and Mental Health Research: A Handbook of Skills and Methods*. London: Lawrence Erlbaum.

Parry, G. (1992) 'Improving psychotherapy services: applications of research, audit and evaluation', *British Journal of Clinical Psychology*, 31: 3–19.

Parry, G. and Watts, F.N. (eds) (1996) *Behavioural and Mental Health Research: A Handbook of Skills and Methods* (2nd edn). London: Lawrence Erlbaum.

Paterson, C. (1996) 'Measuring outcomes in primary care: a patient generated measure, MYMOP, compared with the SF-36 health survey', *British Medical Journal*, 312: 1016–20.

Patton, M.Q. (1990) *Qualitative Evaluation and Research Methods* (2nd edn). New York: Sage.

Persons, J.B. and Silberschatz, G. (1998) 'Are results of randomized controlled trials useful to psychotherapists?' *Journal of Consulting and Clinical Psychology*, 66: 126–35.

Phillips, J.P.N. (1986) 'Shapiro Personal Questionnaire and generalized personal questionnaire techniques: a repeated measures individualized outcome measurement', in L.S. Greenberg and W.M. Pinsof (eds), *The Psychotherapeutic Process: A Research Handbook*. New York: Guilford Press.

Pilcher, D.M. (1990) *Data Analysis for the Helping Professions: A Practical Guide*. London: Sage.

Pilgrim, D. (ed.) (1983) *Psychology and Psychotherapy: Current Trends and Issues*. London: Routledge and Kegan Paul.

Poertner, J. (1986) 'The use of client feedback to improve practice: defining the supervisor's role', *The Clinical Supervisor*, 4 (4): 57–67.

Polkinghorne, D.E. (1989) 'Phenomenological research methods', in R.S. Valle and S. Halling (eds), *Existential-Phenomenological Perspectives in Psychology*. New York: Plenum Press.

Polkinghorne, D.E. (1991) 'Qualitative procedures for counseling research', in C.E. Watkins and L.J. Schneider (eds), *Research in Counseling*. Hillsdale, NJ: Lawrence Erlbaum.

Pope, K.S. (1991) 'Dual relationships in psychotherapy', *Ethics and Behavior*, 1: 21–34.

Pope, K.S. and Bouhoutsos, J.C. (1986) *Sexual Intimacy between Therapists and Patients*. New York: Praeger.

Powell, G.E. (1989) 'Selecting and developing measures', in G. Parry and F.N. Watts (eds), *Behavioural and Mental Health Research: A Handbook of Skills and Methods*. London: Lawrence Erlbaum.

Radley, A., Cramer, D. and Kennedy, M. (1997) 'Specialist counsellors in primary care: the experience and preferences of general practitioners', *Counselling Psychology Quarterly*, 10: 165–73.

Rainer, T. (1980) *The New Diary*. London: Angus and Robertson.

Reason, P. (ed.) (1988a) *Human Inquiry in Action: Developments in New Paradigm Research*. London: Sage.

Reason, P. (1988b) 'Introduction', in P. Reason (ed.), *Human Inquiry in Action: Developments in New Paradigm Research*. London: Sage.

Reason, P. (1988c) 'Whole person medical practice', in P. Reason (ed.), *Human Inquiry in Action: Developments in New Paradigm Research*. London: Sage.

Reason, P. (ed.) (1994a) *Participation in Human Inquiry*. London: Sage.

Reason, P. (1994b) 'Three approaches to participative inquiry', in N.K. Denzin and Y.S. Lincoln (eds), *Handbook of Qualitative Research*. London: Sage.

Reason, P. and Heron, J. (1986) 'Research with people: the paradigm of cooperative experiential inquiry', *Person-Centered Review*, 1 (4): 456–76.

Reason, P. and Rowan, J. (eds) (1981) *Human Inquiry: A Sourcebook of New Paradigm Research*. Chichester: Wiley.

Reason, P., Chase, H.D., Desser, A., Melhuish, C., Morrison, S., Peters, D., Wallstein, D., Webber, V. and Pietroni, C.P. (1991) *Marylebone Health Centre Research Clinic 1989–90: The Co-operative Inquiry*. London: Marylebone Centre Trust.

Reason, P., Chase, H.D., Desser, A., Melhuish, C., Morrison, S., Peters, D., Wallstein, D., Webber, V. and Pietroni, C.P. (1992) 'Towards a clinical framework for collaboration between general and complementary practitioners: discussion paper', *Journal of the Royal Society of Medicine*, 85: 161–4.

Rennie, D.L. (1990) 'Toward a representation of the client's experience of the psychotherapy hour', in G. Lietaer, J. Rombauts and R. Van Balen (eds), *Client-Centered and Experiential Therapy in the Nineties*. Leuven: University of Leuven Press.

Rennie, D.L. (1992) 'Qualitative analysis of the client's experience of psychotherapy: the unfolding of reflexivity', in S.G. Toukmanian and D.L. Rennie (eds), *Psychotherapy Process Research: Paradigmatic and Narrative Approaches*. London: Sage.

Rennie, D.L. (1994a) 'Clients' deference in psychotherapy', *Journal of Counseling Psychology*, 41: 427–37.

Rennie, D.L. (1994b) 'Storytelling in psychotherapy: the client's subjective experience', *Psychotherapy*, 31: 234–43.

Rennie, D.L. (1994c) 'Clients' accounts of resistance in counselling: a qualitative analysis', *Canadian Journal of Counselling*, 28: 43–57.

Rennie, D.L. (1994d) 'Human science and counselling psychology; closing the gap between science and practice', *Counselling Psychology Quarterly*, 7: 235–50.

Rennie, D.L. (1994e) 'Strategic choices in a qualitative approach to psychotherapy process research: a personal account', in L. Hoshmand and J. Martin (eds), *Method Choice and Inquiry Process: Lessons from Programmatic Research in Therapeutic Practice*. New York: Teachers' Press.

Rennie, D.L. (1996) 'Fifteen years of doing qualitative research on psychotherapy', *British Journal of Guidance and Counselling*, 24: 317–28.

Rennie, D.L. (1998) *'Person-centred Counselling: An Experiential Approach*. London: Sage.

Rennie, D.L. and Toukmanian, S.G. (1992) 'Explanation in psychotherapy process research', in S.G. Toukmanian and D.L. Rennie (eds), *Psychotherapy Process Research*. London: Sage.

Rennie, D.L., Phillips, J.R. and Quartaro, J.K. (1988) 'Grounded theory: a promising approach for conceptualization in psychology?' *Canadian Psychology*, 29: 139–50.

Renzetti, C. and Lee, R. (eds) (1993) *Researching Sensitive Topics*. London: Sage.

Rice, L.N. and Greenberg, L.S. (1984a) 'The new research paradigm', in L.N. Rice and L.S. Greenberg (eds), *Patterns of Change: Intensive Analysis of Psychotherapy Process*. New York: Guilford Press.

Rice, L.N. and Greenberg, L.S. (eds) (1984b) *Patterns of Change: Intensive Analysis of Psychotherapy Process*. New York: Guilford Press.

Rice, L.N. and Kerr, G.P. (1986) 'Measures of client and therapist voice quality', in L.S. Greenberg and W.M. Pinsof (eds), *The Psychotherapeutic Process: A Research Handbook*. New York: Guilford Press.

Rice, L.N and Saperia, E.P. (1984) 'Task analysis of the resolution of problematic reactions', in L.N. Rice and L.S. Greenberg (eds), *Patterns of Change: Intensive Analysis of Psychotherapy Process*. New York: Guilford Press.

Richards, T.J. and Richards, L. (1994) 'Using computers in qualitative research', in N.K. Denzin and Y.S. Lincoln (eds), *Handbook of Qualitative Research*. London: Sage.

Richardson, L. (1991) *Writing Strategies: Reaching Diverse Audiences*. London: Sage.

Richardson, L. (1992) 'The consequences of poetic representation: writing the other, rewriting the self', in C. Ellis and M.G. Flaherty (eds), *Investigating Subjectivity: Research on Lived Experience*. New York: Sage.

Richardson, L. (1994) 'Writing: a method of inquiry', in N.K. Denzin and Y.S. Lincoln (eds), *Handbook of Qualitative Research*. London: Sage.

Riches, G. and Dawson, P. (1996) 'Making stories and taking stories: reflections on researching grief and marital tension following the death of a child', *British Journal of Guidance and Counselling*, 24 (3): 357–66.

Riessman, C.K. (1988) 'Worlds of difference: contrasting experience in marriage and narrative style', in A.D. Todd and S. Fisher (eds), *Gender and Discourse: The Power of Talk*. Norwood, NJ: Ablex.

Riessman, C.K. (1993) *Narrative Analysis*. London: Sage.

Riessman, C.K. (1994a) 'Making sense of marital violence: one woman's narrative', in C.K. Riessman (ed.), *Qualitative Studies in Social Work Research*. London: Sage.

Riessman, C.K. (ed.) (1994b) *Qualitative Studies in Social Work Research*. London: Sage.

Roberts, H. (1981) *Doing Feminist Research*. London: Routledge and Kegan Paul.

Robson, C. (1993) *Real World Research: A Resource for Social Scientists and Practitioner-Researchers*. Oxford: Blackwell.

Rogers, C.R. and Stevens, B. (eds) (1968) *Person to Person: The Problem of Being Human*. Lafayette, CA: Real People Press.

Rorty, R. (1980) *Philosophy and the Mirror of Nature*. Oxford: Blackwell.

Rosenhan, D.L. (1973) 'On being sane in insane places', *Science*, 179: 250–8.

Roth, A. and Fonagy, P. (1996) *What Works for Whom? A Critical Review of Psychotherapy Research*. New York: Guilford Press.

Russell, R.L. (ed.) (1994) *Reassessing Psychotherapy Research*. New York: Guilford Press.

Rust, J. and Golombek, S. (1989) *Modern Psychometrics: The Science of Psychological Assessment*. London: Routledge.·

Safran, J.D., Greenberg, L.S. and Rice, L.N. (1988) 'Integrating psycho-therapy research and practice: modeling the change process', *Psychotherapy*, 25: 1–17.

Sampson, H. and Weiss, J. (1986) 'Testing hypotheses: the approach of the Mount Zion Psychotherapy Research Group', in L.S. Greenberg and W.M. Pinsof (eds), *The Psychotherapeutic Process: A Research Handbook*. New York: Guilford Press.

Schulberg, H.C. and Rush, A.J. (1994) 'Clinical practice guidelines for managing major depression in primary care practice: implications for psychologists', *American Psychologist*, 49: 34–41.

Seligman, M.E.P. (1995) 'The effectiveness of psychotherapy: the *Consumer Reports* study', *American Psychologist*, 50: 965–74.

Semeonoff, B. (1976) *Projective Techniques*. Chichester: Wiley.

Sexton, T.L. (1996) 'The relevance of counseling outcome research: current trends and practical implications', *Journal of Counseling and Development*, 74: 590–600.

Shapiro, D.A., Barkham, M., Hardy, G. and Morrison, L. (1990) 'The Second Sheffield Psychotherapy Project: rationale, design and preliminary outcome data', *British Journal of Medical Psychology*, 63: 97–108.

Shipton, G. (1994) 'Swords into ploughshares: working with resistance to research', *Counselling*, 5: 38–40.

Silberschatz, G., Curtis, J.T. and Nathans, S. (1989) 'Using the patient's plan to assess progress in psychotherapy', *Psychotherapy*, 26: 40–6.

Silberschatz, G., Fretter, P.B. and Curtis, J.T. (1986) 'How do interpretations influence the progress of psychotherapy?' *Journal of Consulting and Clinical Psychology*, 54: 646–52.

Silverman, D. (ed.) (1997) *Qualitative Research: Theory, Method and Practice*. London: Sage.

Skovholt, T.M. and Ronnestad, M.H. (1992) *The Evolving Professional Self: Stages and Themes in Therapist and Counselor Development*. New York: Wiley.

Sloboda, J.A., Hopkins, J.S., Turner, A., Rogers, D. and McLeod, J. (1993) 'An evaluated staff counselling programme in a public sector organization', *Employee Counselling Today*, 5 (5): 4–12.

Smagorinsky, P. (ed.) (1994) *Speaking about Writing: Reflections on Research Methodology*. London: Sage.

Spence, D.P. (1989) 'Rhetoric vs. evidence as a source of persuasion: a critique of the case study genre', in M.J. Packer and R.B. Addison (eds), *Entering the Circle: Hermeneutic Investigation in Psychology*. New York: Addison-Wesley.

Steier, F. (ed.) (1991) *Research and Reflexivity*. London: Sage.

Stewart, D.W. and Shamdasani, P.N. (1990) *Focus Groups: Theory and Practice*. London: Sage.

Stiles, W.B. (1986) 'Development of a taxonomy of verbal response modes', in L.S. Greenberg and W.M. Pinsof (eds), *The Psychothera-peutic Process: A Research Handbook*. New York: Guilford Press.

Stiles, W.B. (1993) 'Quality control in qualitative research', *Clinical Psychology Review*, 13: 593–618.

Stiles, W.B. (1995) 'Stories, tacit knowledge, and psychotherapy research', *Psychotherapy Research*, 5: 125–7.

Stiles, W.B. (1997) 'Consensual qualitative research: some cautions', *Counseling Psychologist*, 25: 586–98.

Stiles, W.B. and Shapiro, D.A. (1989) 'Abuse of the drug metaphor in psychotherapy process-outcome research', *Clinical Psychology Review*, 9: 521–43.

Strain, P. and Kerr, M. (1984) 'Writing grant applications: some general guidelines', in A. Bellack and M. Hersen (eds), *Research Methods in Clinical Psychology*. New York: Pergamon.

Strauss, A. and Corbin, J. (1990) *Basics of Qualitative Research: Grounded Theory Procedures and Techniques*. London: Sage.

Strauss, A. and Corbin, J. (1994) 'Grounded Theory methodology: an overview', in N.K. Denzin and Y.S. Lincoln (eds), *Handbook of Qualitative Research*. London: Sage.

Strupp, H.H. (1989) 'Psychotherapy: can the practitioner learn from the researcher?' *American Psychologist*, 44: 717–24.

Strupp, H.H. and Binder, J.L. (1984) *Psychotherapy in a New Key: A Guide to Time-Limited Dynamic Psychotherapy*. New York: Basic Books.

Talley, P.F., Strupp. H.H. and Butler, S.F. (eds) (1994) *Psychotherapy Research and Practice: Bridging the Gap*. New York: Basic Books.

Tichenor, V. and Hill, C.E. (1989) 'A comparison of six measures of the working alliance', *Psychotherapy*, 26: 195–9.

Tingey, R.C., Lambert, M.J., Burlingame, G.M. and Hansen, N.B. (1996) 'Assessing clinical significance: proposed extensions to method', *Psychotherapy Research*, 6: 109–23.

Tolley, K. and Rowland, N. (1995) *Evaluating the Cost-Effectiveness of Counselling in Health Care*. London: Routledge.

Toukmanian, S.G. and Rennie, D.L. (eds) (1992) *Psychotherapy Process Research: Paradigmatic and Narrative Approaches*. London: Sage.

Treacher, A. (1983) 'On the utility or otherwise of psychotherapy research', in D. Pilgrim (ed.), *Psychology and Psychotherapy: Current Trends and Issues*. London: Routledge and Kegan Paul.

Vachon, D.O., Susman, M., Wynne, M.E., Birringer, J., Olshefsky, L. and Cox, K. (1995) 'Reasons therapists give for refusing to participate in psychotherapy process research', *Journal of Counseling Psychology*, 42: 380–2.

Valle, R.S. and Halling, S. (eds) (1989) *Existential-Phenomenological Perspectives in Psychology: Exploring the Breadth of Human Experience*. New York: Plenum.

Van Hasselt, V.B. and Hersen, M. (eds) (1996) *Sourcebook of Psychological Treatment Manuals for Adult Disorders*. New York: Plenum Press.

van Kaam, A. (1969) *Existential Foundations of Psychology*. New York: Image Books.

Vaughn, S., Schumm, J.S. and Sinagub, J.M. (1996) *Focus Group Interviews in Education and Psychology*. Thousand Oaks, CA: Sage.

von Wright, G.H. (1993) 'Two traditions', in M. Hammersley (ed.), *Social Research: Philosophy, Politics and Practice*. London: Sage.

Walsh, R., Perrucci, A. and Severns, J. (1999) 'What's in a good moment? A hermeneutic study of psychotherapy values across levels of psychotherapy training', *Psychotherapy Research*, 9.

Watkins, jr., C.E. and Campbell, V.L. (eds) (1990) *Testing in Counseling Practice*. Hillsdale, NJ: Lawrence Erlbaum.

Watkins, jr., C.E. and Schneider, L.J. (eds) (1991) *Research in Counseling*. Hillsdale, NJ: Lawrence Erlbaum.

Webb, Y. (1993) 'Consumer surveys: an overview', in R. Lieper and V. Field (eds), *Counting for Something in Mental Health Services: Effective User Feedback*. Aldershot: Avebury.

West, M.A. and Reynolds, S. (1995) 'Employee attitudes to work-based counselling services', *Work and Stress*, 9: 31–44.

West, W.S. (1996) 'Using human inquiry groups in counselling research', *British Journal of Guidance and Counselling*, 24: 347–55.

West, W.S. (1997) 'Integrating counselling, psychotherapy and healing: an inquiry into counsellors and psychotherapists whose work includes healing', *British Journal of Guidance and Counselling*, 25: 291–312.

Wheeler, S. and Turner, L. (1997) 'Counselling problem drinkers: the realm of specialists, Alcoholics Anonymous or generic counsellors?' *British Journal of Guidance and Counselling*, 25: 313–26.

Whitaker, D.S. and Archer, J.L. (1989) *Research by Social Workers: Capitalizing on Experience*. London: CCETSW.

White, M.B., Edwards, S.A. and Russell, C.S. (1997) 'The essential elements of successful marriage and family therapy: a modified Delphi study', *American Journal of Family Therapy*, 25: 213–31.

White, M. and Epston, D. (1990) *Narrative Means to Therapeutic Ends*. New York: Norton.

Wilson, S.B., Mason, T.W. and Eing, M.J.M. (1997) 'Evaluating the impact of receiving university-based counseling services on student retention', *Journal of Counseling Psychology*, 44: 316–20.

Wolcott, H.F. (1990) *Writing up Qualitative Research*. London: Sage.

Wolcott, H.F. (1992) 'Posturing in qualitative research', in M.D. LeCompte, W.L. Millroy and J. Preissle (eds), *The Handbook of Qualitative Research in Education*. New York: Academic Press.

Wolcott, H.F. (1994) *Transforming Qualitative Data: Description, Analysis, Interpretation*. London: Sage.

Wolcott, H.F. (1995) *The Art of Fieldwork*. London: Sage.

Wright, D.B. (1996) *Understanding Statistics: An Introduction for the Social Sciences*. London: Sage.

Yin, R.K. (1989) *Case Study Research: Design and Methods*. London: Sage.

Index